About this Book

Our Common Journey is not only an inspiring insider's account. It is a guide to employing the two most powerful tools of environmental policy: cooperation and innovation.
Jonathan Lash, *President, The World Resources Institute*

Our Common Journey presents a lucid and penetrating blueprint for integrating environmental responsibilities into society. It recognizes policy development as a process in which many actors play critical roles. De Jongh's story has an important message: long-range success requires more than good ideas and leadership, it also requires tenacity and hard work. A 'must read' for anyone who aspires to build a sustainable future.
Molly Harriss Olson, *Director, Eco Futures and Inaugural Executive Director, US President's Council on Sustainable Development*

For decades, the Dutch have been the leaders in implementing sustainable development policies. As someone who has tagged along on this journey from time to time, I greatly value Paul de Jongh's full account of the trip. There isn't a better explanation of what it takes to put environmental policies into practice!
Lawrence Susskind, *Ford Professor of Urban and Environmental Policy, Massachusetts Institute of Technology*

Our Common Journey is the first practical case study of how to build and implement a national sustainable development strategy. It is a 'must read' for anyone attempting to translate the notion of sustainable development into action. The Netherlands is the planetary laboratory for sustainability and Paul de Jongh is one of its principal architects.
David Gershon, *Founder and Chairman, the Global Action Plan and creator of the First Earth Run*

Our Common Journey is an insider account of the formulation and implementation of an innovative, integrated approach to environmental policy, and of the experiences and lessons gained along the way. As importantly, it distils the major principles of the 'cooperative environmental management' approach for their global application.
Dr Klaus Töpfer, *Executive Director, United Nations Environment Programme (UNEP)*

Sustainability is more and more a question of shared responsibilities, good governance, multi-stakeholder cooperation, and integration. *Our Common Journey* is about systemic changes, stakeholder involvement and evolving roles in a policy process. Giving an overview of how such a sophisticated strategy has developed over the years in the Netherlands, it offers a most useful methodological analysis to many players confronted with stakeholder involvement. For the European Union, the time has come to design the European Union's first integrated strategy for sustainable development. And *Our Common Journey* is paving the way for this process.
Raymond van Ermen, *Executive Director, European Partners for the Environment*

About the Authors

Paul E. de Jongh spent some 20 years in the Dutch Environment Ministry, serving as project leader of the first National Environmental Policy Plan and as Deputy Director General for Environment. In 1997, he became the Director for Nature Protection in the Ministry of Agriculture. De Jongh has also been active in international organizations, including the United Nations (where he was a co-chair of the Commission on Sustainable Development), and the Organization for Economic Cooperation and Development (where he serves on the Environment Committee). He co-founded the International Network of Green Planners and is a current member of the Sustainability Challenge Foundation and the Global Action Plan. In his spare time, Paul sings in a German cabaret group and, of course, he likes to go hiking.

Seán Captain is an author, policy analyst, and grant writer who has worked for numerous non-profit organizations in San Francisco. He lived in Germany for several years, which helped him to translate European ideas for an international audience. Seán also likes hiking, as well as cycling and rock climbing.

Zed Titles on Sustainable Development

Too often sustainable development is regarded as an issue primarily of relevance to developing countries. In a range of books, Zed has sought to combat this notion and to contribute to the debate – at the level of shifts in paradigm as well as changes in policy – on the necessity of transforming our present economic and industrial model in order to create systems and institutions in genuine long-term harmony with the environment in the North as well as the South. Recent titles include:

Our Common Journey: A Pioneering Approach to Cooperative Environmental Management
PAUL E. DE JONGH WITH SEÁN CAPTAIN

The Eco Principle: Ecology and Economics in Symbiosis
ARTHUR DAHL

In the Servitude of Power: Energy and Civilization through the Ages
J. DEBEIR ET AL.

From the Ground Up: Rethinking Industrial Agriculture
PETER GOERING, HELENA NORBERG HODGE AND JOHN PAGE

World of Waste: Dilemmas of Industrial Development
K. A. GOURLAY

Ecological Economics: A Practical Programme for Global Reform
GROUP OF GREEN ECONOMISTS

In the Wake of the Affluent Society: An Exploration of Post-Development
SERGE LATOUCHE

Silenced Rivers: The Ecology and Politics of Large Dams
PATRICK McCULLY

Prosperity, Poverty and Pollution: Managing the Approaching Crisis
KLAUS NÜRNBERGER

Strategies for Sustainable Development: Experiences from the Pacific
JOHN OVERTON AND REGINA SCHEYVENS (EDS)

Economists and the Environment: A Diverse Dialogue
CARLA RAVAIOLI

Responding to Global Warming: The Technology, Economics and Politics of Sustainable Energy
PETER READ

Greening the North: A Post-Industrial Blueprint for Ecology and Equity
WOLFGANG SACHS, LOSKE AND LINZ

Eco-Socialism or Eco-Capitalism? A Critical Analysis of Humanity's Fundamental Choices
SARAL SARKAR

State of the World's Mountains: A Global Report
PETER STONE (ED.)

The Conserver Society: Alternatives for Sustainability
TED TRAINER

Earth Politics
ERNST VON WEIZSÄCKER

Ecological Tax Reform: A Policy Proposal for Sustainable Development
ERNST VON WEIZSÄCKER AND JESINGHAUS

For full details about these titles and Zed's general and subject catalogues, please write to:
The Marketing Department, Zed Books, 7 Cynthia Street, London, N1 9JF, UK
or email Sales@zedbooks.demon.co.uk

Visit our website at: http://www.zedbooks.demon.co.uk

PAUL E. DE JONGH · SEÁN CAPTAIN

Our Common Journey

A Pioneering Approach to Cooperative Environmental Management

Foreword by Klaus Töpfer
EXECUTIVE DIRECTOR
UNITED NATIONS ENVIRONMENT PROGRAMME

Z
Zed Books
LONDON & NEW YORK

Our Common Journey
was first published in 1999 by
Zed Books Ltd., 7 Cynthia Street, London N1 9JF, UK and
Room 400, 175 Fifth Avenue, New York, NY 10010, USA

Distributed in the USA exclusively by St Martin's Press, Inc.,
175 Fifth Avenue, New York, NY 10010, USA

Set in 10/11.6 pt Berkeley Book/Comic Sans
by Long House, Cumbria, UK
Printed and bound in the United Kingdom
by Biddles Ltd, Guildford and King's Lynn

A catalogue record for this book
is available from the British Library

ISBN   Hb 1 85649 738 0
Pb 1 85649 739 9

Contents

Figures

Images by Stefan Verwey appear on pages 4, 211, 222
Images by Peter Brabbée appear on pages 68, 86, 87

Tables

To our teachers and mentors

Wim ter Keurs and John McNeill

Authors' Note

This book is based on Paul E. de Jongh's experiences over two decades of environmental policy work in the Netherlands and internationally. The basic material from Paul's recollections is supported by extensive written documentation and interviews conducted primarily by his co-author, Seán Captain. The pronoun 'I' always refers to Paul E. de Jongh. The word 'we' generally refers to Paul and his colleagues in the Netherlands Environment Department, except for the Acknowledgments section, in which both co-authors thank people who have assisted them.

Acknowledgements

One person does not write a book, nor do two or three. It takes dozens of people who help in big and small ways to make a rough idea into a finished text. We are grateful to the many people who helped us along this journey.

Above all, we would like to thank the Netherlands Ministry of Housing, Land Use Planning and the Environment, especially its Director for Strategic Planning, Gerard Keijzers, and the Counsellor for Health and Environment at the Embassy in Washington, Paul Hofhuis. The Ministry provided generous sponsorship for this project, yet left us complete editorial freedom; it also helped initiate the project in the summer of 1996 by granting Paul a paid sabbatical at the Center for Strategic and International Studies (CSIS) in Washington, DC. During this time, Paul was a fellow with the CSIS programme Enterprise for the Environment, under the direction of Dr Karl Hausker.

We are also most grateful to Robert Molteno, our editor at Zed Books, who had the courage to believe in this work, and to his colleagues who cooperated in its production.

Next, we thank those who were gracious enough to grant us an interview (or, in some cases, several interviews):

Anne Alons, Christian Avérous, Berthold Berger-Hennoch, Jan-Willem Biekart, Gustaaf Biezeveld, Jan Bijlsma, Dorothy Bowers, Barbara J. Bramble, Bram Breure, Marjolijn Burggraaff, Jan Cleij, Paul Cough, Brad Crabtree, Terry Davies, Jan Jaap de Graeff, Arie Deelen, Robert Donkers, Oliver Dworak, Marius Enthoven, Jeremy Eppel, Frans Evers, J. William Futrell, Molly Harriss Olson, Jan Henselmans, Paul Hofhuis, Jan Juffermans, Willem Kakebeeke, Gerard Keijzers, Niek Ketting, Karl Kienzl, André Kleinmeulman, Wiel Klerken, Leen Koster, Marie-Therese Lammers, Fred Langeweg, Jonathan Lash, Barbara Lawrence, Ernst Lung, Rob Maas, William McDonough, Cees Moons, Ed Nijpels, Paul Nouwen, Jan Pieters, Stacy Richards, Kees Schröder, James Seif, Richard Smith, Randy Solomon, Jan Suurland, Wolfram Tertschnig, Ton Tukker, Jacob van der Vaart, Hans van der Vlist, Hans van Zijst, William Veerkamp, Pieter Verkerk, Rob

Viser, Teo Wams, Jan Willem Weck, Pieter Winsemius, Kees Zoeteman.

Finally we thank those people who did us a myriad of favours – critiquing text, advising on content and publishing, or any number of other 'little things' that were essential to completing this project.

Alan AtKisson, Peter Brabbée, Marlene Captain, Sandi Captain, Clifford Cobb, Brigitte de Vries, Eileen Ecklund, Lona Frauenfelder, Julie Frieder, Leah Genone, David Gershon, Jonathan Golub, Ursula Haggen, Allen Hickling, Huey Johnson, Florian Klein, Pini Koerts, Peggy Lauer, Laura Livoti, Paul Mantel, John McNeill, Jennifer Murray, Hans Opschoor, Zjan Pee, Andrew Peters, Schusma Ramdal, A.J. Rylaarsdam, Patricia Schölvinck, Melinda Smith, Paul Smith, Lawrence Susskind, Belinda van der Vet, Carolina Van Stuijvenberg-Brabbée, Jeannettine Veldhuijzen.

All these individuals played critical roles in completing this project, and we could not have done it without them. Nevertheless, we take full responsibility for the tone of the work and its factual accuracy.

Paul E. de Jongh and Seán Captain

One person's memories would never have been a sufficient foundation for this book. Seán's involvement in the project was crucial, not only as a refiner of texts and ideas, but also as the poser of critical questions that demanded reflection and clarity of thought. I am very grateful to Seán for all his help, and for driving this project to completion.

Paul E. de Jongh

Abbreviations and Acronyms

ALARA	As low as reasonably achievable
ANWB	Royal Netherlands Touring Association
BMRO	Environment and Land Use Planning Office of VNO/NCW (Netherlands)
CAP	Common Agricultural Policy (European Union)
CEC	Central Economic Committee (Netherlands)
CEO	Chief Executive Officer
CEP	Company Environmental Plan
CFC	Chlorofluorocarbon
CH_4	Methane
CO_2	Carbon dioxide
CPB	Central Planning Bureau (Netherlands)
CSD	United Nations Commission on Sustainable Development
CSI	Common Sense Initiative
CSIS	Center for Strategic and International Studies (US)
DGM	Netherlands Environment Department (Directoraat-Generaal Milieu beheer)
ECE	United Nations Economic Commission for Europe
EH&S	Environment, health and safety
EIA	Environmental impact assessment
EMA	Environmental Management Act (Netherlands)
EPA	Environmental Protection Agency (US)
EU	European Union (formerly the European Community)
GDP	Gross domestic product
GNP	Gross national product
HCFC	Hydrochlorofluorocarbon
HFC	Hydrofluorocarbon
IETP	Integral Environmental Target Plan
IMP	Indicative Multi-year Environmental Plan (Netherlands)
IPCC	Intergovernmental Panel on Climate Change
IPO	Inter-provincial Council (Netherlands)
ISO (9000, 14000)	International Standards Organization – standards for business and environmental management systems, respectively.
KWS 2000	Hydrocarbons 2000 project (Netherlands)
LIFE	Community Financial Instrument for the Environment

LPG	Liquified petroleum gas
MAI	Multilateral Agreement on Investment
NASA	National Aeronautics and Space Administration
NCW	Netherlands Christian Employers' Association
NEPP	National Environmental Policy Plan (Netherlands)
NGO	Non-governmental organization
NH_3	Ammonia
NO_x	Oxides of Nitrogen
NUP	National Environmental Plan (Austria)
OECD	Organization for Economic Cooperation and Development
OPPE	Office of Policy, Planning, and Evaluation (US EPA)
PCBs	Polychlorinated biphenyls
RIVM	National Institute for Health and Environment (Netherlands)
RMC	National Environmental Council (Netherlands)
ROM	Area-specific policy for land use planning and environment (Netherlands)
Sep	Cooperative Association of Electricity Producers (Netherlands)
SMEs	Small and medium-size enterprises
SNM	Foundation for Nature and Environment (Netherlands)
SO_2	Sulphur dioxide
TNO	National Institute for Applied Sciences (Netherlands)
UN	United Nations
UNDP	United Nations Development Programme
UNEP	United Nations Environment Programme
VAT	Value-added tax
VMD	Vereniging Milieudefensie (Friends of the Earth Netherlands)
VNG	Association of Netherlands Municipalities
VNO	Netherlands Federation of Industry
VNO/NCW	Confederation of Netherlands Industry and Employers
VOC	Volatile organic compound
VROM	Ministry of Housing, Land Use Planning, and the Environment (Netherlands)

Foreword

The development and subsequent implementation of the National Environmental Policy Plan of the Netherlands is perhaps the most striking example of long-range policy making in environmental management at the national level. This policy analyzes the challenges posed by environmental problems and sets out ambitious policy goals, cutting across administrative boundaries, economic sectors and levels of activity from the local to the international.

What is even more significant is the process through which the policy was assembled and revised. As *Our Common Journey* reveals, this policy was the product of extensive networking and consensus building. It was an approach characterized by negotiations with important agents of economic change and oriented towards market forces; at the same time, however, it set out to safeguard the future of the environment in the national interest.

Our Common Journey is thus an insider account of the formulation and implementation of an innovative, integrated approach to environmental policy, and of the experiences and lessons gained along the way. As importantly, it distils the major principles of the 'cooperative environmental management' approach for their global application.

There is no doubt that *Our Common Journey* is a timely intervention. So far, the idea of integrated environmental management has been internalized very unevenly at various levels of government around the world. The book shows that, if they are to succeed, integrated environmental policies must open new lines of communication on environmental issues between public and private agencies and governments. The aim must be to eliminate or reduce emissions at the source rather than at the end of production processes. Policy must focus on developing 'closed loop' management of industrial processes to minimize waste and emissions and reduce energy needs. And it must emphasize the value of public education programmes to raise awareness of corporate and individual responsibility for cleaning up the environment. Most importantly, this approach sees the target groups as negotiating partners to be involved in the development of environmental management plans, rather than as adversaries, or groups on which policies are to be imposed.

Policy making for sustainable development and environmental protection is not a simple exercise. I commend this publication to governments, NGOs and donors in the hope that it will help foster a renaissance in planning and action for a sustainable future.

Klaus Töpfer

Executive Director of the United Nations Environment Programme
Former Federal Minister for the Environment of Germany
Former Chairman of the United Nations Commission on Sustainable Development

Our Common Journey
Towards Cooperative Environmental Management

I began this book in 1996, partly as a retrospect on progress since the 1992 Earth Summit in Rio de Janeiro. By most accounts, the results of Rio have been disappointing. Though the world community pledged a huge increase in development aid for the environment, scarcely any countries have kept their promises. While we signed a convention to limit deforestation, figures show that the loss of tropical and temperate forests continues at a brisk pace. And while we pledged to integrate environmental and economic concerns under the rubric of 'sustainable development', we've seen the growth of a massive global trade and investment regime which scarcely registers environmental concerns.

These and many other criticisms surfaced in the spring of 1997 when the United Nations held a five-year review of the Earth Summit, billed as Rio Plus Five. This was an opportunity for environmental organizations to criticize inaction by the world's political leaders, and for everyone to criticize the United States in the hope of eliciting a positive response before the Kyoto Protocol negotiations on climate change in December. Then a funny thing happened: the industrialized countries, which account for most of the world's current carbon dioxide emissions, actually signed an agreement to begin reducing those emissions.

The bright promise of Kyoto has been dimmed somewhat, however, by the re-emergence of tensions in environmental policy making. Many environmentalists dismissed the agreement as a totally ineffective strategy for limiting climate change (which is probably true). Many, but not all, business interests predicted that the protocol would have severe negative effects on the world economy. Some politicians from the United States blasted the agreement for not including commitments from developing nations, while those nations counter-blasted the wealthy countries for making unfair demands of their impoverished Southern neighbours.

Such tensions result from the established approach to environmental policy making as a constant battle. Governments, businesses and non-governmental organizations (NGOs) each define what policy should be, and each fights to impose its agenda on the others. Instead of moving forward together, the parties all go their own ways. If I were to compare environmental policy to hiking, I might observe that this approach resembles a poorly organized group outing. Everyone thinks he or she has the right destination in mind and the best information on how to get there. This approach looks more like a boxing match than a hiking trip, and it is destined to fail.

A New Framework

Reaching sustainability will be a very long, difficult journey. On their own, a select few members of the 'hiking party' – such as designated government bureaux or NGOs – cannot hope to reach the target. They must find ways to involve all the participants, including other government departments and businesses. In this book, I want to discuss a new policy approach – one in which the parties discuss environmental, economic and social concerns, cooperating to resolve their differences. This approach is based on my experience in dealing with environmental issues in the Dutch government. Through years of trial and error, my colleagues and I have worked towards a new framework for policy, based not on constant conflict but on what I call *cooperative environmental management*. This framework is sometimes called 'the Dutch approach', although it is being applied, in varying degrees, around the world.

I do not claim that the Dutch have all the answers, or that they lead in all aspects of environmental protection. Through a lot of hard work, however, and in collaboration with colleagues in other countries, we have identified some key lessons of the policy process. We have learned, first, how to clarify government thinking on the nature of environmental problems and the actions needed to address them. We have found ways, for example, to undertake sophisticated data collection and modelling of environmental problems, while presenting the results in concise terms that people readily understand. We have also streamlined our Environment Department* so that other parts of the government, as well as businesses, understand our mission. Second, we have found a framework for discussing environmental issues which government and most companies and NGOs can agree upon. There will always be day-to-day arguments about specific actions or policies, and these may be quite fierce. But most parties in the Netherlands have reached a basic understanding of the ground rules for debate and have learned to appreciate each other's perspectives.

* This is officially known as the Directorate General for the Environment, one of four such directorates in the Ministry of Housing, Spatial Planning and Environment. The make-up of this and other key ministries is explained in Chapter Three.

My aim is not simply to describe developments in the Netherlands. Instead, I will use the Dutch experience as a case study to illustrate the elements of cooperative environmental management, an alternative to the frustration and stalemate of the adversarial approach. I will then apply these elements to an analysis of policy developments around the world. Before describing this new framework, however, I would like to review the old one.

A Critique of the Old Framework

Although obvious in theory, it is not always clear in real-life policy making that each issue has both a cause and an effect. Instead, policy has focused on either causes or effects, with different programmes oriented to one or the other and little coordination among them. This begins to explain why environmental progress has often been so slow, and why policies can be so bureaucratic and expensive.

Efforts to address environmental deterioration began in earnest during the late 1960s and early 1970s. By the mid-1980s there was a fairly clear picture of what was wrong – that is, a catalogue of effects. Problems like deforestation, acid rain, urban smog and waste disposal are obvious to any observer. Policy in the Netherlands and in other countries has been geared to 'dealing with' these problems – or, more specifically, these effects. For example, scientists have studied the acidification of the soil and its impacts on forests and agriculture. Meanwhile, government agencies have cleaned up past damage, such as toxic waste sites.

At the same time, there was a general concept of what might be causing environmental problems. Just as acid rain or waste disposal are obvious effects, factory smokestacks, car exhausts and increased use of disposable products are obvious causes. Accordingly, there were policies to deal with these causes. Engineers developed expensive new end-of-pipe technologies for sources of air pollution, such as scrubbers to remove sulphur from smokestacks and catalytic converters to reduce automobile emissions.

There are causes and effects, but the relationships between them are not fully explored in the old framework. There is little effort to determine the impact, in terms of effects, of measures targeting environmental causes. The old framework also has difficulty examining interrelationships among environmental issues. Although many problems are related, scientists have tended to approach them separately, often appearing to repeat the same research again and again. There is a great deal of information – often duplicated – *but no framework to organize it as a clear, integrated picture.* Without a comparative framework, it is difficult to check the validity of a particular study or finding. It is often easy, however, to design a 'scientific' study which supports any position in a political debate as required, a tactic sometimes called 'junk science'.

Without hard information on causes and effects, policy makers are left to try piecemeal approaches to one or the other. In political terms, it is generally easier to address effects. Cleaning up a polluted site can show that a government is 'doing something' about the environment. Addressing causes is more difficult, since it requires re-evaluating economic structures and production methods. Rather than taking the difficult approach of integrating environmental concerns into the economy, governments generally take the easier approach of cleaning up the damage. Although often costly, such end-of-pipe measures have little or no impact on the overall economic structure. They rarely encourage systemic changes such as reducing energy intensity, conserving resources or moving toward high-quality, long-life products.

The easy approach to environmental causes relies on a regulatory structure known as 'command and control', which creates a war mentality of suspicion and hostility. Because it does not trust business, government – sometimes with support from NGOs – produces strict legislation and highly specific regulations to police the enemy. Because it does not trust government, business responds by skirting environmental responsibilities when it can, or by fiercely opposing government policy through political and legal challenges. Because they trust neither government nor business, often environmental NGOs are confined to criticizing both parties rather than working to propose real solutions.

This war mentality was probably a necessary stage in the development of environmental policy, and it has borne fruit. Levels of pollution have dropped, absolutely or at least relative to economic growth, in many places around the world. In the Netherlands, for example, sulphur dioxide emissions are at their lowest point since 1970, yet the economy has grown by 67 per cent since then.[1] In addition, companies have come to accept, though often grudgingly, that they are responsible for the environmental effects of their activities. The fruits we have harvested, however, were the lowest on the tree, the easiest to reach, and we have reached nearly all of them.

As technology and the economy continue to expand ever more quickly, government regulators are losing the ability to keep up with their prescriptions. Furthermore, the era of quick, end-of-pipe solutions may be coming to an end. Afterthought techno-fixes yield continually diminishing returns, yet great improvements are still needed to sustain a healthy environment for our children and grandchildren.

These improvements will not come if government authority continues to walk its own lonely policy path. The old approach has produced many specialized institutions – government offices, research centres, consulting firms. Their focus is generally on the ends of policy, not the means. Thus success is sometimes measured in terms of new laws, regulations and institutions created, rather than in terms of real environmental improvement. But systemic change can only come from a results-oriented integration of environmental responsibility into other branches of government and the private sector.

The bureaucratic approach is leading to growing frustration in many societies. There is great frustration, for example, on the effects side, as the American David Brower explains: 'as environmentalists, all we have been able to do is to slow down the rate at which things have been getting worse'.[2] Furthermore, new effects seem to 'pop up' constantly. Recent concerns include biotechnology, cloning and the growing suspicion that common synthetic chemicals may act as endocrine disrupters which interfere with development and reproduction. These are the latest in a lineage of crises, such as the *Exxon Valdez* oil spill, the Chernobyl nuclear accident or the chemical releases at Bhopal, India and Seveso, Italy. Each crisis results in new demands to 'deal with' environmental problems, and policy makers are caught in a game of catch-up to find a quick response.

There has also been frustration on the cause side, which basically involves the private sector. Companies have invested billions of dollars in pollution control technologies and spent billions more on fines and legal action; yet they are still told that they are not doing enough. Not only are they constantly attacked on their lack of progress in addressing existing problems, but as frequently they are confronted with demands to address new problems.

These frustrations fuel a *never-ending series of policy conflicts*. Sometimes scientists win, if their research is 'taken seriously' and governments devise a policy response. Sometimes government and environmentalists win, if they manage to pass a strict new environmental law. Sometimes business wins, if it prevents a law from being implemented or successfully challenges a regulation in court. Yet, if everyone wins sometimes, everyone must also lose. The result is a stalemate in which most problems are never solved. Furthermore, *there is little continuity in the policy process*, since the players are constantly trying to undo each other's actions.

In the meantime, the environment continues to deteriorate. This should be a concern not only for traditional 'environmentalists', but for everyone. It has become increasingly clear, for example, that the success of companies depends on a sustainably healthy environment. Without a secure resource base, they will not have the materials to manufacture their products; and without healthy, decent living standards, they will not have customers able to buy their products and services.

Cooperative Environmental Management: the Dutch Example

Although we have not 'solved' environmental problems in the Netherlands, I believe we have devised a useful alternative framework, one that has been developing over two decades of trial and error and is as much the product of sophisticated thinking as of good luck. Cooperative environmental management was not born like the goddess Athena, who sprang fully grown and fully armed from the head of Zeus. Instead, it's a baby that we nursed through years of late-night feeding and nappy changing, lost teeth and skinned knees. For that reason, I think I can best describe the new framework by explaining its historical context and evolution.

While the Dutch approach was originally meant for the specific problems and circumstances in the Netherlands, the experience is valuable for many other settings. Similar political struggles and institutional difficulties are faced in many nations, and similar personal dynamics are involved. I hope readers will see this book not simply as an historical account from one country, but as a case study with lessons that can be applied to their circumstances. This can be done more easily through the example of a small country like the Netherlands, where the scale of issues is more manageable and the people involved are more accessible. We can open the Dutch case study with a preview of the main lessons on offer.

Business-as-usual is no longer an option for government or the private sector, or for the environment. Effective solutions to environmental problems will require some radical rethinking of technology and economics. This can only be achieved if government and business, as well as citizens and NGOs, join forces in a concerted effort rather than waste their energies and ingenuity in endless skirmishing. Bringing about this change, of course, is no small feat. It requires government regulators and NGOs to be clear about what they want – not just on individual, day-to-day issues, but comprehensively and over the long term. It also requires business to be clear on what it can deliver, under what time frames and circumstances.

If the adversarial approach resembles a very disorderly hike, the co-operative approach may resemble a more successful outing. A group expedition, for example, begins with the desire to go hiking and a vague idea of where you want to go. Next, you need to get some information about the territory and how you might reach your goal. Furthermore, you are travelling in a group, so you have to foster a dialogue to which all those involved can contribute. Everyone will not have the same reason for hiking. Some will want to get exercise, some will go for the scenery and fresh air. Others may not be so sure they want to go hiking at all, as is often the case with children. The trick is to help everyone find a reason to participate and objectives they can agree on. Finally, you must assess everyone's abilities so that you can choose an appropriate route and assign duties fairly.

Five Elements

Cooperative environmental management is a strategy to fulfil the tasks mentioned above. It can be described in terms of five main elements:

1 Integrating environmental responsibilities into society as a whole;

2 Presenting clear information, understandable and acceptable for all parties;

3 Recognizing policy as process, in which many actors play critical roles;

4 Framing the policy debate in terms acceptable to all participants;

5 Working for long-term continuity in policies.

Integrating environmental responsibilities
Under the old approach, government plods along the path of compartmentalized, sector-specific policies. In the beginning, this is perhaps inevitable, since new environmental problems seem to keep popping up, demanding immediate responses. As a result, governments develop policies, and bureaucracies, to address each specific problem or problem area – such as waste, or pollution of the air, the water, the soil. After a while, this leads to an inefficient duplication of effort. It resembles a hiking trip in which everyone is carrying his or her own equipment; there may be five tents or frying pans, when the group only needs one or two. They also have different maps and different ideas of how to reach the destination. In the policy field, that means separate bureaucracies for air, soil, water, toxics, and so on. Each has its own scientists and budgets; each issue has its own corresponding laws and regulations.

Not only do the environmental authorities pack their own baggage poorly, they also try to pack for everyone else. The superfluous baggage that government carries, in terms of regulations and bureaucratic procedures, is also forced on business. One day, companies are inspected for emissions to the air, another day for emissions into water. Later they might have to deal with soil pollution or waste disposal. For each area there is generally a separate law and set of regulations, and another ream of pages in a facility's licence. This process ignores the fact that often the same activity, or set of activities, produces each of these problems.

It is also possible that policy on one environmental medium, such as air, can undo policy on another medium, such as water. A good example is the gasoline additive methyl tertiary butyl ether (MTBE) which helps the fuel to burn more cleanly and produce fewer smog-forming pollutants. The problem is, MTBE is itself a potent water pollutant. Through spills and automobile emissions, it is finding its way into drinking water, where even minute quantities of MTBE can make the water taste like turpentine.

Another result of this fragmented approach is that environmental policy makers define problems in different terms from other branches of government or the private sector. In the Netherlands, for example, the Ministry of Economic Affairs dealt with distinct sectors of business, such as industry or refineries, while another ministry dealt with agriculture. The Environment Department, however, was focused on various environmental media, such as air, water, or soil. It was organized according to *effects*, whereas its counterparts in other ministries and the private sector were organized into different sectors of *causes*.

After some time, policy makers may realize the need to reconsider unilateral action and to integrate their work with other branches of government and the private sector. In the Netherlands, the impetus to integrate actually came from business, which demanded a clearer picture of the Environment Department's long-term goals and the responsibilities of different economic sectors. The Department responded by grouping the thousands of different environmental issues into a handful of general themes, such as waste generation or the release of toxics, which recognized the interrelationships among various effects. The themes were complemented by the designation of specific target groups, such as industry or agriculture, which were responsible for causing the problems in the various theme categories. This gave an overall picture, at least, of what was wrong (effects, or themes) and who was responsible (causes, or target groups).

The themes and target groups eventually fed into the development of a National Environmental Policy Plan (NEPP) in 1989. The NEPP, which is updated every four years, tracks progress towards long-term, comprehensive goals. It is the starting point for discussions of how to integrate environmental policy into society as a whole.

Integration in hiking :
Everyone knows where we are going

Integration in cooperative environmental management :
Common targets for all parties involved

Presenting clear information
A hike is not much fun if the group keeps getting lost. The hikers should have a clear idea of where they are heading and how to get there. A trail map is generally an essential tool, but some maps are more helpful than others. An extremely detailed topographical map with every geological feature, for example, can be more confusing than useful. The hiking party may prefer a simpler map with a clearly marked route. The same holds true for scientific information in the policy process.

Solving the information problem requires a unified study of causes and effects to provide clear, useful information. In the Netherlands, the government achieved this by commissioning its National Institute for Health and Environment (RIVM) to prepare a comprehensive study. *Concern for Tomorrow* began by examining environmental quality, but differed from other studies in three important ways. First, it was a truly *comprehensive* study: the Dutch scientific community worked together to examine environmental problems and their interrelationships. The broad scientific consensus behind *Concern for Tomorrow* closed off the opportunity to challenge its findings with junk science. Second, *Concern for Tomorrow* made an effort to trace environmental effects back to their causes and actually quantified the pollution reductions that would be needed. Third, the study took a long-term (25-year) perspective, which allowed sufficient time for making the considerable systemic changes that are necessary.

Clear information in hiking :
Using a good map and compass

Clear information in cooperative environmental management :
Comprehensive cause-effect analysis

Recognizing policy as process, with many roles
Comprehensive environmental solutions will not be devised by one person sitting behind a desk in a government bureaucracy. Nor is public policy like a computer which takes in data at one end and feeds out logical measures at the other. Instead, policy is a human process among people representing different interests in government, business, the press, the scientific community and societal groups. To succeed, the process requires guidance and communication.

There is no single leadership role in the policy process. This is clear when we return to the example of a group hiking trip. One person should not do everything; different people must take the lead in fulfilling different functions. Someone has the original idea to go on a hike. Someone has to get a group of people together and see that they are kept informed about plans. Someone also facilitates logistics, such as dividing baggage to be carried or finding a safe place to cross a stream. It would be unusual for one person to perform all these functions on a group hike, and it is impossible in policy making.

In the Netherlands, for example, the Queen and Prime Minister played the role of *sponsor* by stressing the importance of developing an environmental plan. RIVM acted as an *informer* by presenting objective scientific information on which to base the plan. The Director General of the Environment Department acted as a *process manager* by convening negotiations, and I often served as *driving force* by pushing the discussions toward concrete conclusions. There are several other roles in the policy process, and many other people who played them, which I will describe in later chapters.

Recognizing roles in hiking :
Everyone has duties

Recognizing roles in cooperative environmental management :
Parties have different functions

Framing the policy debate

If you begin a discussion by treating someone like your enemy, that person will become your enemy, and you are unlikely to resolve your differences. If you treat the other person as a potential ally, you may be able to negotiate an acceptable solution. Regardless of the differences among parties, there are almost always some areas on which they agree, and these should be the starting point for discussion. In hiking, the first step in framing discussions is to recognize what everyone has in common. Presumably they like the outdoors and exercise, and they don't mind being a little hot, cold or wet. That doesn't mean they all have the same goals or reasons for wanting to hike, but at least they can respect and understand each other's concerns.

Each party has certain priorities which cannot be compromised, and these must be recognized in framing a policy discussion. The priority of business, for example, is to make money. A company can compromise on many issues, but it will never accept a scenario which substantially affects its bottom line. The primary concern for government officials is to preserve their legal and administrative authority. They may agree to share responsibilities with other sectors of society, but they will never accept a scenario which cedes their power to others. Environmental NGOs will never accept a situation which threatens the integrity of natural systems, or their integrity as independent, critical voices in society.

A major problem with the adversarial approach is that it assumes the parties' priorities are always at stake. If the environmentalists 'win', a company will go bankrupt. If a company 'wins', the environment will be poisoned. These are possible results if policy is approached as a zero-sum game; but there are other possibilities. In hiking, for example, two people can have different reasons for being on the trail but still agree on a route that meets both their needs. If someone wants a lot of exercise and someone else wants to take pictures, they can choose a route which is both rigorous and scenic. Each may give a little, but they should be able to agree on objectives for the hike that satisfy their priorities.

But why compromise at all when setting objectives? In the early days of the adversarial approach, compromise was not very popular. Environmental issues were win–lose propositions, and all the parties thought they could win. After decades of stalemate, however, business and government have begun to see that neither is likely to win a decisive victory, and both are more amenable to making a deal which satisfies their basic concerns.

NGOs are less likely to make deals, since their primary mission is to act as independent critics of business and government. I don't think that cooperative environmental management requires a full buy-in by the NGOs. Perhaps it is best for them not to compromise, but to remain as strong critics, thus driving the public discussion of environmental issues and checking the integrity of other parties.

In the Netherlands, the basis for deal making between government and business was the new concept of 'sustainable development'. The term was coined in 1987 by the report of the World Commission on Environment and Development, which is generally named for its chairperson, Ms Gro Harlem Brundtland, Prime Minister of Norway.* The Brundtland Report said that the goal of both environmental and economic policies should be *sustainable* development, which 'meets the needs of the present generation without compromising the ability of future generations to meet their own needs'.[3]

Interpreting this definition can be difficult, since the present generation does not know how future ones will structure their societies and cannot, thus, determine what future needs will be. Rather than arguing endlessly on this hypothetical point, we in the Netherlands came to a simple conclusion: since we do not know the needs of future generations, we must leave all options open to them. This means that the current generation cannot pass any environmental problems on to the next. Every generation must clean up its own mess.

This concept has helped unify both economic and environmental concerns by introducing the element of time. On one hand, this generation has to clean up its act, so it cannot postpone action indefinitely. On the other hand, a generation (which we defined as a 25-year period) allows the formulation of long-term policies. We no longer had to insist, for example, that business make sweeping changes *immediately*. We were able to set long-term (25-year) goals which were far more ambitious than those we had required before, yet these were more acceptable to business. Companies finally had a clear picture of their long-term responsibilities and a

* In July 1998 Ms Brundtland became Director General of the World Health Organization (WHO).

reasonable amount of time to incorporate the necessary measures into their overall business strategies. The time element was the basis for a deal between government and the private sector on environmental policy.

Framing the hiking process:
Something for everyone's interest

Framing in cooperative environmental management :
Find a deal that respects the parties' interests

Long-term continuity
Once the hikers have agreed on the route, they expect it to be followed as closely as possible. They should recognize, however, that unexpected events will come up: the weather may change, a fallen tree or washed out section of trail may force a detour. Barring catastrophe, however, they expect that the hike will proceed more or less as everyone has agreed.

Those in the policy process also require continuity. Government, in setting long-term environmental goals, must stick to them. Businesses will insist that sweeping new demands are not made, while environmentalists will insist that objectives are not watered down. Business, for its part, must provide the same continuity it demands from government.* Once they have agreed to targets, companies are bound to meet them. At the same time, everyone must recognize the inherent uncertainty of long-term policies and the legitimate reasons for reopening negotiations. On one hand, scientists may discover substantial new environmental threats which were not known when the long-term agreements were set. Technological hurdles, on the other hand, may require that some interim targets for business be adjusted.

Preparing an environmental plan on paper is fairly easy; the real work comes in implementing it. In the Netherlands, for example, it required lengthy discussions with the private sector to set concrete goals that were aggressive enough to fulfil government objectives but flexible enough to accommodate inherent uncertainties and unexpected difficulties. Appropriate, realistic goal setting is essential to the continuity of policies, since measures which are either too lenient or too strict will eventually cause a breakdown of the process.

Continuity is strengthened by building trust among the parties, an assurance that everyone is negotiating in good faith. The personal factor is quite important here. In the final stages of agreements in the Netherlands,

---

* Continuity is most difficult for governments, perhaps, because they are subject to frequent changes of leadership and ideology through the electoral process.

top officials, such as environment ministers and corporate chief executive officers, were involved personally in negotiations. A handshake and a promise are not, in themselves, a basis for making policy, but they go a long way towards instilling confidence on both sides.

Ten years after approval of the first National Environmental Policy Plan, I believe we have established some continuity in policy. As we were completing the NEPP, many other countries were also developing their own national sustainable development strategies. The NEPP, however, is the only one of these plans which has been maintained and updated. NEPP 2 was approved in 1994, NEPP 3 in 1998. In addition, many other reports and plans are produced on a yearly basis to reinforce the development of consistent long-term policies.

Long-term continuity in hiking :
Regular targets, evaluations

Long-term continuity in cooperative environmental management :
Step-wise approach and feedback

Broader Applications

As I have said, cooperative environmental management is more than a theoretical model. Theories have emerged from looking back at what happened and drawing lessons from it. The first part of this book recounts developments in the Netherlands through a series of narrative chapters. It also includes a series of 'interchapters' which describe the five elements of cooperative environmental management in greater detail, partly through examples from the Dutch case study.

The second part specifically addresses the international context of cooperative environmental management. While developing new policies in the Netherlands, my colleagues and I learned of similar efforts in other countries. This led to a considerable exchange of ideas with individuals and institutions around the world. In some cases, the Dutch have incorporated ideas from other countries. In other cases, countries have borrowed ideas from the Dutch. In the last four chapters, I recount some of the exchanges which have already occurred and analyze current and possible future developments toward cooperative environmental management around the world.

Notes

1   Organization for Economic Cooperation and Development (OECD), *Environmental Performance Review: the Netherlands* (Paris: OECD, 1995), 111.
2   David R. Brower and Steve Chapple, *Let the Mountains Talk, Let the Rivers Run* (New York: Harper Collins West, 1995), 19.
3   World Commission on Environment and Development, *Our Common Future* (Oxford: Oxford University Press, 1987), 43.

First Steps
The Beginning of Environmental Awareness

The Dutch Environment

I grew up a short walk from the North Sea, on a coastline of sand dunes at the edge of The Hague. I learned to appreciate nature when I was very young; I also learned it was in danger. Each stroll on the beach, for example, ended with cleaning oil off my shoes. And the sky was often clouded by heavy smog from the industries at the port of Rotterdam, twenty kilometres to the south.

I speak of 'nature', but that is a curious topic in the Netherlands, where so little is still natural. About half the country, the western and most populous part, is one to three metres below sea level. Originally, this was a vast region of wetlands, something like the Florida Everglades. The only 'land' was a scattering of sand bars which people first settled in the time of the Romans. By the late Middle Ages, space on the sand bars was running out, and the inhabitants expanded their settlements by building dikes to hold back the waters, eventually establishing the *polders* of 'reclaimed' land. To keep the land dry, the Dutch built drainage canals to collect run-off water, which they then pumped into the surrounding rivers and marshes. That was the purpose of many of our old windmills. A few of them, in fact, are still moving water; although these days that task is performed mainly by electric pumps. If the power were cut off, the waters would slowly come back, and half of the Netherlands would revert to marshland.

This peculiar and ever precarious situation was a major force in shaping Dutch culture. We never had a great 'frontier', like the American West or the Argentine Pampas, with vast open spaces settled by rugged individualists. From the beginning, the Dutch had to cooperate to scrape together even a tiny bit of land on which to live. Despite the shortage of land, however, there are plenty of people. The Netherlands has the second highest population density in the world, trailing only Bangladesh. The 15.3 million people now squeezed into our small country have no choice but to find ways of working together amicably.[1]

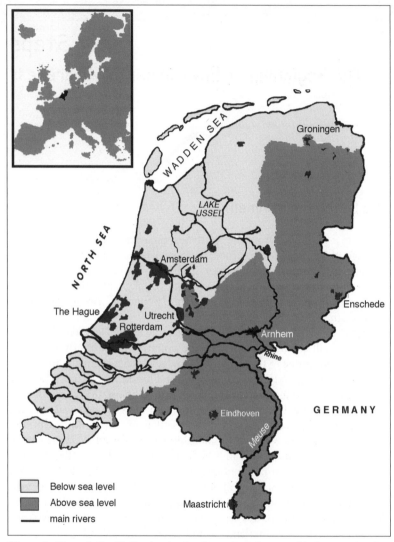

Figure 1 Map of the Netherlands showing areas above and below sea level
Source: Netherlands Ministry of Foreign Affairs.

This tradition of cooperation is now called the '*polder* model', and it explains many of our governmental and societal structures. Managing the *polders*, for example, was the task of our oldest governing bodies, the water boards (*waterschappen*). Since the Middle Ages, they have been charged with maintaining the dikes, levees and canals that hold back the sea. In the past few years, the water boards have also taken on some responsibility for managing water quality. A more recent example of the *polder* model is the

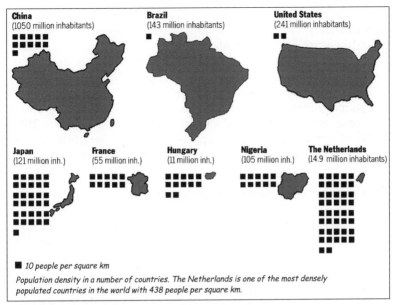

Figure 2 Population density in the Netherlands compared with other countries
Source: Netherlands Ministry of Foreign Affairs.

cooperative approach used to resolve many of our social and economic problems in the 1970s and 1980s. This approach, considered a key to the Netherlands' economic success in the 1990s, is attracting visitors from around the world, a phenomenon dubbed '*polder* tourism' in a 1997 Dutch newspaper article:

> In the past few months, an army of journalists, politicians, union leaders, policy makers, and academics have visited the Netherlands because of their keen interest in the *polder* model. They have labelled it the Dutch model, *le Miracle Hollandaise*, the *poldermodello*, or the third way.[2]

The Dutch know that working together is essential to the welfare of their country. Many societies, especially those of the great frontier nations, have not needed such close cooperation in the past; but times are changing. An ever-growing population, a spiralling global economy and modern systems of transportation and communication mean that no place is isolated anymore. The rise of not only regional but global environmental problems also means that people will have to pool their resources to find global solutions.

The Dutch also have a strong tradition of managing the environment, in the most literal sense. There is scarcely a part of the Netherlands which is still *natural*. Even the sand dunes where I grew up are largely artificial. Many of them are covered with forests planted by entrepreneurs in the last century as a source of timber. People now consider these forests to be a 'natural' environment, which they work to protect. The IJsselmeer is a vast fresh-water lake northeast of Amsterdam which is now an important wildlife habitat. Until 1932, however, it was a salt-water bay called the Zuyder Zee. To control flooding, the government built a huge dike which cuts this bay off from the open sea.

I am not advocating that others should 'follow our good example' in 'preserving nature'; but we can all learn from the experiences of others. These may be of most value to large metropolitan areas which seek to preserve or recreate pockets of nature amidst densely developed urban settings.

Growing Environmental Awareness

By the 1960s it was becoming clear in the Netherlands, as in many other countries, that if indeed we had created a peace with nature, it was breaking down. My own motivation as an environmentalist began after entering senior high school in 1962, where I was fortunate to encounter teachers who taught us about the latest developments in ecology. My fellow students and I were told, for example, about Rachel Carson's *Silent Spring* (published in 1962), which explored the vulnerability of wildlife, and possibly humans, to synthetic chemicals. We also learned about the possible negative impacts of the Green Revolution in mechanized, chemical-intensive agriculture. We discussed the dangers of nuclear power, the loss of biodiversity, and the energy shortage we might face in the future.

I remember reading *The Earth Will Pay: The Spectre of Overpopulation and Famine*, a book about resource scarcity published as early as 1948. Indeed, all the environmental arguments had been voiced long before the first wave of awareness reached the general public in the early 1970s. Language from *The Earth Will Pay*, for example, sounds quite contemporary, except that today's environmental statistics are far more dramatic:

> The earth is home to over *two billion* people. The poor old planet must provide all that these ever-demanding people require for their nourishment and comfort on the weathered crust of the earth. How long can this continue? The world's population has doubled in just a century. Millions of people have been living for years on the edge of starvation. Great quantities of non-renewable industrial resources are running out.[3]

Despite what some diplomats may say about facing new challenges, many of the issues raised at Rio have been known at least since the 1960s. In fact, I studied them in high school. Saying that 'we didn't know' or that 'reliable information was not available' is not an acceptable excuse for shirking our environmental responsibilities.

In 1967 I began my studies in biology at the State University of Leyden, about fifteen kilometres north of The Hague. When I arrived, I was surprised to find that most of my professors and fellow students did not have the appreciation of environmental issues that I had developed in high school. It seemed few of them realized that developments taking place in the world could destroy the very species and systems we were studying. The curriculum in the first years bore no relation to the environmental problems which were becoming more and more visible, such as the extension of industrial developments into natural habitats.

The situation began to change around 1970, and in the vanguard was a small group headed by Professor Donald Kuenen who taught in the Zoology Department and was also Director of the State Institute for Nature Management. Another member of the group was Wim ter Keurs, who became the supervisor of my research on how agricultural developments affect plant and animal populations. The group organized seminars on environmental problems and did studies of harmful developments (urban sprawl, freeway construction, water extraction from the dunes) in the region around The Hague and Leyden. In a 1973 seminar, I found myself involved in my first academic discussion of political and economic strategies to overcome environmental problems.

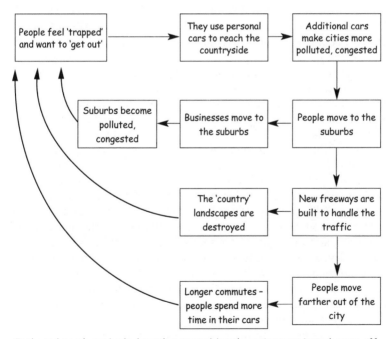

In the end, people are back where they started, but the environment is much worse off.

Figure 3 The vicious circle of the motor car

These changes at the university corresponded to important events in the broader society. It was becoming clear by this time that economic growth was threatening the very quality of life it was supposed to be improving. One powerful example was the role of private motor cars, which were used increasingly to explore the 'natural' landscapes of the Netherlands. People came to realize that the ongoing construction of freeways, for example, would destroy the very nature they wanted to visit. A number of such developments were planned nearby, including a freeway that would have cut through the dunes to create a faster link between The Hague and Leyden. Many of these freeways were stopped, thanks in part to the activism of students and staff from the University of Leyden. The dunes next to The Hague, for example, are now a park protected from future urban development. They were saved because people's concerns over the *effects* of road building prompted them to address the *causes* by entering the political debate.

Different Levels of Action

An important discussion of the early 1970s – and since – has been about the level at which the environmental sciences should focus, with action on a global scale and action on a local scale as the two extremes. One view in the Leyden group said environmental problems were so fundamental and widespread that solutions could only be found on a global scale. An important trigger for this view was the 1972 report *The Limits to Growth*, prepared by Jay Forrester and Dennis Meadows for a coalition of scientists and industrialists called the Club of Rome. This 'club', originally convened in 1968 by the Italian industrialist Aurelio Peccei and the Scottish scientist Alexander King, included prominent thinkers who were concerned about the impacts of continuing economic growth on the environment, specifically on the availability of natural resources. *The Limits to Growth* was fairly pessimistic, implying that the depletion of natural resources would limit the world economy. The report failed to consider innovative ways to overcome resource scarcity, such as greater efficiency or the substitution of renewable and more plentiful resources for those which were especially scarce. Nevertheless, the report was an important first step in considering the relationship between the environment and the economy.* The global view was also given a boost in 1972 by the United Nations Conference on the Human Environment in Stockholm, the forerunner to the UNCED conference in Rio de Janeiro twenty years later.

The opposing view in the seminar held that all positive and negative changes to the environment were ultimately changes on a local scale. People

* The Club of Rome still exists, though its high point of influence was certainly in the early 1970s.

were affected, for example, by freeway construction, noise, or industrial hazards. Pollution was also seen as having its first impact on society at the local level. So, it was argued, the motivation to change harmful activities would be greater here than at higher levels of the scale.* The actions against freeway construction in The Hague area, for example, showed that local motivation could indeed be a powerful force to influence decisions.

While both perspectives are valuable, working at the local scale gave a clearer picture of the contrast between environmental and socio-economic well-being, and it helped us to envision some balance between them. The case of urban sprawl, for example, would not lead to an abstract contrast like 'nature versus housing' on the local level. Rather, it led to more concrete considerations, such as 'building more densely in the cities' versus 'building in the suburbs'. This local approach helped us to bridge the contrasts between environmental and economic perspectives, by examining real situations rather than abstract theories.

I think a widespread 'environmental' consciousness began with concern about local activities. This is a very natural process, since people are first motivated by developments in their neighbourhoods. Each person has a certain level, or threshhold, beyond which he or she can no longer tolerate environmental degradation. For one person, this might be the removal of a familiar old tree because the road is being widened. Another might be concerned that the drinking water is no longer safe. Many people reached such thresholds in the late 1960s and early 1970s. Naturally, most of them were motivated by particular *single issues* rather than by an overall sense of 'the environment', and this would shape the structure of environmental policy for years to come.

Whatever individual motivations people have, everyone goes through a similar cycle in reaching a personal threshold for action. First comes *awareness* of environmental effects, which may result from problems becoming more obvious (like the smog drifting up from Rotterdam) or from better education on environmental issues. Most likely, it is a combination of both. Next, of course, comes *anger* at the situation which people see as threatening their health or well-being. This anger eventually coalesces into the *motivation* to 'do something' about the problem; people begin studying issues and talking with others about what they can do. Finally comes *action* aimed (one hopes) at the causes of environmental problems. People join protests, sign petitions, boycott companies, or make personal commitments to change their lifestyles and 'tread lightly' on the Earth.

Relating causes and effects was considerably harder at the national level, as I saw in 1974 during the construction of a dam in Oosterschelde, an estuary in the southwestern Netherlands. Environmentalists argued that

---

* This argument often surfaces today in discussions about global warming. Although it may be a potentially devastating phenomenon people will not see or feel the effects of global warming for some time. Thus, it is not a major public concern.

just improving the existing dikes would be sufficient to prevent the risk of flooding (which was probably true). The Ministry of Transport and Waterworks, however, insisted that a dam was necessary. After an intense debate, it was decided to build a dam with gates that normally would be left open to preserve the flow of salt water into the estuary. In case of a storm surge, however, the gates could be closed. Here was a *compromise* aimed at mitigating environmental effects (on the region's salt-water ecology), but no real *consensus* on causes (the need to build a dam in the first place). The proponents of the dam pointed to the high cost of the compromise, essentially saying that the money spent showed they were doing enough for the environment. There was no discussion, however, of what 'enough' really was, or how economic causes led to environmental effects.

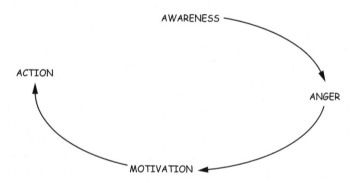

Figure 4 Reaching a personal threshold

Segregating Effects

In the Netherlands, many political disputes on the environment were framed by the procedural regulations of *ruimtelijke ordening*, which can be translated as 'land use planning,' or perhaps 'zoning'. It should not be surprising that the concept of land use planning has been so influential in a country which was literally *created* by such measures. The result for the environment, however, was that we dealt mostly with the effects from harmful activities, without addressing their causes.

The most coherent force shaping environmental policy for many years was the Land Use Planning Act (Wet op de Ruimtelijke Ordening) of 1965. Certainly the Act has been very useful in some areas, such as controlling urban sprawl. In the post-war economic boom, major cities such as Rotterdam, Amsterdam and The Hague were expanding rapidly. Many feared that the cities would spread into each other, creating a Dutch version of Los

Angeles. The solution offered by land use planning was the creation of the *Randstad*, or ring of cities around the centre of the country. Development has been focused on the periphery of the ring, while its centre is preserved as the 'green heart' of the Netherlands.

Along with its successes, however, the Land Use Planning Act has also obscured the relationship between environmental causes and effects. In the framework of *ecological mapping*, for example, ecologists were asked to value the natural elements in rural areas so that planners could minimize negative impacts by choosing to give up the least valuable elements. This system assumed we should, and could, just give up the natural values of one area without affecting others. When considering a 'nature area' and a factory, for example, the land use planning solution would be to keep the natural area far enough away from the factory so that it would not be polluted. By doing this, planners assume all pollution is local, and 'give up' any natural values in the box where the factory is located.

Another flawed assumption is that planners and ecologists cannot directly influence the activities which cause environmental damage. They can segregate harmful activities, but *the way those activities are performed* (such as the level of emissions) is taken for granted. Land use planning accepts, for example, that a factory will continue to pollute as it always has, instead of asking whether that pollution itself can be eliminated.

The Leyden Approach

The Leyden University group took a very different approach. Our examination of concrete local problems led to the view that continued current developments should not be taken for granted. Furthermore, restrictions on certain activities should be seen not as limits, *per se,* but as stimuli for finding creative, alternative ways to meet societal needs. Thus, we shifted our attention from (helplessly) observing environmental threats towards re-examining the activities that cause them.

Analyzing causes, instead of effects alone, led to interdisciplinary work among biologists, economists, urban planners and many other professionals. Had we restricted ourselves to one discipline, such as biology, we would have limited our ability to understand and influence the complex processes causing environmental damage. Many other scientists are more comfortable staying within their specialism, which is understandable. As experts in their fields, they are in positions of strength. It would be hard for outsiders to argue with an expert on the facts of his or her special field. Outsiders can choose, however, simply to ignore the experts. Scientists may feel they are in a strong position by sticking with what they know. But they will be ineffective if they don't make the effort to see that their work has relevance in the 'real world'.

In contrast, the Leyden group may have appeared to be in a position of weakness at first. We ventured from the safety of our specialisms into the wider world of examining and proposing alternative policy options.* Giving up the position of 'strength', however, allowed the Leyden group to explore many new approaches to environmental issues. In gathering new information, we had to talk to all kinds of people, even to those who might have been considered 'the enemy', such as developers or government officials. We started to appreciate their perspectives and understand their motivations. We learned that discussions about development need not come down to yes/no decisions. It was possible to find creative solutions which satisfied differing concerns.

I am not talking about a 'compromise' merely, which often means that everyone gives up something. Instead, we discovered the possibility of building *joint visions* that everyone can support. Take the example of a housing development. The typical debate would be between developers (and growing families), who want more housing, and environmentalists, who want to preserve open space for habitats. A compromise might be a stand-off, in which the development is halted at the half-way point. A joint vision, in contrast, might not simply influence *how many* houses are built, but the *way* in which they are built. For example, denser urban development, with more houses per hectare, would preserve at least as much land as the stalemate option; but it could also provide higher quality housing. Furthermore, by working together, environmentalists and developers might be able to change the design of developed areas, so that even they could provide species habitats.

Our position of 'weakness' at Leyden turned out to be much stronger than one might have thought. My fellow student, Paul Mantel, discovered this 'strength' when he was asked to look at urbanization in the western Netherlands. There had been large-scale plans for suburban growth at the time, while the inner cities were deteriorating. Paul teamed up with Wim ter Keurs to examine transportation plans in the area around The Hague. Two new roads were dropped from the provincial building plans simply because they had asked 'Why?' and '*Why not alternatives*, like public transportation and bicycle paths?'

The Development of Environmental Concern

I now realize my good fortune in being exposed to thinking on the environment that was quite ahead of its time, although it sometimes led to

---

* When I was a student, for example, there were no official provisions for interdisciplinary work; and it was difficult for Wim ter Keurs and I to get approval for my study on the environmental impacts of agriculture. In defending my masters thesis, I had to drop any mention of my economic research and pretend it had simply been a traditional biological study.

frustration and confusion. As I've said, I had an excellent introduction to environmental issues in high school, and was surprised to find that what I had learned did not seem to have made much impact on the curriculum at the University of Leyden. The University eventually discovered this new perspective, however, and ended up being ahead of its time on environmental issues.

I was equally surprised when I left Leyden and was exposed to the attitudes prevailing in government. In the Department of Land Use Planning I continued to consider the question of nature conservation and agricultural development. I was hindered, however, by the prevailing view that these problems could only be dealt with by segregating activities through zoning. I felt we had developed a much more sophisticated view of such issues at Leyden.

The most important lessons from Leyden were about the development of environmental concern. In the beginning, people naturally focus on effects, often in the form of individual, local problems. In looking for solutions, however, people must ultimately trace these effects back to their fundamental political, social, and economic causes. This requires a leap of logic, and a leap of faith. Fortunately, I soon met people in government who were ready to take this leap.

A hiking trip often starts when friends get together and make plans for their holidays. My education in high school and university was like sitting around a warm fire with friends while thinking ahead to the trip we would make. We had no more than a rough idea based on rough information, but we knew there would be no plane or car to take us there. We would have to walk towards a goal – one which we now call sustainable development – and we knew we would walk together.

Notes

1 Organization for Economic Cooperation and Development, *Environmental Performance Review: the Netherlands* (Paris: OECD, 1995), 21.
2 Edith Schoots, 'Poldermodel trekt veel bekijks', *NRC Handelsblad*, 25 July 1997.
3 Egbert de Vries, *De Aarde Betaalt: Het Spook der Overbevolking en Hongersnood* (The Hague: Albani Press, 1951).

CHAPTER 2

A True Sport
Building a Strong Institution

Some people may find it odd to describe hiking as a sport or hobby. It's just walking, they may reply. Everyone does that. Those who take hiking seriously, however, know it's more than 'just walking'. To be effective, a hiker must have the right equipment – good boots, a backpack, tent, compass, and so on. He or she must also train to build up endurance and skills. Above all, the hiker must think about hiking: what it will mean in terms of skills, equipment, pitfalls and roles.

Our first experience with policy making in the Netherlands was like that of a new hiker. In the beginning, people didn't see much need for a separate environmental authority in the government. 'Environmental' issues were handled routinely, just like walking, by various departments through such instruments as zoning or nuisance law. Managing the environment was not seen as a separate 'sport' in its own right, but as an add-on to other government work, or even a short-lived fad. I remember a conversation I had in 1977 with the Director General of the Department for Land Use Planning. When I told him I was working in the directorate's study group on environmental protection, he said, 'Oh, you're going to work on the environment. I suspect that's just the current hot topic, but it will probably go away in due course. If I were you, I would focus on water recreation instead.'

Today, most people realize that 'managing the environment' is far more than an add-on responsibility or a fad. In the early years, however, a lot of work was needed simply to define our responsibilities and establish our role in government policy. As one comes to realize that hiking is more than just walking, we came to realize that environmental policy was more than just responding to individual crises on an *ad hoc* basis. Like the hiker, we had to collect the equipment and learn the skills needed for a long haul. In our case, this meant building up a strong, efficient environmental institution within the government.

The *Ad Hoc* Phase of Environmental Policy

The first Dutch Environment Department* was established by the government of Prime Minister Biesheuvel in the autumn of 1971. It was combined with the more prominent Department of Health to form the new Ministry of Health and Environmental Hygiene. The Department's first Director General,† Willem Reij, attracted very talented people and built a top-notch team of scientific specialists. Within a short time, the Department had a strong reputation for scientific and technical competence, not only within government, but also in the private sector.

The Department had many policies oriented to specific problems, but no overall policy vision. This was probably inevitable, since the early 1970s marked the *ad hoc* phase of environmental policy. New problems seemed to 'pop up' constantly, and the public demanded a quick response to each one. This led to a fragmented, issue-by-issue approach. The only overall vision was that environmental policy meant 'better scientific work' or 'knowing more than polluters'.

The first major product of the *ad hoc* phase was the 1972 *Urgentienota*, generally called the *Memorandum on Urgent Environmental Issues* in English. A *nota* is more than a mere memorandum, however; it is a specific policy proposal which is submitted to Parliament and subject to the same debate and approval as an item of legislation. Being a product of its times, the *Urgentienota* was largely an enumeration of individual problems and scientific fields based on environmental sectors. It called for the development of legislation on specific environmental media, such as air, water, and soil, and specific issues, such as noise pollution or radiation hazards.

Somewhat later, another important environmental *nota* actually came from the Ministry of Economic Affairs. The Minister at the time, Ruud Lubbers, had rather progressive views on integrating environmental and economic concerns, which he described in a 1976 *nota* on 'Selective Economic Growth'.†† This *nota* could have been an opportunity to begin reconciling environmental and economic policies; but a culture of conflict between the two policy spheres prevented such a dialogue at the time.

---

* The Netherlands has never had a specific ministry for the environment, but rather a *Directoraat Generaal,* or Department, housed within a more general ministry. With little regard for the confusion this causes, this directorate general has been divided into individual directorates which are responsible for more specialized aspects of policy. The *Directoraat Generaal* for the Environment, for example, has individual directorates for issues such as air and water pollution, among others. To limit the confusion, I   generally use the term 'department' when referring to the directorate general.

† This person is generally the senior civil servant in a department, second in authority to ministers or deputy ministers, who are political appointees.

†† Ministry of Economic Affairs, *Nota Selectieve Economische Groei* (Den Haag, 1976).

Strategic Thinkers

Willem Reij gave his staff a great deal of freedom to experiment with new ideas. Set many people to work on many things, he reasoned, and something good was bound to come of it. One innovative thinker in the Department was Jos Staatsen, who previously had been a council member in the northern city of Groningen. In 1975, Reij invited Staatsen to join the department and carve out an area of work best suited to his skills and interests. Giving Jos Staatsen this freedom to experiment was a good idea, because he had a lot to contribute, especially managerial skills and a good understanding of politics. Staatsen laid the groundwork for a strategic policy approach by helping to establish a new directorate for general policy affairs.

Meanwhile, a cadre of innovative thinkers was coming together in the directorate for noise pollution. The group was headed by Marius Enthoven, an aeronautical engineer, and also included Frans Evers and Ruud van Noort. None of them were experts in noise pollution, but they were all talented in managing complex programmes. The team members developed some of the strictest and most detailed legislation on noise pollution in the world; and their ideas helped shape the noise policies of the European Commission. Perhaps the legislation they developed was too strict, as often happens when people are trying to establish the authority of a new government department.

Bestuurszaken

I began my government career in 1977 at the Directorate for Land Use Planning; but I soon realized that zoning could not be the best instrument for handling environmental problems. Essentially, zoning is a way to separate activities and land uses which don't seem to fit together, such as residential areas and industrial developments. In so doing, the incentive to ameliorate harmful activities like pollution is taken away. It was hard to introduce new ideas like mixing agriculture and nature protection in this directorate, which was already a well-established institution, resistant to ideas that would complicate its world view.

I transferred to the Environment Department in 1980 and was assigned to the new directorate for general policy development. I began the same day as a young economist named Robert Donkers, and we were both introduced to the head of the directorate, Frans Evers. After shaking hands with both of us, Frans said, 'So, you guys are here to get your careers off the ground, right?' As a child of the 1960s and 1970s, the word 'career' rang very strangely in my ears. I guess I started thinking more about it, however, because I bought my first suit the next week.

The new directorate included a mix of policy makers concerned with such diverse issues as environmental impact assessment, nuisance law, risk assessment and financial instruments. The directorate was called *Bestuurs-zaken*, which translates as General Policy Development, although it is more than that. The Dutch word *besturen* means to guide or govern, and this was an important concept for the Department. The idea was that other parties in society should be responsible for protecting the environment, and that the government should guide them in doing this job. It required thinking about the other hikers who could, and should, join the journey.

So, after some time in the initial, *ad hoc* phase of policy development, we started thinking about how to manage environmental policy better and work more efficiently. Someone like Jos Staatsen, for example, was brought into the Department largely for his experience with *besturen* when he'd held elected office. 'Every new environmental policy starts to attack the individual symptoms of problems, instead of their root causes,' explains Frans Evers. 'So you have specialists in their fields, but no policy experts.'[1] Without such experts, the Department could not set goals and articulate its policies to those who would have to implement them: other government departments, businesses and the local governments.

We began by experimenting with any ideas that looked promising. One was to develop a procedure for environmental impact assessment (EIA). Today EIAs are quite common in many countries and are frequently done before any major development project. In the early 1980s, however, few countries were using them: we had to look abroad for guidance. The three countries we studied were the United States and Canada, where EIAs were required by law, and Britain, where they were routinely performed, although there was no legal mandate.

Looking back, I can recognize EIA as a first step in developing a logical, standardized framework for decision making. Before this, there would be many opinions about a new development, such as a factory expansion. The opinions were often supported by different studies – using different methodologies to determine how harmful, or not harmful, the development would be. The question was always, what study (or opinion) is right? The answer, then, was to block or promote developments in a 'yes/no' political debate.

Without a standard system to weigh the information and compare different impacts, decisions about future developments were largely guided by emotions and the relative political influence of the different sides in a dispute. The challenge of EIA was to promote a political debate about alternatives (and not only zoning alternatives), consider their impacts on environment and society, and frame a regulatory deal. The work certainly had intellectual benefits for a newcomer in the field.

Another benefit of the EIA work was the opportunity to collaborate with our colleagues in the US, Canada, and Britain. We considered the

HOW TO DEAL WITH UNCERTAINTIES

1　Examine each uncertainty to determine its importance to the decision at hand, as well as your ability to reduce this uncertainty. Some of this may only be guesswork.

2　Decide whether it is worthwhile to work at reducing this uncertainty, or whether it is safe to take your assumptions for granted. If the latter is true, you may make immediate decisions based on your explicit assumptions.

3　If you choose to reduce an uncertainty, you will have to conduct some type of research. Before beginning this research, try to anticipate the different outcomes you may expect, and how these will influence your decisions. (If they won't have much influence, perhaps you don't need to do the research!)

4　Decide on future actions to be taken, based on the outcomes of your research. The research should lead to an explicit decision about policy actions.

5　Anticipate what may happen if your assumptions – or your research results – prove to be false. Develop contingency plans for such situations.

Americans, for example, to be ahead of us in their environmental policies; and we borrowed many ideas from them that later influenced the Dutch approach. This collaborative work also prompted us to play a larger international role in environmental policy. Frans Evers, for example, advocated translating many of our documents into foreign languages, such as English.* Today, the Netherlands publishes full-text translations in several languages for most environmental laws, policy plans and reports. This allows us to have more international influence and to conduct discussions with other countries on a much higher level than would have been possible otherwise.

Environmental impact assessments proved valuable as tools for reducing uncertainty in decision making. We further explored this issue in a 1981 seminar with Allen Hickling, a consultant from the Tavistock Institute for Urban Planning in Britain. Allen's main point was that uncertainties are often denied or avoided by decision makers who want a speedy resolution to a situation. The problems presented by uncertainties are bound to surface in the future, however, at which time they may be even more difficult to

---

* Frans had a special affinity for English because he had worked previously as a flight attendant on KLM's service to the United States.

resolve. It is much better, Hickling explained, to face uncertainty head-on at the beginning of the decision-making process.

Allen listed three types of uncertainties: those about cause and effect (essentially scientific uncertainty), those about values (essentially differences of opinion), and those about the side effects of one decision on other decisions. In many cases, people deny the uncertainties about values, instead labelling them as uncertainties of cause and effect. Thus each side in an argument conducts scientific studies to prove it is right. These studies cannot arrive at the objective truth, however, because they are designed from the start to support a particular opinion. In the seminar, Allen presented a few simple steps to manage all three uncertainties (see opposite page).

Taking these steps results in a 'commitment package' of immediate actions, areas for research, actions to be taken on the basis of this research, and contingency plans. The value of this system was to link science to other research in environmental policy making. Science should be part of a properly managed policy-making process, not a means to justify political decisions which have already been made (I will discuss the commitment package at length in Interchapter 2).

The New Ministry

While our work on EIA, uncertainty and other issues was proceeding, major changes were taking place in the Dutch and international political scene. There was a renewed focus on free market ideologies, which we felt were opposed to the common values of social welfare and environmental protection. At first, we saw these changes as a great landslide which threatened to block our way or even sweep us off the trail. In the end, however, I think the political developments put us on a better path.

The Dutch elections of 1982 brought in a rightist government of the Christian Democrats, led by Prime Minister Ruud Lubbers (the former Minister of Economic Affairs), and the pro-business Liberal Party.* Lubbers's victory coincided with the rise of other conservative leaders around the world, such as Margaret Thatcher in Britain, Ronald Reagan in the United States and Helmut Kohl in Germany. A common theme of their governments was a 'no-nonsense' approach which called for deregulation, scaling-back government spending, privatization and other market reforms. These changes were not met kindly by those concerned about the environment; and we certainly had our worries. In the end, however, we were able

---

* In the European sense, 'liberal' refers to a party which strongly supports a free market economy (which was considered a *liberal* economic policy when the term was coined). In modern social and fiscal policies, however, a 'liberal' party is actually quite conservative.

to harness the momentum of these reforms to produce more effective policies, thanks largely to insightful political leaders.

One of these leaders was Pieter Winsemius, although we did not recognize him as such at first. Winsemius clearly came from the business world, which many of us still considered to be the undeniable 'enemy' of the environment. Pieter's father, the Director General for Industry in the late 1940s, was instrumental in directing the Netherlands' tremendous post-war industrialization and economic growth.* The young Winsemius earned a PhD in physics from the University of Leyden and then a Masters degree in business administration (MBA) from Stanford University. After Stanford, he became a partner in the European branch of McKinsey and Company, one of the world's most respected business consulting firms.

In the summer of 1982, Winsemius was asked to a give a speech on deregulation and the environment to the Netherlands Federation of Industry (VNO), the largest and most influential employers' association at the time.† He agreed to do the speech, with one condition: it would not be negative. 'If you had been a student in the 1960s and the 1970s you couldn't be *against* the environment,' Winsemius explains. 'We were past that.'[2] As it turned out, VNO did not want to hear a negative speech, anyway. Their members wanted to appear supportive of environmental measures, but they were concerned about costs and administrative burdens.

Winsemius addressed their concerns by discussing 'an inventory' of measures which would be more efficient for business or more effective for the environment, or preferably both – 'and I wasn't hampered by "knowing too much" or by the fact that I didn't trust NGOs or business or government.' He explains: 'My approach was basically solution-oriented, and that's what the businesspeople saw.' In fact, the Liberal Party decided he would make a good Environment Minister in the new Cabinet.

Politics was something new for Winsemius, who first joined the Liberals the day they chose to nominate him as minister. But his role as an 'outsider' gave him some distinct advantages in the job. 'I was never married to it,' he explains. 'There was no risk for *me*. The real risk was that I might step out any time ... because if my principles were touched too strongly, I would have left.' Winsemius also brought an enthusiasm that career politicians often lack. His experience in McKinsey gave him what he calls an 'American sense of optimism' that problems were there to be solved.

Winsemius also encouraged a very open, personal dialogue with his staff. One of the first things he said to me was, 'Please, call me Pieter.' Before that, I had never addressed a senior official – let alone a minister – by his or her

* The support of the US Marshall Plan was critical to this process.
† In 1994, VNO merged with the Dutch Association of Christian Business (NCW) and became VNO/NCW, an 80,000-member association which represents virtually every large company in the Netherlands and over half of all small businesses (10–100 employees).

first name. Pieter's openness, enthusiasm and humour helped him to manage the many challenges of his years in government.

The first challenge was the formation of a new ministry, since the Lubbers Cabinet had decided to split up the old Ministry of Health and Environmental Hygiene. The health directorates were transferred to the Ministry of Social Welfare, Culture, and Recreation, which itself had just lost the Directorate for Nature Protection. That directorate was transferred to the Ministry of Agriculture and Fisheries, which was commonly seen as the enemy of nature conservation. Fortunately, the Environment Department stayed together; and it joined three other departments to form the new Ministry of Housing, Land Use Planning and Environment (abbreviated VROM, in Dutch).* At first, we feared that the older Land Use Planning Department would dominate the environmental directorates, but in fact the environmental directorates have grown stronger.

Shortly after taking office, Winsemius made a New Year speech in which he challenged his staff to 'do everything quicker and lower' – that is, to make decisions lower on the bureaucratic ladder. 'If you can do something faster than before, do it,' he told them, 'and if you can do it lower down, do it. And don't ask me for permission. I've given you permission.' And the environmental directorates took him seriously. By that summer, they had produced 900 pages of planning documents in the form of Indicative Multi-Year Programmes (IMPs).† 'And I had to go to the Parliament,' Winsemius recalls, 'and say, "Please, please don't get too upset. There's 900 pages coming, but they're so enthusiastic" … and that was a breakthrough inside the Ministry.'

Such enthusiasm was part of the 'organized chaos' Pieter discovered in his new job. We had to develop new strategies to solve environmental problems and we had to try whatever ideas might work. Pieter loved this chaos, and he encouraged us to take responsibility for new initiatives. He and Willem Reij often dispatched fairly junior staff members, as I was then, to high-level negotiations with other departments. Pieter knew that our young enthusiasm would be persuasive.

The Policy Life Cycle

Pieter's position as an outsider was very valuable, because he was not afraid to ask the question 'Why?' Why is the department involved in this area of policy? Why is this considered a critical issue for us to address? Why do we have this organizational structure or bureaucratic procedure? After so many years in government, we had forgotten about these questions; and we hated it, at first, when Winsemius posed them to us. Eventually, though, he forced

---

* Ministerie van Volkshuisvesting, Ruimtelijke Ordening en Milieubeheer.
† Indicatief Meerjarenprogramma Milieubeheer.

us to really think about what we were doing, what we were capable of doing, and what we were ultimately responsible for. Answering these questions was a prerequisite for rational policy development.

Winsemius approached his new job not as a politician, but as a manager. Before he could proceed he had to answer the question, what is *my* job? (And what's the job of my department?) That is a very difficult question for ministers, because they have so many people coming to them demanding attention to so many different problems. Winsemius realized he could not possibly address them all, because he had neither the resources nor the authority. So what was his job? He sensed he could answer this question by applying business principles to the policy process, but it took a long plane ride for him to figure out how.

Winsemius had been invited to speak before a prestigious gathering of American businesspeople in New York in the spring of 1984; but he didn't know what to say. He knew they would not care to listen to the details of Dutch environmental policy. 'It would be like a novelty act,' he thought. Instead, he wanted to engage them in a discussion about the 'problem' of environmental policy, and he sought the right metaphor to capture this.

In February, a few months before his New York speech, Winsemius made a business trip to Singapore. During his 18-hour flight, the idea came to him. He had long known the value of the product life cycle in business. This theory essentially states that every product has a lifetime, after which it is no longer needed or beneficial to the producers. Some products, like table salt, have been in use forever. Others, like ice boxes or black and white TVs, are already extinct. Companies make products because of their added value – in other words, because they are desired and can be sold for a profit. When

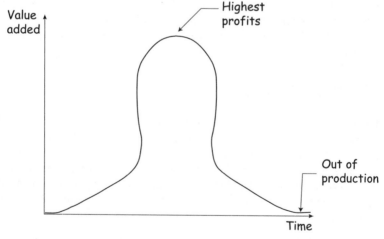

Figure 5 The product life cycle

the added value of a product drops to zero, it is no longer manufactured.

The product life cycle recognizes that everything will eventually go out of production, and it plots the different levels of added value for a product over its lifetime. This can be represented with a simple graph, on which 'time' is the horizontal axis and 'value added' is the vertical axis.

Winsemius realized that government, too, is essentially selling a product: a body of policies to solve various problems. These 'products', he realized, must also have their own life cycles. Policies should eventually solve the problems they address and go 'out of production'. When he tried to graph it, Winsemius realized he could still place time on the horizontal axis, but he did not know how to label the vertical.

During his flight to Singapore, Winsemius thought about the motivations that drive business and politics. The goal of business is to gain profits. It makes money by developing the right products and selling them. The goal of a government is to gain public attention and approval, ultimately in the form of votes. For government, the added value is the political attention it gets by showing it is addressing societal problems. Once these problems are solved, government looks for new problems to address. When Winsemius realized this, he knew what to place on the vertical access: political attention.

He had started out thinking only about his speech in New York, but this model truly excited him. After arriving in Singapore, Pieter continued his work while sitting in the morning sun. Three hours later, he had a good sunburn; but he had also outlined a concept of the policy life cycle. Pieter later asked me to work this draft into a fully fledged speech he could present in New York. It explains the two axes of the policy life cycle, and it divides the cycle into four stages. These stages form the crucial metaphor that changed our thinking about the policy process.

The first phase is called *policy recognition*, in which an environmental problem (or any other problem) first 'pops up' and is noticed by scientists, academics and environmental groups. The problem is not well known or understood by the general public, however, so government doesn't take action. In the case of toxic substances, for example, scientists like Rachel Carson, and some activists, saw the possible dangers of DDT and other pesticides long before most people were aware of them.

The next phase is *policy formulation*. By this time, the public has learned about a problem, and it is very concerned. After enough people had read *Silent Spring* or seen other evidence about toxins, for example, they demanded action. In other words, enough people had reached a personal threshold to speak out. Public attention can skyrocket in this phase, and government sees it is now 'profitable' to step in. The government may do studies and conduct hearings, for example, or propose some piece of 'landmark' legislation banning or restricting the use of certain chemicals.

In the phase of *implementation*, public attention drops off, since many consider the problem to be solved. By this point, they may well be engaged in a completely new problem which is gaining recognition. The real work has just begun, though, since considerable changes are probably needed to make new government policies effective. Because it is no longer a hot issue, however, the problem is not of much interest to politicians. Implementation goes on quietly, behind the scenes, and there is some danger that, without public scrutiny, it may not be carried out properly.

Implementation generally requires the delegation of responsibilities to many parties, such as other ministries, provincial and local governments, or even NGOs and the private sector. Returning to the toxins example, implementation may be turned over to local governments which, in the Netherlands, are responsible for licensing facilities. They may design new inspection methods to see that chemicals are not produced or that they are handled and applied in different ways. The private sector will also start developing less harmful substances or practices as alternatives to using the toxic chemicals.

Until this phase, the policy may have been one department's 'baby', and it can be difficult for parents to send their children into the world. This is essential, however, if the policy is to be implemented and if the original department is to handle the new issues which demand attention. This phase can be especially frustrating for public officials, such as ministers, who want to demonstrate their accomplishments. Such accomplishments will not be appreciated for many years; and future officials will probably be the first to profit from the results. Of course, the current officials do profit from the work of *their* predecessors.

Assuming a good policy has been developed and implemented, the fourth – and final – phase of *control* can begin. It generally takes many years,

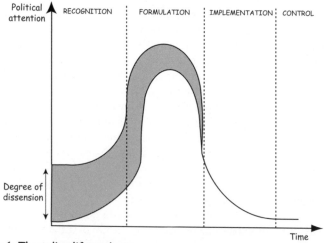

Figure 6 The policy life cycle

but eventually a problem should be brought under control. Policies may still be continued to keep a handle on the issue, but essentially the 'problem' has been solved. In the case of DDT or other toxins, they may not even be produced anymore, at least officially; but regulators have to ensure that they are not secretly manufactured or smuggled in.

The policy life cycle was a revelation because it finally answered the question, 'What is my job?' As policy makers, we are only responsible for phase two of the cycle, the actual formulation of polices. We may have some involvement in the recognition phase, but we are essentially standing on the sidelines, waiting for our turn to come. After phase two, our main work is done, and we must hand the problem on to other parties for the implementation and control phases.

Knowing this, we can see what issues are ripe for action, and which ones are still forming. The Environment Department will be wasting its energies if it tries to tackle a problem which is still in the recognition stage. We can take more subtle actions, however, like funding research or encouraging environmental groups to pursue the issue and bring it towards phase two. We can also start thinking about how we will deal with an issue when it does reach this phase. We first take action, however, in the policy formulation phase, and we must act quickly and decisively. This is often a narrow window of political opportunity to create strong policies.

The life cycle concept also showed us how important, and difficult, implementation can be. Implementation requires integrated work with other parties, including those sometimes considered 'the enemy', such as rival ministries or the private sector. Implementation is also hampered by the lack of public support.

Although it has been a valuable tool, I did have some criticisms of the policy life cycle, particularly regarding the notion that problems just 'pop up'. By waiting for the *effects* of environmental problems to appear, we are almost suggesting that these problems are good, since addressing them keeps us in business. I think it is much more important to look into the root *causes* of problems, and perhaps prevent the effects from occurring in the first place.

I mentioned my concerns to Pieter Winsemius. Although he was a minister and I was only a junior-level staffer, he was happy to have a discussion with me and even listen to my critique. Regardless of the conversation's outcome, simply knowing that the boss was really listening strengthened the culture of the Environment Department. It turned out that the policy life cycle became an appropriate model of how things really work, and therefore a valuable tool for environmental policy development. It was one of the first models to describe our profession, and it provided a language to discuss our work both among ourselves and with others.

A fortunate coincidence ensured that the policy life cycle quickly gained national and international recognition. Before his presentation in New York,

Winsemius stopped in Washington, DC to deliver the closing remarks at a three-day meeting with the US Environmental Protection Agency (EPA). The meeting was one in a series of exchanges which the Dutch and American environmental authorities have held over the years. It featured a diverse Dutch contingent including government officials, parliamentarians, business people and members of NGOs – individuals who would rarely be in the same room together back in The Hague. They provided a rare audience for Winsemius, who chose to present the policy life cycle.

The Dutch who heard him that day, as well as the Americans, were quite impressed, and many asked Winsemius for a copy of his speech. It was distributed throughout the Netherlands in the government, business and NGO communities – all of which invited him to give presentations on the policy life cycle. This was the beginning of what he called 'management by speech'. He began every address with the policy life cycle and applied it to the particular topics he was discussing.

Being a Guest in Your Own Home

In 1986, we helped Pieter work these speeches into a series of essays for the book *Guests in Our Own Home*.* The essays covered important aspects of environmental policy and also explained Pieter's philosophy on integrating environmental protection and free market principles. The book's title came from a speech he had given near the end of his term as minister. Parliament was discussing a law on contaminated soil† and debating the extent of clean-up to require. Should soil be cleaned to minimal standards, enough to allow future industrial development, but not returned to pristine quality? Or should it be restored to its original condition before pollution began?

Winsemius argued for the second option, under the principle of *multi-functionality*. He believed that natural resources should be returned to their original condition, so that future generations could choose any function for them and not be restricted by what the present generation had done. This same belief was proclaimed just a few years later in the Brundtland Report's theory of sustainable development: that today's developments should not compromise the ability of future generations to meet their needs.

Winsemius persuaded Parliament to approve the stricter clean-up policy by recalling an old slogan of the Netherlands Tourist Board: 'Don't thank the keeper of the forest for a pleasant stay by leaving him your trash.' Pieter took this phrase, which was still well known, and gave a speech about the Dutch being 'guests' on their own soil. He told them, essentially, that people in the present generation could not own the land and do with it as they please.

---

* *Gast in Eigen Huis*, published by McKinsey, Amsterdam. English translations are available.
† Wet Bodembescherming, Soil Protection Act.

They are only guests on the land during their lifetimes, and they should treat it accordingly. Winsemius later described the speech as having an 'almost religious' appeal.

As Pieter gave his speech, he began to believe that there could be an over-arching vision to support environmental policies. With such a vision, it would be possible to manage environmental issues strategically – and actually solve them – rather than simply responding to new crises.* This change marked the shift from an *ad hoc* to an institutional phase of policy.

An essential element of building a strong institution was learning how to think about our proper roles and functions. It was not about getting more people in our department, nor about taking over others' responsibilities. The same holds true when preparing a hiking trip. Every hiker has to walk for himself/herself, but people also have to assign roles (who is responsible for what aspect of the total endeavour). The hikers have to gather the right equipment (as we did in developing the EIA regulations) and anticipate the pitfalls (like dealing with uncertainties).

* After leaving the government, Winsemius became known in the press as the 'management guru', and he was frequently asked to give presentations on his experience while serving as Environment Minister.

Notes

1 All Frans Evers quotations are from an interview with the author, 's-Graveland, Netherlands, 3 March 1997.
2 All Pieter Winsemius quotations are from an interview with the author, Amsterdam, 8 March 1997.

CHAPTER 3

How to Pack
Starting to Integrate Environmental Policies

If I were to compare policy making to a hike, I might say that Winsemius's life cycle showed us how to pace ourselves. It explained when to hit the trail and how much ground we could cover in a day. We were not yet ready to depart, however, because we were still carrying too much baggage. The trick is to decide on the absolute essentials and have the courage to pack nothing else. By dividing this equipment among the other hikers, we distribute the weight, and recognize that we all depend on each other.

Environmental policies, and the bureaucracies that administered them, were still divided into sectors for specific environmental media; and each sector carried its own 'equipment', in the form of laws, regulations or bureaucratic structures. A little extra baggage is not much of a problem for a day hike; but it can become an excessive burden on a long trip. The *ad hoc* phase of policy was something akin to a day hike. Devising quick responses to individual problems, we only saw a small part of the trail ahead and didn't worry about what was over the next hill. With a more strategic approach to policy, we started to focus on long-term goals and realized we were in for a long journey. Now the weight of our many *ad hoc* policy tools became noticeable. To lighten the load, we had to share our equipment by integrating our work with the different governmental sectors.

The need to integrate became clear after 1982 and the political realization that we would never have one all-encompassing ministry (or even department) with authority over every aspect of the environment. Some key environmental competencies were destined to remain with other departments, such as Agriculture, Transport, Nature Protection, Waterworks and Economic Affairs. If we wanted to make comprehensive policies, we had to work with these other departments.

Alongside the need to integrate our work at the national level was the realization that we had to harmonize policies with the provinces as well. Though the Netherlands is a small country, it still has some significant regional differences, and each province is responsible for licensing procedures in its territory. In policy terms, this meant different environmental standards in the 12 provinces, something which greatly frustrated companies with operations throughout the country.

In 1982, the Directorate for *Bestuurszaken* began working with the other departments on a plan to coordinate policy at both the national and provincial levels. The original mission was to develop a strategic plan providing a timetable of new policies and regulations that the provinces could expect from the national government. We soon discovered, however, that the Environment Department had to coordinate its own internal operations before it could start working with provinces or other national departments.

More than the Sum of Its Parts

In 1982, Frans Evers convened a working group to develop a new *nota* (policy proposal) for long-term strategic planning in the Environment Department. The group was led by Gustaaf Biezeveld, an attorney who had previously worked in municipal government. Having seen first-hand the difficulties in implementing *ad hoc* national policies, Gustaaf was acutely aware of the inefficiency in fragmented policy making. Eliminating this inefficiency became a personal mission for him.

Gustaaf worked together with Jacob 'Koos' van der Vaart, who was especially concerned with the scientific aspects of environmental policy, and with Marjolijn Burggraaff, whom I knew from my time in Land Use Planning. One strength of that department was, indeed, the ability to do long-term planning. The Environment Department was sorely lacking in this respect; and we believed that someone from our rival department, where ten-year plans were common, could be a very good influence on our work. Marjolijn had originally been loaned to us for a three-year assignment to develop the *nota*, but she has remained in the Environment Department ever since.

In the spring of 1984, Gustaaf's team had intensive discussions with Minister Winsemius on the *nota*, which was later sent to Parliament under the title *More than the Sum of Its Parts* (*Meer dan de Som der Delen*). It was not simply a timetable of regulations, but a new philosophy for environmental policy. The *nota* explained, in very convincing terms, the need for integrating the work of government authorities on environmental policies. The proposed vehicle for integration would be a long-term *National Environmental Policy Plan* (NEPP)* to be prepared by the four ministries with legal responsibilities for the environment: VROM, Economic Affairs,†

---

* The Dutch name is *Nationaal Milieubeleidsplan*, or NMP.

† Curiously, Economic Affairs was not originally involved because of the connection between economic development and the environment (which seems so apparent today). Instead, it was brought in on a legal technicality, in that it administered a fairly obscure mining law with environmental provisions.

Transport and Waterworks, and Agriculture, Nature Protection and Fisheries.

Such policy reforms could not be achieved overnight, of course; and a transition phase was proposed. We began with a series of Indicative Multi-Year Environmental Programmes (IMPs). Each was a four-year plan which set out fairly concrete goals for the first year, and an indication of how policy would proceed in the following three years. This hybrid of yearly and multi-year planning was intended to lay the foundation for a unified National Environmental Policy Plan. The first IMP was prepared by Gustaaf's team on the heels of the *nota,* and was released in September 1984. The two documents can be viewed together as a preliminary statement on the theory of integration. 'In *More than the Sum of Its Parts* we developed a new concept, but it was not complete,' Gustaaf later recalled. 'And in the first IMP, we made a step forward, but it was also incomplete.'[1]

The Language of Integration

The first IMP was not 'complete', Gustaaf realized, because it was impossible simply to coordinate the different directorates in the Environment Department with a 'master plan'. The directorates conflicted by the very nature of their 'compartmentalized' approaches, and Gustaaf's team found considerable overlap among them. This led not only to the duplication, but sometimes even to the negation, of one department's work by another. For example, incineration of garbage helped solve the problem of waste disposal, which was handled by one directorate; but it created a new problem of air pollution, which was handled by another directorate. The staff of the waste directorate wanted to reduce the amount of trash, and incineration seemed to be a solution. It did cause air pollution, but that was not their problem. Directorates within the same Environment Department viewed each other as hindrances, or even enemies.

In time, it became clear that integration was a process involving several steps. The first was to get our own house in order by integrating the work of the various directorates within the Environment Department. Then we could integrate our department's work with the other government departments. Once the national government had a clear picture of its environmental policies, we could take the third step of integrating with the provincial level of government.

Gustaaf's group began its work on integration by redefining environmental problems. Previously, they had been considered as a collection of disturbances to particular environmental media. Polluted lakes and rivers, for example, were grouped under water pollution; emissions from automobiles, factories or fires were all forms of air pollution. Thus each medium,

WHY MAKE A PLAN?

Planning is such a common practice in government institutions (and most other organizations) that its *purpose* is rarely discussed. Planning is just accepted as an inherently good thing to do – a mentality reinforced by the environmental planning requirements of the World Bank or Agenda 21. In the Dutch Environment Department, *More than the Sum of Its Parts* and the IMPs finally forced us to think about why we were making plans in the first place. Looking back, I can think of three reasons, which can be applied to all national environmental policy making:

1 **To coordinate** the work of central government institutions that are responsible for aspects of environmental policy.

2 **To guide** the other levels of government (provincial and municipal) and thereby produce a unified national policy.

3 **To avoid restructuring** the government, for example through the creation of a super Environment Ministry responsible for all aspects of policy on the national and local level. This may still be the dream of many policy makers, but it is arguably more of a political and bureaucratic nightmare.

The National Environmental Policy Plan would go on to serve a fourth function – providing the basis for a social contract on integrating environmental responsibilities into society.

or environmental sector, defined a different *kind* of problem. Gustaaf's group rejected this conventional approach and instead focused on the two aspects of all problems: those of *quality* (effects) and those of *sources* (causes).

- *Quality aspects* deal with environmental effects. This perspective includes all the sectoral issues, such as air, soil, or water pollution; but it recognizes what they have in common – an environmental resource is degraded by some human activity. The release of a toxic substance such as DDT, for example, pollutes air, water, and land; but all these effects are results of the same problem.

- *Source aspects* deal with the economic activities that cause environmental degradation. Policy had previously grouped these sources according to what environmental media they affect. There were water polluters, soil polluters, air polluters, waste generators, and so on. In reality, though, any one economic activity causes several types of pollution. Power plants, for example, produce air, water, and soil pollution; and they also generate waste. The same could generally be said for a pig farm, but the two facilities are very different.

Under the environmental sector approach, the power plant is not treated as one entity, but as three, four, five or however many environmental sectors it affects. As a result, the plant must deal with many different authorities. One day it may be visited by air regulators, on another by water regulators, and on another by officials concerned with toxic releases. For each regulator, the plant will have to complete a licensing procedure, often duplicating the same paperwork.

Furthermore, there is no guarantee that media-specific policies will be consistent with each other. The plant, for example, may be forced to install better equipment to remove sulphur from its emissions and reduce its contribution to acid rain. But desulphurization equipment reduces the efficiency of power plants. Therefore they use more energy, consume more fuel and release more carbon dioxide into the atmosphere (a cause of climate change).

The sectoral approach also lumps together such unlikely bedfellows as power plants and pig farms. They may both cause water pollution, but they have almost nothing else in common. By speaking in terms of environmental sectors, the department used a different language from that used by the rest of society. Businesses are often organized by the type of activity they perform, and other branches of government deal with them in this manner. Thus, the Dutch Ministry of Economic Affairs, for example, has certain staff and policies for energy providers, and the Ministry of Agriculture has its staff and policies for farmers. Furthermore, each economic sector has its own distinct culture and political networks.

Competencies should not be divided according to environmental sectors, but rather in relation to the cause and effect chain. The Environment Department should be responsible for setting policy on environmental *quality* (the effects side). These policies are implemented, however, by departments which are responsible for the various *sources* (or causes). In some cases, this includes the Environment Department. In others, the department must share responsibility with the provinces or with other national departments, such as Agriculture, Nature Protection or Waterworks.

Integration begins with a common language to describe environmental problems – the language of cause and effect. The different actors then divide their responsibilities according to where each can best influence the cause and effect chain. The actors do not give up their existing powers or authorities, but they work at using them in a way which is most effective for an integrated approach.

A Clear Message

These theories of integration were a great step forward, but they were still incomplete. What they lacked was a clear, concise logic which could be explained not only to theorists, but also to politicians and the general public. Pieter Winsemius urged us to avoid undue complexity in our language. 'If you can't explain an environmental problem to your next-door neighbour in five minutes, ' he told us, 'your story isn't good enough.' The theory of integration of source and quality problems, while elegant, was not clear enough for anyone but dedicated policy buffs. We needed to extract the moral of the story, the essential points. Winsemius told us these could not number more than the fingers on one hand.

Breaking problems down into sources and quality, or cause and effect, made policy much more manageable than the previous sectoral designations. The next step, then, was to attack the issues under the headings of 'cause' and 'effect'. Designating policies on harmful substances, for example, helped to clarify quality problems, but we were still dealing with tens of thousands of substances. By 1997, for instance, there were over 75,000 synthetic chemicals in use every day, with another 2,000 being introduced each year.[2] We needed to combine the plethora of environmental causes and effects under a few general categories, an idea we borrowed from our colleagues in the United States.

Our department and the US Environmental Protection Agency (EPA) have had close ties since the 1970s via 'Memoranda of Understanding' which provide for regular meetings and exchanges. At one such meeting in 1984, Frans Evers learned that the EPA had devised a new 'priority list' which narrowed its vast number of responsibilities down to thirty key issues. Frans, who had recently been named Deputy Director General, was grappling with the problem of setting priorities in the Environment Department.

Frans took a copy of the US priorities back to the Netherlands and started to re-evaluate our policies. Later, he came to Winsemius with a list of 56 topics, ranked by priority, which summarized Dutch environmental concerns. The list was quite an accomplishment, but Winsemius knew they could do better. His first advice was not to rank the items, or the ones near the bottom of the list would never be addressed. Furthermore, he knew they could make the list much simpler. Looking again to business principles, he remembered the general rule that people can only juggle about half a dozen concepts at one time. 'So I set up a standing rule: five items,' Winsemius recalls. 'I told them I will fight about number six, but there will be no seven!' And then he added, 'But the moment I leave office, I know you will go over seven.'*

Together, Pieter and Frans worked through the priority list. They did not drop any problem areas, but they looked for similarities which allowed them to combine items under a few general headings. After only two days, they had fitted all problems under five categories, which they termed *environmental themes*. These were:

---

* The National Environmental Policy Plan, approved by Parliament in 1989, recognized eight problem fields. NEPP 3, approved in 1998, added a ninth.

Figure 7 Acid rain campaign: 'Yesterday. Today. Tomorrow?'

- *Acidification (Verzuring)* – the introduction of substances which form acids in the environment, generally via the 'acid rain' which has destroyed forests and aquatic ecosystems in northern Europe and many other places around the world. The main acidifying substances are sulphur dioxide (SO_2) and nitrogen oxide (NO_x) from combustion, ammonia (NH_3) from agriculture, and volatile organic compounds (VOCs) from various industrial processes.

- *Eutrophication (Vermesting)* – the overloading of soil and waters with a high level of nutrients, especially phosphates and nitrates. Eutrophication is caused by run-off from agriculture (synthetic fertilizers and manure) and from improperly treated sewage.

- *Dispersion (Verspreiding)* – the widespread introduction of foreign substances, such as toxic chemicals, heavy metals and genetically modified organisms.

- *Waste disposal (Verwijdering)* – both traditional 'household' waste and toxic materials. Policy should aim to reduce and recycle waste as much as possible, and to dispose safely of whatever remains.

- *Local disturbance (Verstoring)* – the quality of the residential environment. It covers many local problems, such as noise pollution, odour, local air pollution, and industrial accidents.

Winsemius chose his words carefully (he even invented one) so the themes would be very clear to the general public. One clever technique in Dutch was using the prefix *ver-* in each word. This adds a negative connotation, implying that something has gone too far. The word *zuur*, for example, means acid. The term *ver-zuring* implies that the balance of acid in the environment has been disturbed, as in the case of acid rain.

The most colourful word is *vermesting*. This is generally translated as eutrophication, the pollution of water resources by high levels of nutrients, such as nitrogen and phosphorous. This term, however, hides the unpleasant fact that most of the nutrients come from faeces, both human and animal. By the 1980s, we had relieved the human waste problem through modern sewage treatment plants; but animal waste was, and still is, a major environmental concern. Despite its considerable industrial development, the Netherlands also has a large agricultural sector. In fact, it is the world's fourth largest agricultural exporter, specializing in meat, dairy products and flowers.

Dutch farmers import a considerable amount of fodder from other countries. The meat or cheese is exported; but the *mest*, or manure, remains on the ground, causing a serious imbalance of nutrient flows into the country. To better describe the problem, Winsemius rejected the technical term eutrophication, which we also have in Dutch. Instead, he coined the word *vermesting*, which can be translated, a bit awkwardly, as 'manure-fication'. Because it has such a meaning, in this book I use the word *vermesting* rather than eutrophication.

Winsemius worked with other government departments and went to Parliament to win approval of the themes as accepted terminology for the environmental debate. As he explains, 'You can't frame a new discussion with old terms.' The process was very time-consuming, and there was a long debate about the invented word *vermesting*. In the end, however, everyone began to speak the same language.

One of the strongest features of the themes is that they refer specifically to problem areas. This was not the case with the old sector-specific terminology that divided the environment into categories such as air, water or soil. It is not very accurate, for example, to say that 'air' is a problem. A term like acidification, in contrast, clearly refers to an imbalance. Furthermore, it shows how this problem affects several sectors, such as air, water, forest ecology and the urban environment.

While grouping environmental effects under the theme headings, we also sought a better system to group environmental causes (economic sectors). The old media-specific environmental policies approached these sectors by the pollution they produced. Thus a power plant and a pig farm might be lumped together, if they both caused water pollution. Instead of approaching businesses according to environmental criteria, Winsemius chose to designate target groups of companies which corresponded with existing business sectors. We restructured our approach to economic causes by combining tens of thousands of businesses into a handful of distinct target groups. In 1985, we chose to focus on the four most problematic:

- *Refineries* – the Netherlands processes large quantities of crude oil from other countries. Refineries can cause serious environmental problems, such as air pollution and spills which poison the soil and water.

- *Transportation* – cars, buses and trucks pollute the air with their exhausts and the water with fuels and lubricants that spill. The transportation infrastructure also consumes large amounts of land, breaking up natural habitats and bringing development into new areas.

- *Energy production* – generally relies on fossil fuels (coal, gas and oil) which cause air and water pollution.

- *Agriculture* – modern farming methods rely heavily on synthetic chemicals, such as pesticides and fertilizers. In addition, high-density 'factory farming' produces animal waste in quantities which cannot be absorbed by the environment.

Note that the manufacturing industry was not on the original list. Although this sector certainly has serious environmental impacts, we felt that the existing legal and regulatory framework was adequate for addressing them. As time went on, we developed more ambitious environmental goals and a better understanding of interrelationships among economic sectors. In the process, we eventually expanded the list of target groups to include all sectors of the economy.*

It was very unusual to think about the environment in business terms. Until then, we had usually dealt with the private sector indirectly through other ministries, especially the powerful Ministry of Economic Affairs. 'Previously, the other ministries told us about their constituencies,' Winsemius recalls. 'And we said, "No way, they're our constituencies, as well." They are not enemies, but constituencies.' Of course, Pieter's contacts with business leaders helped us to approach the major companies directly.

The other government departments, such as Economic Affairs, were pleased with the themes and target groups. Jan-Willem Weck, who was Deputy Secretary General of Economic Affairs at the time, describes the new terminology as 'an instrument that was very suitable for discussing how to tackle environmental problems'.[3] The main value of the new approach, according to Weck, was being able to engage economic sectors in devising environmental solutions: 'After some discussion, there was a clear conviction that … if you do not involve the persons and the institutions and the companies that will have to do the job of cleaning up the environment, then you can just forget about it.'

---

* The current list includes the original four, plus industry, construction, water cycle, waste processing, the retail trade and consumers.

The IMPs

The basic concepts of themes and target groups were developed in the first two IMPs (of 1984 and 1985). The latter was seen as the first interministerial environmental plan, having involved not only VROM but also the Ministry of Transport and Waterworks and the Ministry of Agriculture, Fisheries and Nature Protection. These ministries signed a joint letter presenting the IMP to Parliament, a practice we would continue and expand with the National Environmental Policy Plan.

Gustaaf Biezeveld was project leader for the first two IMPs. In the summer of 1985, Minister Winsemius asked Biezeveld to assist him in editing the book *Guests in Our Own Home*, and Frans Evers asked me to take over as project leader for the third IMP. Just a few weeks into the project, I realized that we needed to make substantial progress in translating the theories of the earlier plans into concrete policies. Everyone understood the basic concepts of dividing environmental problems into sources and qualities, as well as the relationship between the two via the cause-and-effect chain. This thinking, however, did not carry over to most people's daily work. Although we now recognized both source-oriented and quality-oriented policies, I felt that too much emphasis was still placed on the latter. We basically continued the earlier approaches which set quality standards for effects without always taking adequate measures on the cause side to ensure they could be attained. Even when dealing with environmental causes, we seemed too committed to command-and-control emission standards, without considering other policy measures.

I felt that standards, whether geared to causes or effects, are not sufficient tools by themselves. I had first realized this at Leyden when confronted with ecological mapping as a policy tool. Some scientists liked standard setting because they could define an ideal world on paper, and they assumed that the policies to create this world would just take care of themselves. By limiting their role to setting standards, however, scientist gave up on opportunities to actually influence the activities that were causing environmental deterioration.

We also discussed the definitions of themes and target groups, which were often difficult to fit in with the existing structure of the Department. The work of the Directorate for Radiation Protection, for example, fell under three themes: Waste Production, Dispersion of Toxics, and Local Disturbance. The Radiation Directorate, as well as the other directorates, resented having its work 'spread out' among several themes. We needed long negotiations to convince the directors that the themes and target groups would not dissipate their authority, but rather encourage more interdisciplinary work in the Department.

While the IMP caused some trouble in our own Department, it also helped relations with others. The Ministry of Economic Affairs was pleased with the report, for instance, because it included improved cost calculations for environmental policy. The third IMP was also the first document to use the term 'environmental efficiency'. This concept, combined with the cost calculations, was an early effort to incorporate cost-benefit analysis into environmental policy.

Major Changes in 1986

Despite our efforts to manage policy development carefully, we were soon reminded that new crises can still 'pop up' unexpectedly. On 24 April 1986 the number four reactor at the Chernobyl nuclear plant in the Ukraine exploded, sending a radioactive cloud over most of Europe. For perhaps the first time, the public realized that environmental problems are truly global in scale, that an event thousands of kilometres away can threaten their own safety. This did a lot to strengthen public concern and build the political support for stronger environmental policies.

Of course, we had no choice but to prepare an *ad hoc* response to a sudden crisis like Chernobyl. Our work on improving policy making allowed us, however, to 'manage' even this crisis more strategically. Pieter Winsemius decided that we should take the lead on Chernobyl, nominating the Chief Environmental Inspector, Marius Enthoven, to head up the response. So, within a few days, the government had collected extensive information on radioactive fall-out and embargoed foodstuffs from regions of the country which had been contaminated. Our research was so thorough, in fact, that we advised other European nations on how the fall-out was affecting them. For his service, Marius received the Medal of Honour from Her Majesty the Queen, which was quite exceptional, given his young age.

The crisis turned Dutch nuclear policies on end. The lower house of Parliament had recently voted, by a slim majority, to expand the country's nuclear energy programme. After Chernobyl, and a thorough study programme, the government decided that the risks of nuclear power were too high, and it halted future development of the industry.*

Despite his successes, which culminated in the decisive response to Chernobyl, Pieter Winsemius chose not to serve another term as Minister. He may not have had the option, anyway. In the elections of 1986, the Liberals lost ten parliamentary seats to the Christian Democrats. Although the two parties continued in a ruling coalition, the Liberals were definitely the junior partner, and fewer Cabinet posts were left for them. As a 'punishment' for the electoral defeat, the Liberals removed their party

---

* I was involved in devising the post-Chernobyl policies as Deputy Director for Radiation Protection from 1986 to 1988.

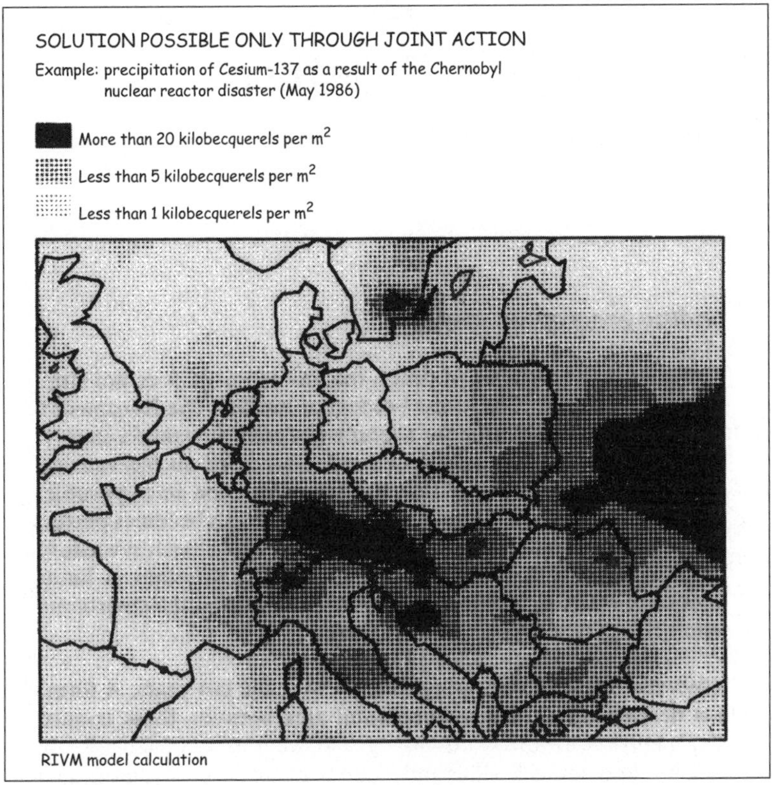

SOLUTION POSSIBLE ONLY THROUGH JOINT ACTION

Example: precipitation of Cesium-137 as a result of the Chernobyl
nuclear reactor disaster (May 1986)

More than 20 kilobecquerels per m^2

Less than 5 kilobecquerels per m^2

Less than 1 kilobecquerels per m^2

RIVM model calculation

Figure 8 Contamination of Europe by Chernobyl
Source: RIVM

leader, Ed Nijpels, although they did choose him as the new Environment
Minister. Under Winsemius, we had laid the foundation for strong and
efficient new environmental policies. Ed Nijpels built on this work by
helping guide the political process that culminated in the first National
Environmental Policy Plan.

In Winsemius's time as Minister, we learned how to pack for the journey.
The prioritization by environmental themes made it clear where we had to
go. The target groups clarified who was walking with us. Both models are
still the basis for integrating environmental concerns into other policy areas.

Notes

1 All Gustaaf Biezeveld quotations are from an interview with the author, The Hague, 5 March
   1997.
2 US Environment Protection Agency, *EPA Strategic Plan* (Washington: GPO, 1997), 37.
3 All Jan Willem Weck quotations are from an interview with the author, The Hague, 15 August
   1997.

Getting a Team Together
Towards Integration

The Process Towards Integration

Environmental policies do not begin with an integrated structure. Instead, integration emerges from a long process with four key phases. Let me introduce them with an example from my favourite sport. I started hiking as a boy exploring the sand dunes of The Hague. All hikers begin the same way, with a basic desire to explore the countryside, to walk just for the sake of walking. They are probably not well prepared for the sport. They may not know the hiking trails or have the right equipment, like a comfortable backpack, a jacket for bad weather, or good hiking boots.

Later, people learn the word 'hiking' and see it as a particular sport or hobby. They find out what skills and equipment are necessary, motivated in part by the wet feet, sore shoulders, and blisters from their earlier days. They start planning ahead, studying trail maps, and buying better equipment. They will still have problems, however, if they travel alone. They have to carry all their own equipment and struggle with tasks that are awkward for one person, like pitching a tent in bad weather. And if they get lost or injured, they have no one to ask for help.

Long excursions into the wilderness should not be undertaken alone. Carrying all the equipment will slow the hiker considerably, and an injury in the wild can be very dangerous. People minimize burdens and risks by hiking in groups. Adding more hikers, however, involves new skills and tasks. The team members must get to know each other and determine how best to utilize everyone's talents. And they have to communicate well – to agree on the route and the pace of the hike.

After a while, a real team may emerge. Decision making will become easier as the hikers come to know each other. They can spend less time planning, since people's interests and abilities are already known. The group may not talk as much, at least not as much about hiking. Its members will develop a group instinct.

The progression of environmental policy resembles the stages of hiking. As hikers must eliminate excess baggage and improve their communication in the group, policy makers must integrate their operations by eliminating overlaps in responsibilities and communicating clearly with other government departments and society at large. I consider integration to be one of four phases in the development of environment policy. Two important phases precede it; and there is a final phase beyond integration in which policies have fully matured and environmental thinking becomes instinctive. The four phases are: *Ad hoc* response, Institutionalization, Integration, and Imbuing.

The *Ad Hoc* Response

As in hiking, environmental policy began by reacting to situations without any planning or theory, just getting out and walking. People started by responding to individual, local matters, such as the contamination of drinking water, the loss of forests for firewood, or smoke and odours from early factories. At the time, people did not see the connections among local issues or their broader relationships to the earth's natural systems. Some laws or regulations for local issues emerged centuries ago, but the first systemic efforts began with nineteenth-century nuisance law. The Dutch, for example, introduced the 1875 Nuisance Act to control a number of local disturbances, such as odour or noise from factories, which were not regulated by other ordinances.

In the post-war years, rapid industrialization and population growth created a number of environmental crises for the Netherlands and other countries. The Dutch government responded with specific laws to protect certain resources like water, forestry and cropland. In the 1960s, the development of urban and suburban areas began to concern some citizens. They were generally motivated by particular projects in their communities, such as the new roads proposed for the sand dunes and meadows around The Hague. The government responded with zoning measures such as the 1965 Land Use Planning Act and the 1967 Nature Conservation Act. Once legislation has been set up, the transition between *ad hoc* response and the next phase may take place.

Institutionalization

After enough individual problems arise, people begin to see relationships among them, and a general concept of 'the environment' emerges. This resembles the second stage of hiking, in which people recognize it as an actual sport requiring certain skills and equipment. In the same way, a policy approach is institutionalized within government and society. The word 'environment' first comes into use, and people begin to categorize its elements, such as air, water and soil. People also categorize families of environmental problems, like waste, toxic substances, and noise distur- bance – the environmental sectors that form the basis of institutional policies. Seeing the need for a formal response, governments establish departments or ministries for 'the environment'. This is a significant step from the *ad hoc* phase, in which environmental responsibilities are scattered among different policies and government bureaucracies.

Institutionalization began in the Netherlands with the establishment of an Environment Department in 1971. The first years of the department were spent building up a qualified staff of specialists in different sectoral issues. This specialized approach characterized early policies and laws, such as the 1972 *Memorandum on Urgent Environmental Issues* with its enumera- tion of individual problems. Specialization, while necessary to some extent, has inherent flaws. It leans toward the 'strong' position we identified at the University of Leyden, in which scientists use their expertise to dictate policy directions. Specialists trust that their scientific 'truths' will determine policy, but they do not engage the actual political debate. The specialists waste too much energy discussing issues among themselves, rather than communi- cating with other parts of government and society. They develop their own language, which others cannot readily understand.

Such poor communication can lead to a 'state of war' with other parts of government. The Dutch Environment Department, for example, fought especially hard battles with the Ministry of Economic Affairs, often considered the natural enemy of the environment. Our department usually took the 'strong' (but also very risky) position of combating this ministry on the basis of scientific truths, such as toxicology studies. Meanwhile, our opponents were arguing on the basis of economic truths, such as models of industrial growth. At the time, there was no way to relate and compare the two sets of truths. Thus, the argument was expressed in simplistic terms of 'the environment' versus 'the economy', a situation in which the economy always wins.

Along with improving communication, a hiker can also become more efficient by eliminating excess equipment. The 'equipment' used by an environmental authority includes its overlapping sector-specific laws, regulations, bureaucracies and plans. Policies may be streamlined within an environmental department to strengthen the institution's position toward other sectors of government and society.* The Directorate for General Policy (*Bestuurszaken*) was a mechanism for streamlining the institutional structure of the Dutch Environment Department. This directorate was

---

* The streamlining of policies was discussed in some countries, such as the United States, as an abstract term even in the early 1980s, but little practical action has been taken until recently.

outside the sector-specific framework of the department and was free to work on coordinating the activities of the other directorates.

The appointment of a minister who was an outsider to both government and environmental policy also helped, because he brought in a fresh viewpoint to critique the old way of doing business. The policy life cycle, for example, challenged the chaotic, *ad hoc* development of policies. We learned that there is a certain stage for every issue at which government needs to enter the political debate, and that we should not chase a problem before it is ripe for attention. We could then focus more on strategic planning for the institution. Important Dutch milestones in institutionalizing environmental policy were the memorandum *More than the Sum of Its Parts*, the IMPs and the National Environmental Policy Plan. These documents, and the processes they engendered, showed us the overlaps and conflicts in our department.

Building strong institutions is still the goal for many environmental authorities around the world, a trend which began with the 1972 Stockholm conference and continued with the 1992 United Nations Conference on Environment and Development in Rio de Janeiro. UNCED, especially, fuelled institutionalization in developing countries, since many of them created their first environmental authorities in order to participate in the conference.

An institution can be strengthened when its operations are streamlined, thus reducing many of its duplicative, sector-specific policies. It should also reduce bureaucracy and complexity in regulations, which may engender some good will with businesses and other branches of government. Institutionalization, however, is still based on a win–lose mentality. By building a stronger institution, 'we' – in the environmental authority – seek to strengthen our position and win more battles against 'them' – the rest of society.

An environmental authority may win more battles this way, but it will not come much closer to winning the 'war'. In the first place, the opponents are still too strong. An environmental authority is unlikely ever to have the staff, budget and political clout single-handedly to defeat government economic authorities and the private sector. Second, institutionalization may become a trap which actually makes an environmental authority *less* effective. Policy makers may increasingly define their mission as strengthening the institution and winning political battles, rather than really solving environmental problems. In this case, the *means* of implementing policy – such as laws and regulations – may become *ends* in themselves. Third, any measures which environmental authorities can force on their opponents will only be implemented half-heartedly, at best. Truly solving environmental problems – moving toward sustainability – requires abandoning the war mentality and making a more concerted effort to work with other parties.

Integration

Policy makers can avoid the institutionalization trap by recognizing that they cannot succeed on their own. The environment is integrated into every aspect of the economy and society. Thus, environmental policy must be integrated into all aspects of government policy, business operations and societal attitudes. This certainly is not an easy task, but it is the only approach that can succeed.

If environmental policy makers listen hard enough, they may hear some positive overtures from their old enemies. In the mid-1980s, for example, some companies approached the Dutch Environment Department with a view to establishing environmental care systems. These were generally not the companies with the best environmental records, but they were under considerable political pressure to clean up their operations. They hoped that working with the government to develop environmental care systems would be a good way to get out of trouble with regulators.

Integration begins with better communication, both among employees within the institution, and with society at large. In the beginning, the Dutch Environment Department was not speaking the same language as most other sectors in society. We began to remedy this language gap with the policy life cycle, which was also adopted by other departments, businesses and NGOs as a common vision of how the policy process develops. Then the themes helped forge consensus both within the government and among other sectors on the description of environmental issues. Formulating the themes with the other departments was important because it led to agreement on the terms of the environmental debate. Moreover, the themes provided a structure for developing common goals: we could work out targets with the parties that were involved for each theme.

The designation of target groups had even broader reach than the themes. Here, the Environment Department did not try to define new structures, but to utilize existing ones. It proved very difficult to approach environmental causes according to the different media they impacted, since this was an artificial structure created by our department. It made more sense to address causes through existing business sectors which were already organized and practised in negotiating. This approach helped us communicate with other government entities which already used these designations, such as the Ministry of Economic Affairs. At the same time, we were better prepared to approach economic sectors directly.

New cooperation with other government departments emerged in the joint preparation of the IMPs, allowing us to work with other entities which were responsible for aspects of the environment: the Department of Agriculture and the Department of Waterworks. In the National Environmental Policy Plan, we expanded these contacts to include the Ministry of

Foreign Affairs and bodies that traditionally were not involved in environmental policy: the ministries of Finance and Economic Affairs. Preparing a joint policy plan, however, is not an end in itself; it is only one of the means to integration. Laying out priorities in a plan helped the Dutch Environment Department to clarify its own thinking and to open discussions with other parties. True integration, however, results from a process, not a plan. The process requires continual dialogue and engagement.

We are still working on integration in the Netherlands. Significant conflicts persist among various departments in the government. The infrastructure plans of the Department of Transportation, for example, often seem to contradict the Environment Department's goals for the transport sector. The daily struggles within the government and with the private sector will probably continue for many years; but concrete instruments for integration have been developed. These include negotiated contracts, or *covenants,* with target groups to implement environmental goals. Several structures have also been set up within the government to integrate its environmental policies. For example, all government departments must report the environmental implications of their annual budgets.

Imbuing

After a lot of teamwork, hikers can get so good at working together that they do it instinctively. This is also the goal of integrated environmental policies. The last phase of policy development, still some way off, is for environmental sensibilities to be *imbued* in society's regular behaviour. 'The environment' will disappear as a separate area of policy, but environmental concerns and information will direct people's actions as much as economic factors do today.

While this new behaviour will come partly from better public education and awareness, political and economic structures can also help integrate environmental concerns into everyday decisions. Relying entirely on good will is not only unrealistic but unfair. Very few people will put themselves at a financial disadvantage or endure additional hardships in order to live sustainably, and they should not have to. In some cases, the environmental choice is already the economic and convenient one. In many crowded cities, for example, it is easier and cheaper not to have a car and instead to travel by alternative means, such as walking, cycling or public transportation. This is only possible, however, where there is an infrastructure which supports alternative means (and perhaps also discourages car use).

In most cases, however, the environmental choice is still the hard one, and government policies should steer economic, social and technological developments toward sustainability. Environmental protection measures, for example, have encouraged many businesses to develop 'clean technologies' which substitute benign materials or processes for ones which are harmful to the environment. In recent years the electronics industry, for example, has phased out the use of ozone-destroying CFCs as cleaning solvents and replaced them with water-based solutions.

Yet technological fixes will not suffice. Consumer and producer behaviour will have to change as well; and financial instruments can be powerful tools to hasten these changes. One method is to remove price distortions which encourage environmentally harmful behaviour, such as subsidies for extractive industries, automobile use, or suburban sprawl. Other methods include 'internalizing' the environmental costs of harmful activities through taxes or user fees, or providing tax breaks and subsidies to more environmentally friendly practices.

Financial measures are difficult to implement, since they challenge the existing power structure of the economy. Good financial instruments should produce more 'winners' than 'losers,' but potential losers often provide formidable opposition to change. The challenge for policy makers is to stack up enough political support to make such changes possible. Some governments, for example, are eagerly looking for ways to reduce public expenditures and balance their budgets; and environmentally harmful subsidies provide an attractive target. In addition, major institutions like the European Union, the Organization for Economic Cooperation and Development and the World Bank are now examining the environmental impacts of current subsidy programmes.

Overlaps in Reality

Like any policy model, the four phases are only an approximation of how things actually happen. In reality, policy developments cannot be neatly divided into different stages; there will be considerable overlap. In addition, some aspects of policy are at later stages of development than others, as is the case with recycling and climate change. In the Netherlands, recycling is well on its way to being imbued into society; people are starting to do it instinctively. The response to climate change, in contrast, is rather *ad hoc*. A few measures exist to promote efficiency or alternative energy, but there is still disagreement over the extent of the problem; or whether it even is a problem. Institutionalization is just emerging. Integration and imbuing are yet further off.

Table 1 The four stages of environmental policy

Phase	Ad hoc	Institutionalization	Integration	Imbuing
Goals	Per issue	Per department	Common goals among parties	Overall societal objectives
Responsibility	Government section	Government department/ ministry	Target groups	Producers/ consumers
Means	Decrees, subsidies	Legislation	Joint planning, covenants	Economic instruments

CHAPTER 4

Wandering in the Woods
Beginning the National Environmental Policy Plan

By the time Pieter Winsemius left office, there was a general feeling in the Department that producing the National Environmental Policy Plan would be a fairly routine task. The IMPs had broken the back of the job, we reasoned; the NEPP would merely require some refined analysis based on the environmental themes. We felt we had covered most of the NEPP trail after leaving the IMPs behind us, and we expected to reach our destination by nightfall. But we realized later that we still had a very long way to go — and that we didn't even know what direction to take.

Getting Started

The first initiative to start the NEPP was taken by Jan Suurland, who became the Director of *Bestuurszaken* in 1983 after Frans Evers was promoted to Deputy Director General. In early 1986, Jan assembled a small working group for the NEPP: Gustaaf Biezeveld, Koos van der Vaart, Wim Iestra and myself. Koos had been a member of Gustaaf Biezeveld's team developing *More that the Sum of Its Parts* and he was currently heading a section in the *Bestuurszaken* directorate which examined the economic aspects of policy. Wim Iestra also worked in this section.

We had made considerable progress on the integration of policies by the time of the third IMP, which was due to be released in September 1986. Jan Suurland felt we had a sufficient foundation for the NEPP and that such a plan would be critical in capturing political support to restructure environmental policies. 'It would create political awareness of the need for far-reaching environmental measures,' Jan explains, 'if we could make it clear that "business as usual" scenarios would result in severe environmental degradation.'[1] At the time, I do not think that anyone realized how difficult developing this plan would be, which may have been fortunate. Had we known what to expect, we might never have begun.

Jan proposed starting with a workshop of stakeholders from the

Department, other government departments, industry, local and provincial governments, and environmentalists. The meeting was convened in the village of Veldhoven in May 1986. There were about forty participants who discussed two topics: what issues should be covered under the NEPP and what conditions were necessary to develop substantive policies. The first question drew a wide spectrum of replies, but most of them focused on local issues, including very minor problems like litter and dirty sidewalks! Despite the years spent trying to integrate our work in the Environment Department, we found that thinking was still rooted in the *ad hoc* phase of environmental policy.

The discussion on conditions for substantive policies included such suggestions as: providing clear scientific evidence of problems, considering economic and ecological impacts, and reaching agreement on solutions among the stakeholders. The criteria resembled those we had used for environmental impact assessments, and they were eventually incorporated into the Dutch approach. At the time, however, I feared that the list we were formulating might prove discouraging. It made the process look quite complicated right from the beginning, since we had no idea how to accomplish most of these tasks. I also felt that making such a list put too much emphasis on bureaucratic mechanisms and not enough on the political process that would be needed for reform.

Although the group at Veldhoven agreed on the value of a NEPP, they certainly had different images of what it should entail. The Department wanted a comprehensive, long-term plan to further the work on policy integration. Businesses wanted more open communication with the government and the predictability of long-term policies. Local and provincial governments sought more guidance (and funding) from The Hague. And environmentalists wanted a strong plan with far-reaching targets. There was enough common ground among stakeholders to get started, but clearly reconciling people's concerns would be a long process.

There was little agreement within the Department on how the NEPP should be prepared and who should lead the project. Since I was working on the third IMP, which was considered the predecessor to the NEPP, I felt some pressure to serve as project leader again. I had reservations about this, however, partly because the NEPP was a huge task which might end in disaster. I was still mulling over the situation when Frans Evers announced the reorganization of the Directorate for Radiation Protection. He offered me the position of Deputy Director, which looked like an exciting career move given the recent Chernobyl incident. I still felt responsible, however, for the NEPP. When I mentioned this to Frans, he said that he was considering my colleague, Bram Breure, to head that project, which I found to be an excellent choice.

Bram came to the Environment Department in 1981. In 1984, Frans Evers asked him to join a small unit of project managers linked to the

Director General's staff. Evers deployed this team throughout the Department to help push reform efforts. Bram's first assignment was to the Directorate for Waste, where he worked with Allen Hickling to increase stakeholder participation in policies. Through this experience he came to know and greatly respect Hickling's approach. Bram also assisted the Air Directorate on a project called Hydrocarbons 2000, which eventually led to an agreement with industry to reduce emissions of these pollutants vastly by the end of the century.* The goals of the project were met well ahead of schedule, and the agreement served as a model for the covenants with business we would employ a few years later.

Because he was never tied to a specific directorate, Bram seemed well positioned to build broad-based support for the NEPP in the Environment Department. He began this task in the autumn of 1986 by putting together several working groups. His core team consisted of Marjolijn Burggraaff, Paul Nouwen and Michel Janssens. Nouwen was a staffer in the Waste Directorate and, like Bram, a fan of Allen Hickling's strategic choice approach. Janssens had previously served on my IMP team. Bram also invited Allen Hickling and his colleague Arnold de Jong to work as consultants on the NEPP.

Bram put a lot of thought into structuring the process to develop the NEPP; he later described his approach as '70 per cent process and 30 per cent content'.[2] In addition to his core group, he also created a 'philosophy group', an interdepartmental group, and a steering group. The philosophy group consisted of individuals, including myself, who discussed theoretical aspects of the plan. The steering group was a high-level forum chaired by Willem Reij and including his peers from the other ministries that had been involved in the IMPs. Finally, there was an interdepartmental group with representatives from the ministries of Economic Affairs, of Transport and Waterworks, and of Agriculture, Nature Protection and Fisheries. The members of this last group were not given much authority to negotiate. Bram felt that the colleagues from the Ministry of Economic Affairs, for example, were sent mainly as 'gate keepers' to insure that the Environment Department did not cause 'too much trouble'.

Despite the resistance he often encountered, Bram was very committed to soliciting broad involvement in the NEPP process. As he describes it:

> There is a widespread (and still increasing) need to stop acting as 'experts' who push the content from the inside to the outside of an organization. Instead, there is more and more recognition that an organization – like any living organism – can only thrive if it is able to relate to its environment, giving full attention to the input from outside. This essentially 'interactive' approach was in its pioneering stage in 1986. No wonder that the resistance against it was great.[3]

---

* For more information on the Hydrocarbons 2000 agreement, please see Chapter 9.

Bram was concerned, for example, about rivalries between the newly appointed theme and target group coordinators and the heads of the old sectoral directorates in the Environment Department. Marius Enthoven, who was Inspector General at the time, agrees that the conditions within the Department were difficult: 'Many of the directors at that stage didn't feel the need for integration that much and, well, they wanted to limit the damage.'[4] Another difficulty was the NEPP's lack of a high-ranking 'sponsor' in the Department to defend the process in its first vulnerable year.

Leadership Changes in the Ministry

Ed Nijpels had a hard act to follow when he became Environment Minister in 1986, because Pieter Winsemius had grown very popular, especially for his campaign on acid rain and his handling of the Chernobyl crisis. Furthermore, Ed admits that 'the environment was not one of my favourite subjects at that time.'[5] Though Nijpels had no formal experience in environmental policy, he was a tremendously fast learner. Nijpels soon developed a keen understanding not only of 'the environment' but also of the strategic approach we had been pursuing in the Department. It was not until 1987, however, that he could focus his energies on the NEPP.

Perhaps the highest priority for the Ministry, at first, was preparing the fourth *nota* on land use planning. Ed's work on this *nota* taught him some lessons about how to sell a major policy document – lessons he later applied to the NEPP. For instance, Ed worked hard at building multi-party support for the fourth *nota* by holding discussions with all the political parties in Parliament. 'It was very strange that a minister from the right-wing coalition was giving a presentation to the socialists in Parliament,' he recalls. In addition to the fourth *nota,* Ed had to manage a potential crisis in the Department for Government Buildings, which was revealed to have an 800 million guilder ($400 million) budgetary shortfall.

Meanwhile there was a lot of uncertainty about the senior leadership of the Department. Willem Reij was nearing retirement age and Nijpels had to find a successor. Frans Evers, the likely candidate, fell ill shortly after Bram began work on the NEPP. By the time Frans returned, Ed Nijpels had decided it was best to make him the new Director General for Government Buildings in the hope that he would bring some order to the troubled department. Frans's departure was another obstacle for Bram Breure, as Marjolijn Burggraaff recalls: 'That was a problem for Bram. His sponsor in the department was not there anymore.'[6] To make matters worse, Willem Reij was also ill at the time. Frans's successor, Pieter Verkerk, did his best to pick up the pieces; but he was overwhelmed by many pressing tasks, especially the strategy for acid rain. He was unable to work much on the NEPP at first.

Some Ideas Take Shape

We eventually got a clear picture for the content of the NEPP, thanks to the National Institute for Health and Environment (RIVM).* The institute had been created in 1982 during the last days of the old Ministry of Health and Environmental Hygiene by merging three institutes: those for Drinking Water and for Waste, and the large institute for Health in the village of Bilthoven (near Utrecht). The collaboration between RIVM and the Environment Department was built on a few strong personal contacts. Ruud van Noort and Kees Zoeteman, for example, had both worked in the old Ministry of Health and Environmental Hygiene, and they moved to RIVM when it was founded. Van Noort became the institute's Director General while Zoeteman became his deputy director for the environment. The two agreed on the importance of integrating the institute's operations and on the need to produce scientific findings which would be useful to policy makers. Ruud van Noort was actually an economist, an unusual background for the head of a scientific institute, and was to develop a critical emphasis on economic analysis at RIVM.

Another important link was that between Koos van der Vaart and Fred Langeweg. Koos came to the Environment Department's *Bestuurszaken* directorate in 1979; and first joined a long-established project with the Free University of Amsterdam that gathered very precise data on how different sectors of industry were contributing to overall pollution. 'That was all interesting,' Koos recalls, 'but it wasn't very policy-relevant.'[7] To make this information more useful, Koos encouraged the university researchers to link their scientific findings with existing economic data and thereby forecast how economic developments would affect the environment. After its founding in 1982, RIVM took over the forecasting work from the university.

Through his work with the university and the new RIVM, Koos got to know Fred Langeweg, who headed the institute's Laboratory for Waste and Emissions. In 1984, Koos approached Fred and proposed an experiment on integrated resource assessment and planning in the eastern province of Gelderland. Their work introduced RIVM and the Environment Department to the same questions of integration they would soon face on a national scale through the NEPP.

This task began in the spring of 1987 when Jan Suurland commissioned RIVM to prepare an integrated national environmental assessment as a possible guide for the NEPP. Koos, who was in Jan's directorate at the time, worked intensively with RIVM to produce a powerful scientific study which would also have political significance. For Koos, the challenge was to develop a uniform way to express RIVM's voluminous environmental data.

* Rijksinstituut voor Volksgezondheid en Milieuhygiene.

'The difficult thing', he recalls, 'was to get the same kind of prognosis for every theme.' At that time, the most sophisticated research had been done for acidification, because it is such a critical problem, and its causes are so well known. Scientists had succeeded in identifying major sources (such as sulphur dioxide or nitrogen oxides), aggregating them, and studying how certain levels of pollutants would ultimately affect environmental quality. 'They could cover the whole thing' Koos explains, 'from source to the eventual effect.'

Such detailed information did not exist for most other issues. Under the local disturbance theme, for example, noise pollution was based more on subjective research, such as opinion surveys. To express this theme in more precise terms, RIVM had to develop quantitative measurements, such as the number of homes which would be exposed to noise beyond a certain decibel rating in the year 2010. According to Koos, the task was not for RIVM 'merely to use what they already had, but to ensure that every theme had the same *kind* of results, so that you could compare them.'

RIVM's environmental quality report eventually provided the foundation for a strong environmental plan. The NEPP team would not even have RIVM's preliminary findings until early 1988, however, nearly a year after the report was commissioned. The lack of concrete information and 'sponsorship' from the department's leadership were quite demoralizing. In hiking terms, the NEPP team was wandering in circles. Not that I fault them for this wandering. Nothing like the NEPP had ever been done before; they had to make their own trail.

I experienced some of this wandering in November 1987 when Bram asked me to facilitate a day-long meeting of department directors in Scheveningen, a seaside neighbourhood of The Hague. The morning discussions soon revealed a variety of opinions on what the NEPP should accomplish, specifically on how to continue policies for the five environmental themes. Some participants, such as Marius Enthoven, argued that the themes should be approached as five distinct policy areas. In this case, much of our work was done, they argued; and we simply had to work out specific policies for each theme. Other people, such as Jan Suurland and Kees Zoeteman, suggested linking the themes to add new elements, such as the relationship between environmental and energy policies or more emphasis on public health.

From a managerial perspective, it is certainly easier to handle five distinct policy areas than to meld them together. From an intellectual perspective, however, there are clearly many interrelationships among the five themes. Furthermore, if the themes were kept separate, it was likely that environmental policies would continue to be carried out in a compartmentalized fashion – there would simply be five new compartments. Although it would be more difficult, relating the themes to each other seemed the only way to move toward more efficient, integrated policies. Throughout these discussions, I was struggling to bring the group towards a focus for the NEPP which could unite the five themes.

In the late afternoon Jan Suurland came to my rescue: the central issue, he said, was reconciling environmental and economic interests. A long-standing assumption in politics held that the environment and the economy are mutually exclusive; but they are not. The economy is dependent on the environment for its resources and services (like purifying water and neutralizing pollution). Furthermore, it can be argued that a decent living standard and economic efficiency are needed before people have the incentive and ability to focus on environmental concerns.

Jan proposed using the concept of 'sustainable development' to show the interdependence of the environment and the economy. The term had been around for several years, but it gained international recognition after it was included in the Brundtland Commission's report, *Our Common Future*. The original intention of sustainable development was to bridge the gap between industrialized and developing nations. Concerned with limiting the global environmental burden, and perhaps still influenced by *The Limits to Growth*, industrialized countries often denied the legitimate right of developing nations to harness their environmental resources and improve living conditions. Sustainable development implied that economic activity needn't destroy the environment, but could be carried out at a sustainable level which would improve the economy without reducing environmental quality. Suurland argued that the same logic Brundtland applied to developing countries could also be applied to industrialized ones.

It was a vague concept, but it was also late in the day, and almost everyone agreed that sustainable development should be the focus of the NEPP. The one vocal critic was Marius Enthoven, who warned us not to remain on such an abstract level. He already saw how far we had to go to achieve a concrete environmental plan. Sustainable development did become the major *philosophical* underpinning of the NEPP, but our work was not really energized until we had the *scientific* base provided by the RIVM.

Clear Information

RIVM always had top-notch scientists, but they were not accustomed to communicating with anyone but their peers. When they succeeded in packaging their information, even our staff were amazed at the severity of the environmental problems the RIVM study had chronicled. Koos van der Vaart and Fred Langeweg worked intensively to coordinate the study and refine its message. The two men realized that they needed to write, not for scientists, but specifically for government officials. As Fred explains, 'What a policy maker wants to know is: What is the problem? Is it important? And what can I do to solve it, possibly within three or four years?'[8] He chuckles after this last remark, then adds one more question: 'What are the costs and benefits of it?'

This last criterion is extremely important. If scientists rarely examined the political implications of their work, they virtually never evaluated economic impacts.* Fortunately, both the previous Director General of RIVM, Hans Cohen, and his successor, Ruud van Noort, felt the organization should have some capacity in this field. In 1984, the new position of staff economist was filled by Rob Maas, who had previously worked on labour market issues at the Netherlands Economic Institute. An energetic man with a perpetual boyish grin, Rob is also a very bright analyst who understands his work's political implications.

In 1986, Rob developed a computer model that examined the costs and benefits of traditional pollution control methods, often termed 'end-of-pipe' technologies. They simply filter and treat harmful emissions or effluents – without addressing the processes that create pollution. Rob's model showed, as he had expected, that such policies were not very effective. 'Simply using end-of-pipe measures is expensive,' he explains, 'and it wastes material. You are just moving waste from one environmental compartment to another one.' Rob theorized that it would be much better to change production and consumption patterns – for example by reducing or recycling waste products, rather than simply treating and storing them. 'If you could raise the efficiency of the economy or if you could re-use materials, you could save end-of-pipe abatement costs, and you could save the costs of primary materials. You could get better environmental quality *and* better economic growth.'[9]

Later, Rob encountered Donald Huising, an American professor of resource economics who taught at the Erasmus University in Rotterdam. Huising was travelling around Europe lecturing on 'pollution prevention'. He presented case studies of American firms, such as 3M and Monsanto, that had taken measures to rethink their operations and reduce or recycle harmful industrial by-products. Within a short time, these companies could demonstrate genuine cost savings from their efforts, as summed up by what 3M called its 3P strategy: *pollution prevention pays.*

Kees Zoeteman was very excited about the work of Fred Langeweg, Koos van der Vaart and Rob Maas. Langeweg's team had made considerable progress in refining its environmental data and putting it into precise terms for policy makers, but they still lacked an overall philosophy. Kees realized they needed a concise, powerful message to have a real political impact, and he proposed the concept of *environmental scale*. Even with the theme approach developed by Pieter Winsemius, environmental issues were still confusing for most people because of their geographical context. Some

---

* We made a start in economic analysis by including cost estimates in the three integrated IMPs.

THE END-OF-PIPE FALLACY

Environmental protection originally meant cleaning up the effects of pollution, not preventing its causes, and 'pollution' referred to the obvious 'point sources' like factory smokestacks or outflow pipes into rivers. Assuming that the manner of production could not be changed, regulators intervened at the very end of the process – often literally at the end of the pipe – where they mandated some type of filtering system to capture the worst pollutants. It was all right for companies to make a mess, as long as they also cleaned it up.

'Pollution prevention' introduced, for the first time, the idea that it might be cheaper, and better for the environment, not to make a mess in the first place.

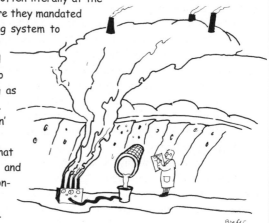

Figure 9 End-of-pipe measures

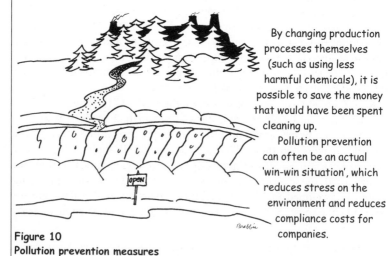

By changing production processes themselves (such as using less harmful chemicals), it is possible to save the money that would have been spent cleaning up.

Pollution prevention can often be an actual 'win-win situation', which reduces stress on the environment and reduces compliance costs for companies.

Figure 10
Pollution prevention measures

problems, such as noise, odours or indoor air pollution, only affect a local area. Other problems, like water pollution, can affect a region or even a whole country; whereas acid rain often effects several countries. Still other problems, like ozone depletion or nuclear fall-out, can affect the whole world – a point made very clearly by Chernobyl. Categorizing environmental issues according to geographic scale would clarify the responsibilities of different public authorities. 'At the lower-scale levels are issues to be dealt with by communities,' Kees explains.[10] 'Other issues, like acid rain, are to be dealt with in the European Union. And something like climate change is actually a United Nations problem.'

RIVM eventually developed a scheme with five levels of scale. They are:

- *Local* – fairly simple problems around the home or in neighbourhoods, such as noise, odour and public safety. These have relatively minor impacts on the environment, and they can often be remedied by urban planning and zoning.

- *Regional* – affect cities and counties. Examples include solid waste disposal and toxic contamination through the water table. Usually, municipal and provincial governments can address such problems.

- *Watershed (Fluvial)* – includes pollution or depletion of entire water systems. They are often international in scale, since major rivers like the Rhine and the Danube pass through several countries. National or international efforts are required in these cases.

- *Continental* – acid rain is a prime example. Of the acidifying substances that reach the Netherlands, 56 per cent originate in other countries, such as Germany, Poland, and Britain, whereas approximately 70 per cent of Dutch emissions are 'exported' to neighbouring countries.[11] Multilateral international efforts are needed for such problems.

- *Global* – problems affecting the entire planet. They can only be handled by international bodies, such as the United Nations. Examples include climate change, stratospheric ozone depletion, and global deforestation.

The scale metaphor was used to completely reorganize the institute's environmental assessment work. 'Everything was there anyway, but we rearranged the stuff,' explains Langeweg. 'As science, that was trivial, but for communication purposes it was an ideal approach.'

RIVM then hired public relations consultants to help consolidate the message further. The consultants told them they would have to catch people's attention in the first three or four sentences. The staff spent about a month looking through their work to find the essential message. They knew, for example, that pollution had to be cut tremendously to prevent further deterioration of the country's environment. The actual amount varied, of course, for different substances and different media. But on

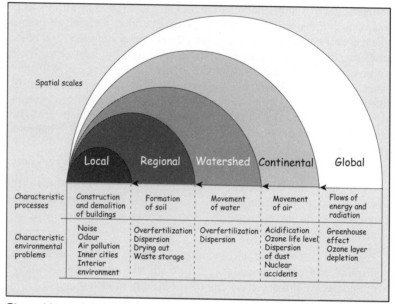

Figure 11 Spatial scales of environmental problems: the characteristics and problems at the local, regional, watershed, continental and global levels
Source: *RIVM*

average, the staff reckoned that pollution had to be cut by somewhere between *70 and 90 per cent* – a tremendous amount! Next, the staff looked at how such reductions could be effected. Rob Maas had shown that conventional end-of-pipe technologies were inefficient, even for the much smaller reductions required by existing regulations. Any further measures would have to address the very structure of processes that were causing emissions, as the new 'pollution prevention' strategies seemed to do.

RIVM condensed these ideas in three sentences:

1 Preserving the Dutch environment will require 70 to 90 per cent reductions of all pollution.*

2 Such reductions cannot be achieved by conventional end-of-pipe technologies.

3 Therefore, a structural change in production and consumption patterns will be required†

* This did not include carbon dioxide (CO_2). Although it was suspected that such reductions would also be required for CO_2, no 'quality standards' were developed for it in the RIVM report.
† This was the first time in the Netherlands (and perhaps in any country) that a government institution endorsed the 'environmentalist' argument of changing production and consumption.

The staff at RIVM developed a standard presentation for any issue. They began with the three sentences and the five levels of scale to provide the overall context. Then they launched into the particular issue they were discussing and explained how it fitted into the big picture. This strategy resembled the 'management by speech' approach of Minister Winsemius, by which he discussed issues in the context of the policy life cycle.

Quite a Shock

Most of us in the Environment Department remained unaware of RIVM's work for some time. We spent a year wandering in the *process* of the NEPP without having much *substance* to direct us. 'RIVM was working on issues,' Marius Enthoven recalls. 'They would come up with something, but it was not entirely clear at that stage. Bram Breure was doing all kinds of exercises with the directors, which were useful, but at some stage didn't make progress.' One day, Marius and the new Deputy Director General, Pieter Verkerk, decided to get together a group of people to discuss the NEPP and the work of RIVM. The group included Kees Zoeteman, Rob Maas, Fred Langeweg, Bram Breure, Marjolijn Burggraaff, Henk Brouwer, Gerard Wolters and myself. We decided to meet on a Tuesday morning in early February 1988 at RIVM's offices in the town of Bilthoven.

I shared a car to the meeting with Marjolijn Burggraaff and Henk Brouwer. Henk had been my boss in the section for environmental impact assessment, and he was still heading that section. He and I were not official members of the NEPP project team, but Marius wanted our input. 'I wonder what Marius has in mind for this meeting?' Henk asked as we drove along the dark and misty fields that morning. 'Certainly he wants to save the idea of having a strong NEPP,' I answered, remembering Enthoven's criticism of the meeting at Scheveningen. 'It's too abstract,' he had told us. 'There's too much reliance on the *process*, and not on the *results* we want to get out of the process.' Marius, we have seen, had been unhappy that we were using a term as vague as sustainable development as the focus of the NEPP. Actually, I shared his concern; but, as the facilitator of that meeting, I was also happy to have reached some conclusion.

When we arrived at RIVM, we were directed into an ice-cold room where the others were waiting. It was a very informal meeting. We wore sweaters and slacks, and we looked more like a bunch of friends going hiking than government officials discussing sensitive political matters. We warmed up with some coffee, and then Marius gave the floor to Kees Zoeteman.

Kees began with the new concept of environmental scale, which was still pretty rough, but we immediately saw its value. The local scale, for example, covered the small problems that often get a lot of attention, but can be fairly easily controlled. The continental scale spoke to the problems that Gerard

Wolters and I were dealing with. Gerard, the director for air policy, was very busy with acid rain, which had become a problem throughout Europe. My work in the directorate for radiation protection obviously dealt with continental, and sometimes even global, issues. The Chernobyl incident was not even two years behind us then.

After Kees had spoken, Fred Langeweg presented the preliminary results of the study. His team had examined two future scenarios: one assuming that current policies would be continued, the other assuming that the best available end-of-pipe technologies would be employed. Both scenarios looked at present trends and extrapolated 25 years into the future (with 1985 as the base year). This was amazing for us, since such long-term modelling had been inconceivable only a few years earlier.

The first scenario demonstrated that current measures were sorely inadequate. Regarding acidification, for example, there was no hope of success. The scenario showed that emissions would drop somewhat if we continued our policies and if other countries honoured their international treaty commitments. RIVM found, however, that acid deposition would not fall below a critical load which the soil could neutralize; so damage would continue. Furthermore, emissions would soon rise again with future economic growth.

We were more surprised by the second scenario. Even using all technical means currently available or expected in the future, we could not preserve the country's environmental quality. In the case of acidification, RIVM found that the deposition on soil would have to drop by 80 per cent, from

Figure 12 Acid deposition in the Netherlands, 1986

Source: *Concern for Tomorrow*, pp. 84, 89.

Figure 13 Predicted acid deposition in the Netherlands, 2010

Source: *Concern for Tomorrow*, pp. 84, 89.

5,000 acid units per hectare per year to 1,000 units. We had considered a 20 per cent reduction as much as we could hope for, and probably would have settled for a levelling off. Furthermore, end-of-pipe technology would never be sufficient. It might be possible to achieve 80 per cent reductions on individual pipes, but that would not necessarily stop the absolute number of pipes from growing, nor the overall level of pollution from growing worse.

Kees Zoeteman then went through the results for other environmental problems and told us that overall pollution had to be cut by 70 to 90 per cent. Everyone from the Environment Department was stunned. We immediately began questioning the results. Had RIVM used the most up-to-date estimates for critical loads? Had they consulted with other scientific institutes in the Netherlands? Were they certain their predictions would hold up in the real world? Fred Langeweg replied that there were definitely some uncertainties, and the numbers might be off by a few percentage points. But there was no doubt that pollution had to be cut far more drastically than we had assumed up to that time, and that conventional methods would not do it.

We broke for lunch then, eating in almost complete silence as everyone thought over the implications of what we had learned. I realized that all the theories and strategies we had developed over the years, though very good, were not good enough to meet the full environmental challenge. I felt as if I were back in the late 1960s, when my friends and I knew that something 'revolutionary' had to be done to save the environment. Always I had sensed that things were going terribly wrong, but never had I had the scientific proof to validate my suspicion – not until that morning at RIVM.

'Let's take this seriously,' Marius told everyone after the short lunch break. 'Let's assume that RIVM can stick to these conclusions, even against fierce criticism.' He reminded us that the institute had an impeccable reputation and that its findings would have considerable weight. RIVM was also a health institute, with such duties as producing vaccines; and there is no room for error in that field. 'When RIVM comes out with these conclusions, it will be a political fact which requires an adequate political answer,' he told us. 'So let's use the RIVM report as the basis for the National Environmental Policy Plan.' Finally, we had the right sponsorship for this project in Marius, who was a senior member of the Environment Department, the likely candidate to succeed Willem Reij as Director General, and one of the most respected civil servants in the government. Marius announced that he would brief Minister Nijpels and Director General Reij on the RIVM meeting and ask for their full support.

Marius suggested that we take some time to work through our strategy internally before resuming discussions with the other departments. That very afternoon, we started brainstorming about the structure of the NEPP and drafted a rough table of contents. It should begin, we decided, with a description of the environmental themes and the levels of environmental scale. Next should come a section on the general principles behind all environmental policies, to be followed by chapters describing the long-term goals and the policy measures for different target groups we had defined. Finally would come the cost estimates for the plan.

Rob Maas was helpful here, since he had already made preliminary calculations for the two scenarios in the report. Under the first one, the continuation of current policies, total expenditures would rise from 7 billion guilders (US$3.5 billion) in 1985 to 16 billion guilders (US$8 billion) in the year 2010.[12] With projected economic growth, this meant that expenditures would remain at approximately 2 per cent of the country's gross domestic product (GDP). Under the second scenario, expenditures would rise to a level between 25 and 30 billion guilders ($12.5 to $15 billion), representing about a 3.5 per cent share of GDP.[13] We had no idea what a third scenario might cost.

We pondered how we could convince the public, and business, of the need for such radical reforms; then we decided to let the numbers speak for themselves. We later illustrated the high environmental burden in the Netherlands in the mid-1980s, for example, by comparing it with other industrialized countries.

Table 2 Environmental burdens per square kilometre, mid-1980s

Country	Population	Cars	Industrial production (in $1,000)	Energy consumption (tons of oil)	Head of cattle
Belgium	321	84	593	1,348	248
France	97	28	174	307	84
Germany (West)	248	72	713	986	145
Japan	298	47	446	892	30
Netherlands	**334**	**92**	**568**	**1,595**	**334**
New Zealand	11	4	5	38	226
United Kingdom	229	59	229	833	169
United States	23	12	42	81	12

Source: Organization for Economic Cooperation and Development

We concluded the meeting by assigning duties for the new NEPP, as it was clear that the main tasks would be handled by this very group. I was asked, for example, to prepare a chapter on the principles of future environmental policies. We also urged our colleagues from RIVM to continue working with other scientific institutes, in order to forge a solid consensus behind the report.

I think everyone felt that we were embarking on an historic undertaking that day. We knew it was a daunting task; but we were encouraged by the strength of the information and the high-level sponsorship. We had the same strange calmness as a group of hikers that gets lost far out in the woods. Panicking certainly wouldn't help; and it was impossible to turn back. We just had to push on and believe we would eventually find the way out.

Notes

1 All Jan Suurland quotations are from an interview with the author, The Hague, 4 March 1997.
2 Bram Breure, interview with the author, Leidschendam, 10 March 1997.
3 Bram Breure, personal correspondence with the author, 31 March 1998.
4 All Marius Enthoven quotations are from an interview with the author, Brussels, 11 March 1997.
5 All Ed Nijpels quotations are from interviews with the author, The Hague, 31 July and 8 August 1997.
6 All Marjolijn Burggraaff quotations are from an interview with the author, The Hague, 3 March 1997.
7 All Koos van der Vaart quotations are from an interview with the author, The Hague, 18 August 1997.
8 All Fred Langeweg quotations are from an interview with the author, Bilthoven, 6 March 1997.
9 All Rob Maas quotations are from an interview with the author, Bilthoven, 6 March 1997.
10 All Kees Zoeteman quotations are from an interview with the author, The Hague, 5 March 1997.
11 Organization for Economic Cooperation and Development, *Environmental Performance Review: the Netherlands* (Paris: OECD, 1995), 60.
12 Conversions to US dollars are based on the exchange rate of 26 April 1997.
13 National Institute of Public Health and Environment (RIVM), *Concern for Tomorrow*, English translation (Bilthoven: RIVM, 1989).

CHAPTER 5

Getting Our Bearings
Drafting the First NEPP

Some hikes are easy. There's not much danger of getting lost on a day trip in a public park, for instance. A long hike in a remote wilderness, however, can be much more difficult. It may look easy from afar – maybe the hikers want to go from one mountain to the next: what could be simpler! Once the group sets out, however, things get more complicated. There may be several possible routes, and the group has to decide which is best, given the weather and the abilities of the hikers. Even finding the trail may be difficult in a remote region where the path is poorly marked or overgrown in places.

The size of the party can be a further hindrance to finding the way. Everyone may have his or her own opinion about what route to take. They may all have good ideas, but it may be best for a smaller group to sit down and think out a strategy. We were in the same situation with the NEPP in early 1988. The workshops, brainstorming and interdepartmental groups had flooded the process with ideas, but we needed a few people to sit down and sort through the information before we could proceed. We had to get our bearings before continuing the journey.

Getting Started, Part Two

We made a new start on the National Environmental Policy Plan after the February meeting at RIVM. Willem Reij asked Marius Enthoven to supervise the project, thus filling the sponsorship position that had been empty since Frans Evers left the department about six months earlier. Enthoven's participation was a sign of the NEPP's new importance. Willem Reij would reach retirement age that year, and we were certain that Marius would be nominated as the next Director General of the Environment Department.

Marius began by forming a new team called the NEPP Support Group,*

---

* This was later renamed the NEPP Task Force, and then the Interdepartmental Group – an organization (with different members) which still plays an important role in developing the NEPP's strategies.

which included Bram Breure (who continued as project manager), Marjolijn Burggraaff, Henk Brouwer, Gerard Wolters, Kees Zoeteman, myself and, later, Peter van der Kolk. Enthoven was not an official member, but he chaired all the meetings. The environment directors supported our decision to suspend the interdepartmental work temporarily; and the leadership of the other departments didn't object, either. Frankly, the other departments were probably glad of the break.

It soon became clear that there were significantly different perspectives in the team. Marius, for example, wanted to develop the strongest possible response to the RIVM studies as quickly as possible. Bram and Marjolijn feared we would provoke a backlash from the other government departments if we presented them with a demanding 'take it or leave it' plan. The different opinions were a sign of the new dynamics in the group. Marius had taken over Bram's role of managing the NEPP *process,* and he wanted Bram to drive the development of *content* for the plan. Naturally, Bram tended to continue in his former management role.

While we were working on the first draft of the NEPP, Bram Breure collapsed with a heart ailment; and he remained at home for some time. It seemed that we were suffering casualties before the battle had even started, and we wondered if we were pushing ourselves too hard! Bram's illness forced an important decision on Marius Enthoven, who did not share Bram's vision of how the NEPP should evolve. According to Marius, 'Bram had problems in making the change from the process-oriented stage to talking about all the new RIVM findings. I took the decision that Bram probably was not the best person at this stage to guide the process and that we would need a new project leader.'* I can't say whether or not this was the right decision, but I do know it is generally useful to bring new people into long-term policy projects. The original people will inevitably burn out, and new energy is always helpful.

Marius had been pleased with my work on the third IMP and my general interest in the NEPP. He asked me if I would consider taking over from Bram, but I told him I had to think about it. I did not want to 'steal' the job from my friend Bram. I was also quite happy with my work in the Radiation Protection Directorate. Finally, I was very uncertain of where the NEPP project was going. Would I be leading it up a mountain or off a cliff?

I soon got some reassuring news. Despite the problems we were facing, the directors of the Environment Department clearly wanted to push on with the NEPP. There were also encouraging signs from other government

---

* Bram returned to the department and worked on a project to implement the European Union's directive on international hazardous waste shipments. Later he became a management consultant with the firm of Smeekes, van der Wiel and Partners where he has advised clients on environmental topics, including implementation of the Hydrocarbons 2000 agreement he had helped develop. Recently he has also worked outside the environmental field on projects for large Dutch corporations and government departments.

departments. On 26 and 27 April, we described the RIVM report and our planned response to representatives of the environmental 'inner circle' – the departments of Nature Protection and Waterworks and the coordinating section for environmental policy in the Ministry of Economic Affairs. To our surprise, they were not as negative as we had expected. The RIVM studies were very convincing, and our colleagues liked the concrete nature of the NEPP, including the 70 to 90 per cent pollution reduction goal. Although this was very ambitious, it was at least something tangible. Of course, the colleagues present were also the most 'environmental' people from their respective ministries.

The New Team

With Enthoven's imminent promotion and the positive response from the other directors, it was clear that the project was really going somewhere. At the end of April, I accepted Enthoven's offer. One of the first things I did was change my title from project *manager* to project *leader*. I felt my primary role should be to drive the development of content for the plan, rather than to manage the process (which seemed a better role for Marius). Marius and I always had a good understanding of what we wanted from the NEPP. Our relationship resembled the old dynamic between Bram Breure and Frans Evers.

The first meeting of my new team was on 16 May 1988. It was a small group consisting of Marjolijn Burggraaff, Paul Nouwen, Peter van der Kolk, Alka Bodrij and my new secretary, Marie-Therese Lammers. Paul Nouwen had worked with Bram Breure on various projects in the past, and he had the same enthusiasm for Allen Hickling's strategic choice approach. I knew Peter as a very capable attorney from the *Bestuurszaken* Directorate. Alka was a consultant from TNO, the National Institute for Applied Sciences. Marie-Therese was officially just a typist, but I soon realized she had much more to offer.

Marjolijn was especially valuable because she had been involved for the entire integration process, from the report *More than the Sum of Its Parts*, through all three IMPs and Bram's original NEPP team. 'I wanted very much to do the first NEPP as the culmination of my work,' she explains. 'I wanted to cover the whole range.' Marjolijn is a talented writer, and I especially valued her help in developing and refining the NEPP text. She also started the custom of making hot chocolate in the evenings, which did a lot to keep our spirits up.

In the first weeks, we sequestered ourselves in an intense working group we jokingly called 'the conclave', after the gathering of Cardinals which meets to elect a new Pope. This proved an ironically appropriate term years later, when a frustrated representative of the energy sector called the NEPP a 'Bible' and branded me 'the Pope of the NEPP'. We were almost completely secluded at the time, and privacy was pretty much assured by our location. We met in a deserted office building which had belonged to the defunct Department of Environmental Hygiene. It was a miserable concrete structure from the 1960s, but it was all ours. We had plenty of room to hold meetings, hang up charts and lists of ideas, or just make a mess. Our group worked late each night drafting a new text for the NEPP. My only opportunities to leave the office were brief runs with Marjolijn to a sandwich vendor who had set up just outside our building. He did quite a good business in that time and must have faced ruin after the NEPP was completed in the spring of 1989.

I developed a great appreciation in those days for Marie-Therese Lammers, a former primary school teacher who had taken a temporary position as Bram Breure's secretary. Bram soon realized Marie-Therese's talents, as did I after joining the NEPP project. I generally spent my days in various meetings, returning to the office in the evening to write. It may sound medieval now, but we scarcely had any computers then. I wrote the NEPP with a new fountain pen I had just bought, and I gave the texts to Marie-Therese for typing. In her days as a teacher, she had reviewed and critiqued her pupils' essays, and she did the same for me. Marie-Therese often pointed out sections which were unclear and encouraged me to refine them. She was the first person to edit the NEPP.

Marie-Therese was also very helpful in handling logistics, an especially critical task during our later negotiations with other government departments and stakeholder groups. She had a very good feel for the process, and she understood the need to keep all the participants well informed. Marie-Therese served as a type of 'right hand' for me, seeing to those seemingly mundane, but actually critical, details such as scheduling meetings or ensuring that everyone receives the most recent drafts of documents.

Each Generation's Responsibility

We worked very intensively during the week but generally kept our weekends free, although the NEPP certainly never left my mind. In my free time, I often went hiking with my friend Paul Mantel, whom I had known since student days at the University of Leyden. The exercise and fresh air, and my conversations with Paul, were good opportunities to mull over ideas for the NEPP. After graduating from Leyden, Paul became a high school teacher; and he often challenged me to explain my ideas in terms that his pupils could understand.

One of my tasks was to write the chapter explaining the principles of environmental policies, including the 'sustainable development' conundrum. The Brundtland report defined it as 'development that meets the needs of the present generation without compromising the ability of future generations to meet their own needs'.[1] But what are the 'needs' of future generations? Are they the same as our own? Are they greater, or smaller? We could not answer these questions. In fact, we could not even define our own generation's needs. Are the 'needs' of a European the same as the needs of an African or an Asian?

I remember discussing these questions with Paul on one of our hikes. 'Needs?' he said. 'I thought you were paid for *solving problems!*' I considered his reply. We knew, more or less, what the environmental problems were; the RIVM report told us very clearly. Now, I wondered, how should we go about solving them, and how long would it take? Brundtland clearly stated that each generation was responsible for the welfare of the next. Thus, it was our responsibility to solve the current problems and leave a clean environment to our children. They might mess things up again, but that would be their problem, and their responsibility. This sentiment recalled the philosophy of Pieter Winsemius in his book *Guests in Our Own Home*. Each generation had to behave as a guest on this Earth and leave the 'home' in good shape for future visitors.

Next, I had to define 'a generation', which I estimated at twenty-five years. The NEPP was originally conceived as a mid-term plan, simply describing policy over the next four to five years. With the concept of sustainable development, however, the NEPP could provide a long-term vision of how society would appear in a generation. This was a major shift in our thinking, encouraged by Ms Brundtland and my fellow hiker!

The long-term perspective proved very valuable in our dealings with business. We would still make demands of companies; in fact we would make considerably more than in the past. We could also give them sufficient warning and time, however, to fulfil these demands. As Pieter Winsemius later observed:

> The Ministry and business were fighting on today's issues all the time. If you created an opening [via long-term goals], you could relax a bit more. It became something which was much more negotiable.... And I think it took a lot of pressure off, where it was otherwise an absolute win–lose situation – today, or in the next six months.

We later combined the concepts of integration and scale levels with this long-term perspective to create a more precise definition of sustainable development for the NEPP:

> In principle, every generation must leave behind good environmental quality. This means that existing environmental problems must be solved within the span of a generation (20 to 25 years)* while the creation of new problems must be

* As the NEPP was intended to take effect in 1990, we originally set 25-year goals for the year 2015. Later a colleague from the Ministry of Economic Affairs pointed out that the targets were based on the RIVM report, whose scenarios begin at 1985 and end in the year 2010. Since we

prevented. For the current generation, the environmental legacy from the past must also be reduced to acceptable proportions.[2]

This definition made a strong case for environmental action. RIVM had concluded that overall emission reductions of 70 to 90 per cent were necessary, which required a change in basic consumption and production patterns. For many stakeholders, the time frame of 25 years was long enough to make such radical changes conceivable, yet short enough to make them understand that they themselves had to start contributing. The generational perspective also had a powerful psychological message – the notion of handing a clean, safe world over to our children. Who could argue with that? It was a point of agreement from which to start the discussions on environmental policy.

The term sustainable development also established the link between environmental and socio-economic problems. The examples in the Brundtland report mainly concern developing countries where poverty leads to environmentally harmful activities, which in turn lead to more poverty. An example would be depleting forests of firewood because people cannot obtain more expensive fuels for cooking and heating. Yet in the Netherlands we also have many situations in which deteriorating environmental quality hurts the economy. Contaminated properties, for instance, hamper development of the inner cities, an especially serious problem in a country where space is so limited. There are also concerns about the drinking water supply, high costs for incinerating municipal waste, and overfishing of the North Sea. Tourism is hurt by news stories about polluted beaches. Even foreign investment is jeopardized, since companies demand good living conditions for their employees.

These examples provide a third reason for strong environmental policies. The first two are protecting public health and protecting ecosystems. The third is protecting socio-economic development: the environment is not only demanding from, but also offering something to the economy. The two are not mutually exclusive, as assumed in the 'environment vs the economy' debate. We thus had the right to talk about economic developments in the context of environmental policy, something which had not been politically 'allowed' in the past.

Feedback

Sustainability became a very compelling argument for environmental protection; and the RIVM report showed the extent of changes that would be needed. However, we still had to describe the process that would get us

couldn't change the RIVM research, we moved the NEPP targets up to 2010, shaving five years off our implementation schedule. I subsequently asked if this meant I could collect my pension five years earlier!

from our current state to a sustainable future. One of my biggest fears was that we would study environmental quality (in other words, environmental effects) for years before taking any concrete action on the sources of problems. I thought about the field of nature conservation, for example, in which it was common for scientists to spend years (rather than months) debating ecological objectives while harmful developments in industry, transport and agriculture continued unchallenged. Furthermore, I was convinced that scientists alone could not set environmental goals, because they require political choices by citizens and their elected representatives. Detailed scientific analyses are not much use to them; especially if they don't first have a general sense of the problem.

I wanted to begin the NEPP by describing the fundamental processes which are common to all environmental problems. I did this by introducing the concept of *feedback*, which shows how damage is 'rolled off' from the present time and place and transferred to other environmental sectors, scales, or generations. By rolling off problems, we may hide them for a time; but we can be sure they will come back to haunt us.

Feedback recognizes that the cause and effect chain is not linear, but circular. Agriculture, for example, produces food for humans. If it is pursued too intensively, however, it can cause environmental damage, such as erosion or water pollution from pesticides, insecticides, and fertilizers. Problems are temporarily rolled off from agriculture to other sectors and time periods, such as water resources or next year's crop, but the damage returns to its source via feedback. The soil lost this year will not be available for the next. As the erosion continues, it becomes increasingly difficult to raise the same crops. Water pollution also comes back to haunt the farmer. The pollutants that wash off this year's crop will work their way into the water used for next year's. Through feedback, the sources of environmental problems eventually feel the effects of their own actions.

Feedback provides good evidence to support the sustainable development concept. It shows that the environment and the economy are interdependent because they are both elements in the same system. Whatever affects one will eventually affect the other. Although feedback is based on common sense, it can still be obscured if defined in narrow technical terms. The government, for example, might study the intricacies of ecological processes for years before taking action. Rather than spending a lot of time analyzing exactly what is wrong, I decided to identify a few rules of thumb that illustrate fundamental problems. A bit later, the Swedish physician Karl-Henrik Robèrt developed a similar notion of feedback called 'The Natural Step'. The gist is that actions should be taken right now to tackle the causes of environmental problems by changing production processes – even if the precise effects of activities have not been proved. Rather than talking endlessly about cause–effect relationships, people should just take the natural step of reducing the *potential* causes of problems.

Energy Extensification

The first feedback mechanism that came to mind was the over-use of energy. Until that time, people had argued that energy was not an environmental concern as long as its production was 'clean'. The problem is, no form of conventional energy is entirely clean. End-of-pipe measures on coal-fired power plants, for example, reduce problems but do not solve them. Even the best filters or scrubbers allow some quantities of pollutants, such as sulphur dioxide and nitrogen oxide, to escape. Even if these pollutants could be eliminated totally, the very process of burning coal (or any other material), must produce carbon dioxide (CO_2), which the science of climate change now shows to be an important pollutant. Climate change has been used as an argument in favour of nuclear power. Since it does not involve a smokestack, proponents explain, it is clean. The Chernobyl disaster negates this theory.

Energy is involved in nearly every activity that affects the environment. It is a key component in transportation, industry, agriculture and heating our homes, which all have clear environmental impacts such as air pollution, oil spills and accidents. My case for energy as a feedback mechanism was supported by Jip Lenstra, an expert on the topic in the Environment Department who provided me with countless examples. Some are fairly obvious. Acidification and climate change, for instance, are closely linked to energy use. In a world almost entirely dependent on fossil fuels, less energy means less sulphur dioxide, nitrogen oxides and CO_2. By looking a little harder, though, it is possible to see energy's role in almost all environmental problems, even the *vermesting* theme. The Netherlands can only support its huge number of farm animals by importing fodder from other countries; and the extra nutrients from this fodder eventually end up as manure on the fields. If energy were more expensive, it would not be economical to import so much fodder; and the number of farm animals would naturally drop to a more sustainable level.

There has been a great intensification of energy use in the twentieth century. More and more processes are automated, and reliance on energy is undermining common sense design principles. People build expensive and inefficient air conditioners to cool buildings, for example, when they could often get the same results by planting a few trees, using more insulation, or choosing a lighter shade of paint. Rather than continuing the route of energy *inten*sification, we should strive for extensification, improving efficiency by looking for clever, low-energy alternative technologies.

We can also change the type of energy we do use. In the balanced natural world, nearly all energy comes from the sun – either directly through heat and light or indirectly through wind or photosynthesis in green plants. The same balance should apply to the human world. All energy should be recovered directly from the sun through so-called 'alternative sources' like solar, wind and biomass power.

Integrated Chain Management

In all cases of pollution, the environment is exposed to substances it either cannot absorb at all or cannot absorb in the quantities that are released. As a result, materials are not recycled or neutralized, but instead spill out into the environment as harmful pollution. This violates a key rule of ecology, that all materials travel in closed cycles. In nature, any substance which is produced, even a waste product, is raw material for some other part of the environment. Cycles carry materials to where they are needed. Nothing is lost. The cow, after grazing, drops manure on the soil; and this manure nourishes the growth of more grass. Or, as Shakespeare described it:

> *Hamlet:* A man may fish with the worm that hath eat of a king, and eat of the fish that hath fed of that worm.
> *King:* What dost thou mean by this?
> *Hamlet:* Nothing but to show you how a king may go a progress through the guts of a beggar.[3]

People have an intuitive sense about pollution. No matter what scientific studies can or cannot prove, people just know that smoke and garbage are not healthy. We could argue endlessly about permissible emission levels and the possible toxicity of various substances, and indeed this scientific research is quite valuable. Without having all the numbers, however, it is still clear that breaking material cycles is harmful to the environment.

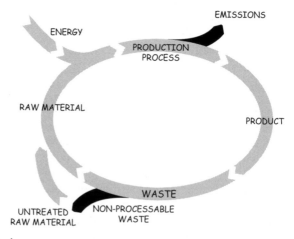

Figure 14 Cycles

Source: Ministry of Housing, Land Use, Planning and the Environment, *National Environmental Policy Plan.*

Balance returns when materials are recycled; but I feared that 'recycling' had become a stale environmental mantra by that time. I wanted a fresher term with a broader definition. The first I proposed was *integrated chain management*, meaning that we have to look integrally at all chains of material use, from raw materials to waste products. Later, I also used the term *integrated life cycle management*, emphasizing the life cycles of products and how to reduce emissions at each step of production.

Quality

I was pleased with these two elements of feedback, but I felt they were a bit too technical to stand on their own. I struggled to think of a third element; but I ultimately needed another hiking trip to figure it out. I had been enjoying these hikes a little less each year because the scenery was deteriorating. Rapid economic development has been filling up the open spaces in the Netherlands since the 1950s, and many of the new buildings are rather unattractive. I have seen more and more poorly constructed concrete boxes which are passed off as homes, schools or offices. I have also seen the rapid mechanization of agriculture.

I was thinking about this one Sunday while Paul and I were hiking through northern Holland. We were walking along a dike that separated the river from the low-lying fields when we met a farmer riding his bicycle towards us. We stopped and made some of the usual small talk: 'Nice day. Are you out for a hike? Have you seen any interesting birds today?'

Then the man started talking about his land. 'Nowadays, I'm pretty busy, and I don't have much time for bird watching,' he told us. 'But I try to get out and inspect my fields on Sundays.'

'Are you looking for anything special?' I asked him.

'Oh, just checking the quality of the land,' he answered. 'And I must say, it's not as good as it used to be. I'm seeing fewer and fewer birds, for example. I'm sure the chemicals have something to do with it. I know all the fertilizer we use is affecting the quality of the soil somehow. But honestly, I don't know how I'd make a living without using all that stuff.'

I thought about the farmer's words as we continued on our hike. 'Affecting the quality,' he had said, but it echoed in my mind as '*neglecting* the quality'. That's it, I realized. Quality is the third element of feedback! Perhaps I cannot prove it, but I can think of many examples showing that something which is really cheap or ugly is also harmful in other ways. Think of the waste in poorly constructed buildings, like the junky office tower where the

NEPP team met. It had bad windows, bad heat, and was unpleasant to work in. Shortly after we completed our project, this building was torn down, like all the cheap products and disposable goods that waste resources and soon end up in the landfill. Or think about the ugly suburban sprawl that is ruining the countryside. I'm not talking about the architectural style but the architectural substance. The bad planning and shoddy work-manship of many develop-ments should be the first clue that something is wrong; and indeed something is. They not only ruin the  landscape, but also waste materials on buildings that won't last and highways that aren't needed. Sprawl forces people to spend more time in their cars – wasting energy, causing air pollution, and diminishing people's quality of life.

Improving the quality of products generally reduces their harmful environmental impacts. A sturdier product, for example, will last longer, and thus will not have to be replaced as often. This saves the resources that would go into making replacements; and it cuts down on the waste produced when a product is discarded. Recycling can reduce this even further. Arguments to lower consumption are certainly controversial, since they challenge most people's definition of 'economic growth'. Yet I feel that this definition is rather outmoded. Increases in efficiency, and the rise of the service sector, show that economic prosperity is not always proportional to raw industrial output.

Thinking about quality helped me understand that technology and economic development are not inherently harmful. Yet they are harmful when used carelessly, without thinking about their consequences or about quality. The American Robert M. Pirsig explained this notion well in his seminal work *Zen and the Art of Motorcycle Maintenance*:

> The ugliness the Sutherlands were fleeing is not inherent in technology. It only seemed that way to them because it's hard to isolate what it is in technology that's so ugly. But technology is simply the making of things and the making of things can't by its own nature be ugly or there would be no possibility for beauty in the arts....
>
> Quality, or its absence, doesn't reside in either the subject or the object. The real ugliness resides in the relationship between the people who produce the technology and the things they produce, which results in a similar relationship between the people who use the technology and the things they use.[4]

I expected plenty of criticism when I brought my theories into the working group. None of them was scientific, and a concept like 'quality' was especially fuzzy. To my surprise, no one objected to the roll-off mechanism as manifested via the three elements of feedback in production and consumption. Even without scientific backing, these theories made evident sense. For me, this was a clear sign that I was on to something. I used roll-off and feedback to explain the changes in production and consumption that would be called for in the NEPP. The final text explained them as follows:

> Feedback at the source prevents the occurrence of the roll off mechanism. This feedback consists of three premises which must always be applied jointly.
>
> 1 *Integrated life cycle management* (including product life cycle management) aimed at closing material cycles as much as possible and keeping residual emissions and waste flows within acceptable limits. The chain from raw material to production process, product, waste, and emissions must be seen integrally in life cycle management.
>
> 2 *Energy extensification* aimed at reducing total energy consumption from finite sources by increasing energy efficiency, utilizing renewable energy sources, and decreasing energy needs.
>
> 3 *Quality improvement* aimed at the quality of raw materials, products, production processes, waste flows, and emissions into the environment, as well as the quality of the natural environment itself. A product is 'high quality' if it can meet needs over a long period, can be repaired, and is suitable for recycling.[5]

The feedback elements and preliminary RIVM findings were included in our next draft of the NEPP, which we sent to colleagues in our department and other departments on 24 June 1988. From this point on, we broke our 'conclave' and began engaging the stakeholders again, starting within the central government. In the first days of July, we went over the draft NEPP with as many of our colleagues in the other departments as we could reach during the summer holiday season. Many colleagues were not too surprised by the NEPP's recommendations, except perhaps by the call for a 50 per cent cut in energy use by the year 2050.* We incorporated their suggestions into a second 'summer' draft of the NEPP which we released on 18 July; among many improvements there was now a more complete description of the environmental themes. It was also distributed to a wider audience, including all government departments, the provinces, the association of municipalities, the Confederation of Netherlands Industry and Employers (VNO/NCW) and some environmental NGOs.

---

* This was taken directly from the Brundtland Report. Marius Enthoven was reluctant to put this goal in the NEPP, but Gerard Wolters advised us to keep it in.

THE PROGRESSION OF ENVIRONMENTAL MEASURES

While developing the NEPP, we identified four types of measures for addressing environmental problems. Only the last type allows an integrated approach to sustainable development.

Effect-oriented measures – taken to fix environmental damage after it has occurred. Examples include cleaning up toxic waste sites and replanting degraded forests. Effect-oriented measures are clearly inadequate for an integrated approach, but they are needed to clean up the 'legacies' of past environmental damage.

Emission-oriented measures – the classic end-of-pipe approach. Such measures do prevent pollutants (at least some of them) from reaching the environment, and they can be implemented fairly quickly. They are essentially band-aid solutions, however, designed to improve the *status quo* and not to reform it.

Volume-oriented measures – seek to reduce the overall extent of products or practices that harm the environment. An example would be a tax on gasoline that induces people to drive less. Volume-oriented measures alone may only delay damage and are not politically viable if they call for a reduction in people's standard of living.

Structural source-oriented measures – alter the technology of production and consumption processes so that harmful effects are reduced without using end-of-pipe methods. If these measures are initiated 'on the drawing board', they can be integrated into normal technological development and business investments, at a much lower cost than emission-oriented measures.

The Third Scenario

The two scenarios of the RIVM report showed us that anything short of structural reforms to the economy would be inadequate, but we needed a thorough, compelling vision of what such changes would look like. Rob Maas had done excellent work developing the first two RIVM scenarios: 'business as usual' and 'all possible end-of-pipe measures'. In the summer of 1988 I arranged for him to join my team and work on a third scenario that would outline a series of measures to change production and consumption along the lines of energy extensification, integrated chain management and quality improvement.

Rob worked together with the Division for Economic Policy Affairs, which had been led by Koos van der Vaart. In 1988 Koos was elected to Parliament to fill the seat left vacant by the death that year of former Prime Minster Den Uyl. Koos's old function in the process was filled by Paul Hofhuis, an economist who worked intensively with Rob to refine our economic modelling during the long Cabinet discussions on the NEPP. Later, Paul led some of our first negotiations with business interests on NEPP implementation. He then served, from 1994 to 1999, as the Environment Department representative at the Netherlands Embassy in Washington.

Fortunately, Paul and Rob did not have to build the third scenario from scratch. Dutch universities and environmental NGOs had already produced many valuable studies which they incorporated into their work. The Centre for Energy Saving, for example, had prepared a proposal on restructuring this sector, called 'The Forgotten Scenario'. A coalition titled 'Wise on the Road' released a study by the same name which called for shifting the emphasis from road to rail transportation. Meanwhile, the University of Utrecht had compiled an extensive inventory of measures to raise industrial energy efficiency. As Rob observes, 'We were lucky that we had some of these "bricks" available to build the third scenario, because otherwise it would have been very difficult.'

On the basis of these studies, Paul and Rob combined the end-of-pipe measures with structural changes geared to the three feedback mechanisms. The result was a third economic scenario (Table 3).

Table 3 The third scenario

Feedback mechanism	Action
Energy extensification	• Big drive for energy conservation in homes and businesses. • Expanding the share of co-generation. • Maximum use of renewable energy sources. • Reduced use of coal and oil. • More efficient generation of electricity. • Sweeping change in transportation pattern from private car use to public transport and bicycles. • Expanding the share of rail and water in the transportation of goods.
Integrated chain management	• More efficient use of minerals in agriculture and reduced use of fertilizers. • Integrated crop protection methods and reduced use of pesticides. • Reduction in waste flows; greater recovery of raw materials. • Large-scale application of process-integrated clean technologies.

Table 3 The third scenario cont.

Feedback mechanism	Action
Quality promotion	• Introduction of cleaner and more economical products. • Increasing the quality of products by raising the added value per unit of raw material. • Replacing (raw) materials such as heavy metals, asbestos, and PVC with alternatives less damaging to the environment. • Maintenance of the current milk quota system and continuing production increases per dairy cow (to improve efficiency).

The RIVM findings, the intergenerational concept of sustainable development, the feedback mechanisms, and the third scenario provided strong content and direction for the NEPP. It took some time to develop these ideas, but the time was well spent. Sometimes the best way for hikers to make progress is to stop for a while and take their bearings. It was as if we finally had a map for our journey, in addition to an objective and a rough time frame. We now had an indication of how to get there, via emission-oriented measures and structural changes in production and consumption – the narrow trail of the third scenario.

Notes

1   World Commission on Environment and Development, *Our Common Future* (Oxford: Oxford University Press, 1987), 43.
2   Ministry of Housing, Land Use Planning and the Environment (VROM), *National Environment Policy Plan*, English translation (The Hague: SDU Publishers, 1989), 75.
3   William Shakespeare, *Hamlet*, Act IV, Scene 2, ll. 27–31.
4   Robert M. Pirsig, *Zen and the Art of Motorcycle Maintenance* (New York: Bantam New Age, 1981), 260.
5   Ministry of Housing, Land Use Planning and the Environment (VROM), *National Environment Policy Plan*, English translation (The Hague: SDU Publishers, 1989), 82.

A Good Map and Common Sense
Presenting Clear Information

Navigating

The first year of work on the NEPP (1987) was like a hiking trip without a map. We had only the vague notion of wanting to go somewhere new, and a feeling that it would be a long journey. Without the RIVM report, however, we lacked the critical information needed to find our way through the woods. A tremendous amount of research had already been done on the environment, but it was not in a useful form. RIVM condensed this earlier research into a clear map showing the path to follow.

A lot of work goes into a map. It is the product of specialists who collect a great deal of information on a region, including climate, topography, plant and animal life. Their research findings could fill a backpack easily, but information in such quantity is not very useful to hikers. Rather than a heap of scientific reports, they need some basic information that fits on a single sheet of paper. A good trail map is an example of how to tailor information to people's needs. Very detailed work is required to assess an area, but the information is condensed into a simpler form which is useful to hikers. Even a good map can be confusing, however, if the hikers get preoccupied with its details. The map may show, for example, that a certain stretch of trail is approximately 7.5 kilometres long. This number is only valuable in relative terms. Is it a distance I can cover before nightfall?

Working through environmental policy resembles navigating on a hike. Information is essential, but it can also be a hindrance if not presented and used properly. The scientific 'map' can become rather confusing for three reasons. First, studies are often highly specialized and thus poorly integrated to provide an overview of environmental problems. Second, research findings are generally written for other scientists, not for policy makers. Third, even the best information rarely provides unequivocal proof of how problems are caused and how they can be solved. Scientists may pursue an issue for years to find perfect explanations, while environmental quality continues to deteriorate. It is often better to start taking action based on preliminary findings and common sense.

Cause and Effect

A policy approach focused only on causes is like a hiker who looks at his feet too much. He may take very good individual steps; but he does not know if his strides are long enough to reach the destination in time, or even if he is headed in the right direction. Without looking up and taking his bearings from time to time, he may walk into a tree or even off a cliff! Something similar happened in our response to acid rain. We focused on the causes, such as various industrial operations which produce sulphur dioxide or nitrogen oxide. Then we designed specific steps, mostly end-of-pipe technologies to remove a certain volume of pollutants from the air. Without thoroughly examining environmental effects, however, we did not have sufficient information about our ultimate goal and whether these 'steps' were adequate to reach it. The RIVM report showed us that the strides we were making in dealing with causes would bring us, at best, to a 20 per cent reduction of acidifying substances, while our target should be 80 per cent.

An approach focused on effects is like a hiker who only looks up and never watches her feet. She may see her goal clearly, but she doesn't know what steps to take. If she is not careful, she may slip in a muddy patch or step in a hole and twist her ankle. This is analogous to a policy that focuses too much on effects, via environmental quality studies. There were, for example, many grim environmental quality reports showing the various effects of acidification in different regions. They were not integrated into a national perspective, however, and they did not provide clear recommendations for addressing environmental concerns.

Hikers cannot focus only on their feet or only on their destination; and policies cannot focus only on causes or only on effects. Hikers must keep an eye on their ultimate destination but must also watch their steps as they proceed toward it. Scientists study environmental effects and assess the extent of damage; but they must also trace these effects back to their causes and identify appropriate steps to remedy them. In the process, they recognize how one activity may lead to several problems and they gain a more integrated view of the environment. Examining cause and effect relationships also demands a long-term perspective, which is needed to assess overall trends in the environment and the results of policies directed at their sources.

Tailoring Information

The success of a message depends on targeting the right audience. While

RIVM is a research institute, its primary audience was not the scientific community. Experts in the field already have a good understanding of environmental problems. The crucial audience for environmental policy includes politicians and the general public; and the message must be clearly presented to them.

Fortunately, RIVM was led by policy makers like Ruud van Noort and Kees Zoeteman, who had originally worked in the Environment Department. Their interests were not in pure science, but in its applications to integrated environmental policy. RIVM was also driven by people like Koos van der Vaart, who insisted on detailed information he could use in his work. As a result, the institute's goal was providing overall guidance for policy makers, not statistics for scientists and bureaucrats.

To maximize the report's value, RIVM and the collaborating scientific institutes had to package it carefully for input into the political process. Government leaders are overwhelmed with information on a broad array of topics, and the policy formulation stage provides only a brief window of opportunity to address an issue. Officials need concise information which is placed in context. A policy maker can't decide to do something about the environment, for example, until he or she knows the economic and social implications of that 'something'.

Unfortunately, government advisers are not always good at tailoring information and putting it in context for policy makers – a problem parodied in Hamlet during a conversation between the king and queen and their minister Polonius:

> Polonius: My liege and madam, to expostulate
> What majesty should be, what duty is,
> Why day is day, night night, and time is time,
> Were nothing but to waste night, day, and time.
> Therefore, since brevity is the soul of wit,
> And tediousness the limbs and outward flourishes,
> I will be brief. Your noble son is mad.
> Mad call I it, for, to define true madness,
> What is't but to be nothing else but mad?
> But let that go.
>
> Queen: More matter, with less art.
>
> Polonius: Madam, I swear I use no art at all.
> That he's mad, 'tis true: 'tis true 'tis pity,
> And pity 'tis 'tis true – a foolish figure.
> But farewell it, for I will use no art.[1]

The art of the RIVM report comprised over *three hundred pages* of scientific details, yet its matter was summarized in only *three sentences*:

1 Preserving the Dutch environment will require 70 to 90 per cent reductions of all pollution.

2 Such reductions cannot be achieved by conventional end-of-pipe technologies.

3 Therefore, a structural change in production and consumption patterns will be required.

In a similar manner, Rob Maas and Paul Hofhuis summed up a fundamental restructuring of the economy – via the NEPP's third economic scenario – with 15 key phrases. Such concise statements played a similar role in streamlining RIVM's message as the themes and target groups had for our message in the Environment Department.

Uncertainty and Intuition

Policy makers and scientists can reduce confusion and controversy by presenting information as clearly and concisely as possible. But there are limits. With few exceptions, science can only provide good estimates, not absolute facts. RIVM's main assertion, that pollution must be cut by 70 to 90 per cent, was very imprecise – a 20 per cent spread! In absolute terms, the report was not very conclusive. In relative terms, however, it was quite clear: our environmental goals were terribly inadequate in many areas, and we had to take strong measures immediately. We had no time to quibble over a few percentage points, as Ed Nijpels explained in his Preface to the report:

> It is my opinion, based on the present report, that a far-reaching adjustment of our environmental management may not be delayed, even if we are still faced with numerous uncertainties. The report convincingly demonstrates that postponing action will result in our environment being exposed to great risks.[2]

Unfortunately, lack of scientific 'proof' is often an excuse to delay action. Even the Environment Department staff fell into this pattern at first. After hearing RIVM's preliminary findings, we immediately began questioning the precision of their calculations. Fred Langeweg replied that, in practical terms, there is no difference between calling for a 75 per cent or an 80 per cent reduction in acidifying emissions, because either quantity is several times larger than the 20 per cent reduction we had previously planned on. That's similar to a group of hikers arguing for hours about whether they are seven-and-one-half or eight kilometres from their daily goal. They could better use their time by just walking there.

Policy makers who are preoccupied with scientific certainty may overestimate the precision of their own work. RIVM's results were just educated guesses about the extent of environmental problems; but our policy response could only be an educated guess about the measures to solve them.

Government cannot change society. It can only enact policies that may influence society in a positive way. Both science and policy involve experimentation. Frequent evaluations and adjustments are needed to achieve good results.

In theory, decisions are based on absolute facts. In reality, they are mostly based on intuition. This was a clear lesson from the workshops Allen Hickling conducted for the Environment Department (see Chapter 2). Allen showed us that uncertainty is an inherent part of the policy process. Decisions can (and often must) be made even when there isn't absolute knowledge. A policy maker should not be expected to eliminate uncertainty altogether, but rather to reduce it as much as possible.

To do this, Allen presented a model of the 'commitment package' consisting of four elements:

1 Actions which can be taken immediately based on facts or current explicit assumptions – because their impacts are fairly certain and the risk of delaying action is too great.

2 Research – on explicit, possible future actions for which uncertainty is still too high to make a decision.

3 Future actions – which will be taken according to the possible outcomes of sufficient research.

4 Contingency plans – in case the original assumptions or the results of the research prove to be wrong.

Suppose some hikers are not sure if they can reach their destination because they don't know whether a particular bridge is still in service. If they cannot use the bridge, the group will have to make a considerable detour, which may cost them an extra day. A commitment package might look something like this:

1 Actions to be taken immediately: the group decides to leave a few hours earlier and buy food for an extra day.

2 Research: if the group encounters people coming from the other direction, they will ask about the bridge. If possible, the group will ask several people, thus not relying on any one person's information.

3 Future actions: if more than three people confirm the bridge is in service, the group can reasonably assume it is. Thus, they plan on camping at a point 'X' on the other side of the river and dumping the extra food when they get there.

4 Contingency: if, after all, the bridge is not in service, the hikers will camp at a point 'Y' on the near side of the river and keep all their food for the extra day of travel.

The three feedback mechanisms in the NEPP (energy extensification, closing material cycles, and improving quality) were an effort to clarify the assumptions on which immediate actions were based. It is very difficult to show the precise consequences of our actions (which we might not know for years), but it is fairly easy to show that many of them are serious. While RIVM provided the scientific underpinning for policies in the NEPP, feedback provided the common sense explanations. As we intensify energy use, the pollution associated with it grows. As we break material cycles and disperse more pollutants into the environment, we witness more damage to ecosystems and human health. As we continue to neglect quality, we waste more resources and produce more trash.

The research element of the NEPP's commitment package consists of frequent scientific evaluations by RIVM and economic assessments conducted jointly by the government and the private sector. This information is then used to guide future actions in subsequent revisions of the NEPP (generally produced every four years).

Of course, the ultimate feedback is to see whether the NEPP's long-term targets are reached after a generation. The only contingency here is to keep monitoring progress along the way and to make adjustments if necessary. Even if the targets are not met in time, we hope that the future generation will learn from our mistakes and devise a better way to reach the goals.

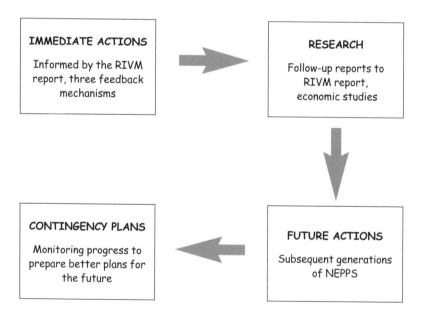

Figure 15 The NEPP commitment package

A good map is of utmost importance in a hiking trip. Nevertheless, the map must be complemented by observations, such as the position of the sun, the angle of shadows, or the location of a church steeple in a nearby village. Ultimately, navigation comes down to intuition. I have often sensed that a hiking trip was going in the wrong direction, and most of the time my feeling was right. Having realized the need to change direction, the map is needed to figure out exactly how.

Notes

1   William Shakespeare, *Hamlet,* Act IV, Scene 2, ll. 86–99.
2   National Institute of Public Health and Environment (RIVM), *Concern for Tomorrow,* English translation (Bilthoven: RIVM, 1989), Preface.

CHAPTER 6

New Members Join the Team
Building Support with Stakeholders

The draft NEPP from the summer of 1988 gave the NEPP team the knowledge to get their bearings and envision the journey ahead. We had to remember, however, that the other government departments, and even most people in our own department, did not have this knowledge. Although we could see the way forward clearly, we couldn't just push ahead and expect the others to follow. They needed some time to check our information and confirm it for themselves before proceeding.

A Wider Audience

In August 1988 our summer draft was reviewed by the NEPP steering group, a key venue for integration. The group was chaired by Marius Enthoven and included government officials such as Jan Willem Weck (the Deputy Secretary General of Economic Affairs), Jur van Zutphen (Director General in the Ministry of Agriculture), and Gerrit Blom (the Director General for Waterworks). After the autumn of 1988, the steering group was occasionally expanded to include important business stakeholders, such as Niek Ketting (Chairman of the Dutch Electricity Generating Board), Peter Vogtländer (President of Shell Netherlands), Hans Blankert (then chairman of VNO's section for the electronics and metal industries), Paul Nouwen (President of ANWB, the Netherlands Tourist Board), and Maarten de Heer (Secretary of the Agriculture Association). By extending the steering group, we avoided the civil servant's instinctive reaction of defending and remaining within the sectors for which his or her ministry feels responsible. Including key people from the real world (those who would have to walk on the hike) allowed us to focus on real threats and opportunities while discussing objectives for environmental policies.

In a small country like the Netherlands, most people in government and business know their counterparts very well. Marius, for example, had been friends with Ketting and Vogtländer since their student days together.

Nevertheless, Marius was as dedicated to his environmental goals as Ketting and Vogtländer were to their business priorities. Neither side expected the other to 'cut them a break', but they didn't expect each other to play tricks, either.

The good news in the summer of 1988 was that the steering group liked the general theories in the first half of the NEPP. The bad news was that they did not wish to proceed with the policy recommendations in the second half. Instead, they wanted first to publish the NEPP as a theoretical white paper and then assess the public reaction to it.

In response, Marius Enthoven called a strategy meeting at Willem Reij's office the day I returned from summer vacation. The upcoming RIVM report, he told us, would create tremendous momentum within government and society for strong environmental policies. We had to maintain this momentum by publishing a full-scale response as quickly as possible. Yet he also acknowledged the steering group's recommendation that we elicit public input. In early September, we decided to present the four theoretical chapters of the draft NEPP to stakeholder groups and solicit their recommendations for specific policies. Then we could hand Parliament a full-scale NEPP that already represented a broad consensus on implementation measures.

Meanwhile, public interest in the NEPP was growing. Elements of the draft plan, which had leaked out somehow, were discussed on the evening news and in the papers, especially the statement that environmental problems had actually become worse since the famed *Memorandum on Urgent Environmental Issues* of 1972. Editorials also praised Minister Nijpels for making such brave, controversial statements on the environment. In fact, the coverage of these 'brave' statements strengthened his hand and actually made his political position somewhat less risky.

Public interest continued to grow, thanks to a series of incidents that kept the spotlight on the environment. It began in early September 1988 with the Queen's opening address to Parliament. The monarchy has a mainly symbolic role in the Dutch system. The Queen's address is actually prepared by the Prime Minister, with input from each of his ministries. Shortly after submitting its report, the Environment Department received a letter from the Prime Minister's office asking for more *positive* statements. Given RIVM's preliminary findings, we felt this was hardly possible.

Unhappy with this response but undeterred by it, Prime Minister Ruud Lubbers inserted the statement that the environment had improved somewhat, *especially* with respect to air and water quality.* The major

---

* Lubbers had used the Dutch expression *met name,* which in common usage means 'especially'. People were outraged at the Queen's (and thus Lubbers's) statement that the environment had improved, *especially* with respect to air and water. Lubbers claimed that, in his dictionary, *met name* meant 'for example'. Thus, air and water were just examples where some progress *had* been made.

environmental groups were outraged by the speech, as were several members of Parliament who had seen drafts of the NEPP or the RIVM report. Opposition parties claimed Lubbers had tricked the Queen into lying. These arguments spilled over into the general budget debate, and the environment suddenly seemed to become a major political issue.

In fact, it had already been a growing concern for some time, sparked by a number of crises such as the Chernobyl accident, the *Exxon Valdez* oil spill, and a dramatic decline in the seal population of the Dutch Wadden Sea.* Word of the NEPP had also been spreading that summer. These were all components of the fuel that the Queen's address finally ignited.

A Sponsor

Lubbers was not too surprised by the upwelling of public concern for the environment, since he had followed the issue at least since his mildly pro-environment stance as Minister of Economic Affairs in the 1970s. In his first term as Prime Minister, Lubbers had to focus almost entirely on the country's dire budget crisis, but by the autumn of 1988 he suspected the environment would be one of his government's new priorities. In a conversation years later, Lubbers told me he had purposely placed the statement in the Queen's speech to see how the public would react.

Seeing that the environment had indeed become a major political issue, Lubbers moved swiftly to address it. During the budget negotiations of 1988, he persuaded Parliament to allocate an extra 100 million guilders (US$50 million) for environmental programmes in the coming year, and he presented RIVM's estimate that environmental measures might cost up to 30 billion guilders (US$15 billion) per year by 2010. Lubbers also told Parliament that the country had to take a major step forward by developing a National Environmental Policy Plan. After we had got over the shock, we realized that we had a very important political sponsor for the process, one who dared to say what was at stake and what the consequences might be.

The Stakeholder Sessions

We held ten meetings with stakeholder groups in October and November 1988. Generally lasting a day, each session focused on a particular segment of stakeholders, which corresponded to a revised list of target groups in the draft NEPP. Most of them were economic sectors, represented by high-level executives and leaders of trade or consumer organizations. The ten stakeholder/target groups were:

---

* The number of seals had been declining from an original population of 16,000 down to a few hundred in 1988. That same year, a distemper epidemic nearly wiped out the few that remained.

- Agriculture
- Chemical industry and refineries
- All other branches of industry
- Construction
- Consumers (combined with environmental NGOs)*
- Energy production and distribution
- Environmental services (waste management and water supply)
- Municipalities
- Provincial governments
- Transport.

The sessions were facilitated by Anne Alons, with assistance from Allen Hickling and Arnold de Jong. Anne's goal was to produce a relaxed atmosphere, where the participants could think creatively, rather than fighting or 'dealing' on small points of policy. He realized that the ambitious goals of the NEPP could only be achieved by breaking the existing trend of economic developments. Stakeholders had to harness their own creativity and think of what they themselves could do differently. 'The government alone could not bring about such changes,' Anne explains. 'That was impossible.'[1]

During the sessions, I realized that a stakeholder group is not monolithic. The secretariats of business associations, for example, usually represent the more conservative views in their organizations. A progressive stance could alienate their conservative members, so it is generally safer for secretariats to be cautious, something I later termed 'secretariat's syndrome'. To make progress, it is often best to bypass the secretariats and go directly to the key decision makers, such as corporate CEOs. They have the freedom and authority to think more creatively and the power to advance more daring proposals.

Although many of the participants were cautious, few were hostile. Only a minority were genuinely against the NEPP, or environmental policies in general. They often complained about the complexity of existing regulations and joked that all the Environment Department really wanted was to block economic development and return us to the Middle Ages. Others admitted that the global environment truly was imperilled, but explained that the Netherlands was so small that we couldn't do anything about it, anyway.

It was impossible simply to deny that there were environmental problems. The 14 November meeting with the transport sector, for example, was on a grey Monday morning when heavy fog stalled traffic and caused

---

* We wanted to have NGOs involved in all the sessions, but the other departments feared there would be 'too much confrontation'. Also, some NGOs, most notably Greenpeace, declined the invitation to participate.

major accidents all over the country.* The transport stakeholders all agreed that something had to be done about congestion, although for different reasons. The Environment Department wanted to limit traffic, especially private car use, for ecological reasons. The transport stakeholders wanted to reduce personal car use in order to free up the roads for more commercial freight transport.

Participants in the sessions were not converted into environmentalists; but many of them moved from being unyielding opponents to being genuine stakeholders because they all agreed to take each other seriously. Our concerns were environmental, as described in the upcoming RIVM report, and we asked that business respond to these concerns. In exchange, we agreed to respond to business concerns. Success came not from criticizing or downplaying people's concerns but from redefining them in an effort to find common ground. The Environment Department, for example, is concerned to eliminate chlorine. The chemical industry is concerned to save money. Instead of casting the environmental goal negatively, as banning chlorine, we could cast it positively, as looking for a safe, *economical* substitute.

Many participants were most creative when proposing what *other* economic sectors should do – a phenomenon I call 'neighbours pollute most'. It is relatively easy to give advice to others, but people have more trouble deciding on changes in their own behaviour. They generally want a lot more information about possible consequences of their decisions.

The stakeholder meetings were mini-versions (but very intensive ones) of the larger debate in society. The introduction to the meetings by senior officials like Marius Enthoven, who had been named Director General by then, reflected the sponsorship of our efforts by the Prime Minister. The facilitators, like Anne Alons, played the same role of managing the process that political leaders like Ed Nijpels would take on during parliamentary debates. The stakeholders (and some adversaries) at the meetings represented general social and economic groups which would be affected by policies. I myself played a role which I now call 'driving force'. Anne's facilitation of the sessions freed me from managing the *process* and allowed me to push the discussions on the *content* of policies. As the NEPP process advanced, this role of driving force was also taken on by other people, eventually even by Prime Minister Lubbers.

Our 'mini' discussion had a much larger audience than I had first realized. About 30 people were invited to each of the ten meetings; so 300 people were involved from the start. Yet each of them had a network of about 20 colleagues with whom he or she discussed the NEPP, meaning that

---

* I remember the date so well because it was exactly a year after I had finally disposed of my car, committing myself to cycling and public transportation.

up to 6,000 key people participated in some way.* This included many influential leaders in the private sector. In fact, we had come much farther in selling the NEPP to the business stakeholders than to our colleagues in the government.

Making Choices

In mid-November we had a two-day conference with the other government departments to go over the results of the stakeholder meetings. Over a thousand ideas had come out of the sessions, and they were posted on sheets of paper covering a wall 20 metres long.

Some were ideas we had encountered before, others were new. The old ideas fell into two categories. The first said that people don't really need the things that harm the environment. We don't need cars if we have good public transport. We don't need to worry about waste disposal if we recycle. The second group said that technology would solve problems by continually providing cleaner and more efficient ways to do things, so there was no need to change people's behaviour. There were also some exciting new ideas, like changing environmentally harmful incentives in the tax system or influencing the behaviour of consumers, rather than just producers.

We had envisaged that representatives of the different government departments would condense the 1,000 ideas into a short list for the NEPP, but holding a discussion with so many people about so many items proved impossible. At the end of the first day, most participants gladly adjourned to the bar for the happy hour, but I stayed behind with Anne Alons to ponder how we could coordinate the decision making of such a large group.

'Just throw the less useful ideas on the floor,' Anne suggested. I expressed my horror at the thought. Someone had to, Anne replied. We couldn't possibly discuss 1,000 ideas in detail in a few days. Anne told me that, as project leader, I was more familiar with the ideas, and the people involved, than anyone. What better person to make the first cut? I was uncomfortable with this reasoning, but I had to admit there was probably no other solution.

We started examining the sheets of paper. 'Is that an innovative idea?' Anne would ask me. 'If not, throw it away.' I proceeded along the wall. 'Could you imagine this being implemented in the next two years?' he would ask. 'Could you imagine your minister announcing this idea to the

---

* In fact, we had begun to reach an even larger audience. In the summer of 1988, the Environment Department initiated an 'Environment Ideas Book' project. We published advertisements in newspapers and magazines asking people to sign on and propose their own ideas for solving environmental problems. The public suggestions were then compiled into an Ideas Book which was published at the same time as the NEPP. Owing to time restraints, we were not able to incorporate the public ideas into the first NEPP, but many of them did make their way into the second NEPP, three years later.

government? If not, throw it away.' It got easier after the first few papers dropped to the ground. I no longer feared tossing out the one brilliant suggestion that could save the Earth. In about two hours, Anne and I had narrowed the list to 100 proposals. I must admit that many of them were from environmental organizations which, after all, had spent years working on creative solutions to environmental problems. There were also, however, many creative ideas from business.

I was nervous about presenting the 100 ideas to the participants the next morning, but no one objected to my unscientific selection method. Most seemed relieved that they only had to deal with 100 ideas, instead of 1,000. We asked the participants to contribute to a more detailed account of the remaining ideas, which we later presented to the NEPP steering group.

The full steering group, with key business leaders, met at a chic restaurant near Leyden. Arnold de Jong began the meeting by explaining how we had solicited ideas and condensed the list of stakeholder suggestions. He was immediately attacked by the steering group members. The sessions were meant to involve stakeholders themselves in devising solutions to environmental problems, they said, instead of having solutions imposed by the Environment Department. We countered that we had, in fact, solicited input from everyone (as evidenced by the 1,000 ideas collected). At some point, however, the ideas from a group exercise have to be condensed into a workable number of items. The same thing can happen in hiking. Everyone may voice his or her ideas about where the group should go, but they will spend all day at the trail head if someone doesn't take the lead and choose a route. This choice should be based on everyone's input, but may not satisfy everyone completely.

Despite their anger at the decision-making process, the steering group members also heard some ideas they liked. I explained, for example, that people should be rewarded for doing good, instead of merely being punished for causing harm. We might be willing to let companies come up with their own solutions to environmental requirements. If these were successful, perhaps we could avoid imposing prescriptive and complicated regulations. I also discussed the need for long-term objectives, and how these would benefit companies by giving them a clear idea of what to expect in future policies. I acknowledged the need to work harder at pursuing reforms in a European context, so that Dutch firms wouldn't be disadvantaged in international competition. I explained that new government funding could be expected to accompany the NEPP. All the costs wouldn't be borne by the private sector. Finally, I said that the government would work on changing consumer behaviour to create more demand for green products and services, and that companies could benefit by fulfilling this demand.

These ideas appealed to the business people present, and we had a good discussion about the most economical ways to achieve environmental objectives. Marius gave me a ride home afterwards, and we reflected on the meeting. It had been a narrow escape, we agreed, but an escape nonetheless. We held firm on developing the NEPP, but we showed the stakeholders our willingness to negotiate specifics and find economical ways to reach our goals. That was enough to keep them involved in the process.

The Pace Speeds Up

Events really accelerated in the winter of 1988/9. There were some negative developments, and a few close calls for the NEPP. Fortunately, these developments were overshadowed by the positive events. By the time spring came around, we had developed unstoppable political momentum, thanks in part to the important new leadership we gained.

First came the trouble. The Ministry of Economic Affairs was increasingly concerned about the NEPP. 'We were, in fact, very, very worried about the consequences of this new National Environmental Policy Plan,' recalls Wiel Klerken, who worked in Economic Affairs at the time. 'What would it mean for industry? Could industry cope with it?... We had the idea that it might be disastrous.'[2] Klerken was a staffer in the Ministry's section on environmental affairs. His boss was Kees Schröder, whom we had already dealt with for many years. I certainly did not always agree with Kees and Wiel; but I trusted them to play fairly. 'I guess you have to make a separation between cooperation at the personal level and on the playing field,' Kees explains. 'We were honest to each other, but we fought the battles we had to fight.'[3]

While our dealings with mid-level officials had been amicable, we learned that they did not represent all the sentiments in their ministry. The higher, and often more conservative, officials become very worried when they saw preliminary estimates for the overall costs of environmental measures. Our Directorate for Air Policy, for example, had done studies which showed that combating acid rain would cost billions of guilders annually. Before this, estimates for environmental expenditures only ran into hundreds of millions, amounts not considered large enough to have macro-economic effects. These new estimates, however, showed that our policies might have a significant impact on the economy, and Economic Affairs assumed it would be a negative one.

The strongest adversary was the Permanent Secretary of Economic Affairs, Dr Frans Rutten, who was also chairperson of the Central Economic Committee (CEC). For years, the CEC was one of the pre-eminent government authorities, and generally had the final say on economic matters before they were presented to the Cabinet. 'The CEC considered themselves to be the brains of the Cabinet,' Marius Enthoven explains.

Rutten's concerns were understandable, given the economic context.

The Netherlands had been in dire financial straits at the beginning of Lubbers's first term in 1982. The economy was in recession and public debt was dangerously high. As a key Lubbers adviser, Frans Rutten had played a critical role in reforming the economy. 'He was very centred on trying to get the deficit down,' Jan Willem Weck recalls. 'I'm sure that after tackling all kinds of elements in wages and the social security sector, he was reluctant to create a new economic cost in the form of a growing environmental sector.'

Other developments were more favourable. On 3 December, the long-awaited RIVM study was published as *Zorgen voor Morgen*. This has been translated as *Concern for Tomorrow*, a title that does not capture the full meaning. The word *Zorgen* means not only 'concern', but also 'care'. The report showed not only why we should be concerned, but also how we could care for our future. RIVM had spent a long time thinking about the name of the report; they even used outside consultants. In the end, however, the clever title was proposed by Rob Maas's wife, Anke.

Concern for Tomorrow had a clear message and powerful language about environmental conditions, along with iron-clad science to back it up. It was strengthened further by the involvement of all major scientific institutes in the country. This was not only one institute's report, but the national consensus. There was no opportunity for 'junk science' to challenge the findings. The formal stakeholder groups could not deny the findings in *Concern for Tomorrow*, and the general public also took great interest. The media covered it in depth, and the report was discussed all over the country.

The next major event was the Queen's address on Christmas Day. Unlike the speech to Parliament in September, this is prepared by the Queen herself and is generally an upbeat, non-political statement. This time, however, she chose to discuss grave matters, the impending collapse of the environment. Clearly, she wanted to save face after her remarks in September, which had caused an embarrassing political dispute. Some policy watchers said the Queen wanted to take revenge on Lubbers but, whatever her feelings, the motivation was surely much deeper. *Concern for Tomorrow* was certainly on her mind, and she had to address the nation's collective fears:

> What we are now seeing is not the destruction of the Earth at a single blow, but its demise in a silent drama. Our world is suffering from deforestation, desertification, the polluting and poisoning of the air, the soil and the water, the extinction of plant and animal species, interference with the ozone layer that protects us from dangerous radiation, and rising temperature with its menacing consequences such as higher sea levels. The Earth is slowly dying and the inconceivable – the end of life itself – is becoming conceivable...
>
> Now we are faced with the challenge of finding a new relationship with nature, characterized by respect for ecological balance, caution, and careful management.[4]

During the Christmas holiday, Ruud Lubbers received a visit from Michel Rocard, the French Prime Minister of the day. Rocard was concerned over environmental matters, particularly climate change, and he was very interested in developments in the Netherlands. Lubbers and Rocard decided to issue a statement calling for international action on climate change, and they invited Prime Minister Brundtland of Norway to join them. Ms Joke Waller of the Environment Department, who had authored the government's response to the Brundtland report a year earlier, drafted a new document, the *Declaration of the Hague*. It was released on 11 March 1989, and signed by the heads of state or government from 24 nations, including both the industrialized and developing worlds.* The declaration may have been the first step leading to the landmark UN Conference on Environment and Development in 1992.

In January 1989, Lubbers also got some positive signs from the private sector when he and Marius Enthoven attended a meeting of the Netherlands Christian Employers' Association (NCW).† 'They were all very much impressed by the Queen's speech,' Marius recalls. 'Because these people are very loyal to the Royal House.... It was as if their values had been changed.' Shortly afterwards, the other major business association, the Netherlands Federation of Industry (VNO), joined the Netherlands Trade Union Confederation (FNV) in a joint statement on the need for employers and employees to work together on protecting the environment. Such joint statements were common features of the *polder* model for economic or social issues; but this was the first time one had been issued for the environment.

Showdown

The positive developments with business indicated that the outside world was changing more rapidly than the world within the government. In early January we received the CEC's long-awaited report on the NEPP. It stated that another 300 million guilders (US$150 million) could be budgeted for the Environment Department, but that the NEPP project should be ended. The CEC's reasoning seemed rather dubious. The report questioned or dismissed all of RIVM's findings, except those for acidification. Somehow the report further concluded that acidification was equivalent to personal automobile use, and that a recent EU directive on catalytic converters would take care of the problem. End of story.

A showdown on the NEPP soon followed. The CEC's chairman, Frans Rutten, phoned Marius Enthoven one morning in late January and,

---

* The signatories were: Australia, Brazil, Canada, Egypt, France, Germany, Hungary, India, Indonesia, Italy, Ivory Coast, Japan, Jordan, Kenya, Malta, New Zealand, the Netherlands, Norway, Senegal, Spain, Sweden, Tunisia, Venezuela and Zimbabwe.

† Nederlandse Christelijke Werkgeversverbond. The association later merged, in 1994, with VNO to form the umbrella Confederation of Netherlands Industry and Employers (VNO/NCW).

according to Marius, 'suddenly summoned' him to appear before the committee that afternoon. Marius was outraged because he suspected that the CEC would take some quick statements from him and then vote to kill the NEPP that very day. 'So I refused to go,' he recounts. 'And that was the first time in his life that someone had *refused* to appear before his committee.'

Marius knew he would have the full support of Ed Nijpels, who had made the NEPP the centrepiece of his political career. Earlier, Nijpels and Marius had worked out a strategy for dealing with the CEC that centred around funding. Nijpels felt the department would need at least an extra 1.5 billion guilders (US$750 million) to implement the NEPP. If he didn't win that funding, Ed decided, he would resign.

In response to the CEC report, Lubbers called the first official Cabinet session to discuss the NEPP. The meeting soon turned into an argument, with Ed Nijpels and Marius Enthoven on one side and Frans Rutten on the other. Then Lubbers stepped in, explaining that Nijpels, as Environment Minister, had primary responsibility for this matter, and that he should be able to speak first without interruptions. Ed took this opportunity to throw down the gauntlet. 'You've now heard what the problems are,' he said. 'I assume there is no disagreement about the goal of cleaning up the environment and the targets indicated by RIVM. We should now focus the discussion on the means to achieve these targets.'* According to Enthoven, no one challenged this statement: 'They were all silent, and we didn't discuss the ambitious goals anymore. We only discussed the policy responses.' Though he chose not to strike back at that moment, Frans Rutten was certainly not ready to admit defeat.

Why did the Cabinet suddenly decide to support a radical – and very risky – restructuring of national policies? First, Minister Nijpels had presented the NEPP in a way that was very hard to criticize. The environment was a huge public concern at the time, and it was not politically viable to appear anti-environmental. Perhaps the most important reason for Ed's success, however, was that he had the one and only ally he really needed, the Prime Minister. If Ruud Lubbers had sided with Frans Rutten and the CEC, the NEPP might have died at that very moment. But Lubbers had decided to make the environment a central theme of his government, and he became the crucial sponsor of the NEPP process.

---

* The Cabinet debate is reconstructed from Marius Enthoven's personal recollections.

Notes

1 All Anne Alons quotations are from an interview with the author, The Hague, 8 August 1997.
2 All Wiel Klerken quotations are from an interview with the author, The Hague, 4 March 1997.
3 All Kees Schröder quotations are from an interview with the author, The Hague, 4 March 1997.
4 Her Majesty Beatrix, Queen of the Netherlands, *Christmas Address*, English translation (The Hague: Ministry of Foreign Affairs, 1988).

From Boxing to Hiking
Roles in the Policy Process

Roles in the Institutional Phase

The institutional phase uses a very simple model of the policy process: 'We vs Them'. Because I'm writing from a civil servant's perspective, I'll say that 'we' refers to government environmental authorities, and 'them' to the rest of society, especially corporations which are regulated by the government. The 'We vs Them' mentality applies, however, to all parties in the adversarial approach to policy: scientists, companies, NGOs. Everyone starts out seeing public policy as a battle with clear winners and losers. This perspective bears little resemblance to a group hike and much more to a boxing match. From the perspective of the Dutch Environment Department, the two contestants in the ring were government regulators, who protect the environment, and corporate villains, who despoil it (Figure 16).

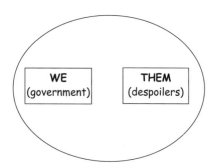

Figure 16 We vs Them

This isn't just a back alley brawl, however; it's a match between famous heavyweight fighters. It will have a very big audience – so big that they will not all fit in the arena. Many people will follow match on TV, on the radio, or in the newspapers. The media must be involved to reach this audience, and journalists will add their own commentaries and interpretations. Such a large event also requires a promoter; someone must bookthe arena, sell tickets and contact the media. In professional sports, there are sponsors with the resources and recognition to publicize the event. Taking these new roles into consideration, we can picture the boxing match as consisting of two concentric rings: the inner ring for the actual match, and the outer ring for the audience, media, and sponsor (Figure 17).

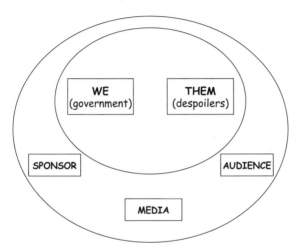

Figure 17 The full boxing match

This is a fairly complete picture of a boxing match, and of the adversarial – or institutional – phase of policy. As public concern for the environment grew, it went from being a back-alley brawl to a major sporting event. When the media became involved, both sides realized the importance of outreach and public relations. They also realized the importance of the sponsor, generally a prominent political or cultural figure. Environmental authorities, for example, looked for sponsorship from a president, prime minister, celebrities or NGOs. Their opponents also tried to win sponsors for their side.

Roles in Integration

It's easy to see why environmental policy often resembles a boxing match. Boxing is straightforward, easy to follow and quite exciting. To achieve sustainable development, however, we must pursue an integrated approach, which is more complicated. The move toward this approach has begun in many places all over the world. I myself first noticed it while at the University of Leyden.

My fellow students and I originally viewed environmental policy as a boxing match, adopting what I have called the 'strong position' – take on the bad guys and beat them. (Of course, the 'bad guys' may have had the same image of us, if they even noticed us.) Later, we began adopting the 'weak position' of trying to bring other parties into a dialogue, the first step in moving from institutional to integrated policies. We realized it was sometimes possible to reach mutually beneficial settlements with the parties we had considered to be enemies. I say 'sometimes' because there were (and perhaps always will be) parties whose interests are too different, or whose attitude is too dogmatic, to permit this outcome. For the time being, at least, they remain adversaries to environmental policies. Those who are willing to enter a dialogue are not necessarily won over to the environmental perspective, but they are willing to *consider* making a deal.

Moving from the adversarial/institutional approach to the integrated approach ruins the nice model of environmental policy based on a boxing match. There is still the role of 'We' – those who want to make new policies; but what about 'Them'? Some of them are adversaries, as in the boxing match. But others are willing to work toward a settlement, provided it respects their (generally economic) stakes in the policy outcome. This group is called the *stakeholders*. Trying to picture these new roles with the old model doesn't work very well (Figure 18).

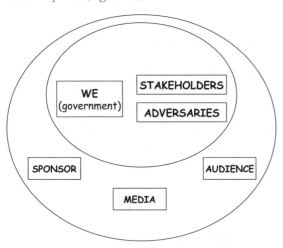

Figure 18 The crowded ring: who is fighting whom?

The centre ring is getting crowded, and it's no longer clear who is fighting whom. Presumably, the government and adversaries are still fighting. But what about the government and the stakeholders, or the stakeholders and the adversaries? What are their relationships to each other?

Although it is already quite full, the centre ring is going to get even more crowded. In the old-style approach, 'We', the government, see ourselves as both the advocates of new policies and the primary source of information to guide policies. We conduct research on environmental problems and formulate solutions, then we tell society what to do. As a party with a definite agenda for the policy outcome, however, government cannot also claim the role of providing objective information. That role should be turned over to a neutral party which has no affiliation to any combatant in the boxing match, or to a coalition representing all the boxers.

The RIVM report *Concern for Tomorrow* was a step toward more objective information, but only a step. RIVM is not the Environment Department, but they are closely associated. To give the report more credibility, RIVM collaborated with all the major scientific institutions in the Netherlands. *Concern for Tomorrow* thus represented the consensus view of the Dutch scientific community, not just the view of one institute. Of course scientists also have an agenda in the policy debate, so their information must be complemented by information from other sources, such as economists. The NEPP's third economic scenario helped to bring in the economic perspective. Later, we also included assessments from a very influential government economic institute and even a joint fact-finding project with the business community.* The stakeholder sessions in the autumn of 1988 were also very important sources of information. They gave many more parties, especially local governments and companies, a chance to provide input.

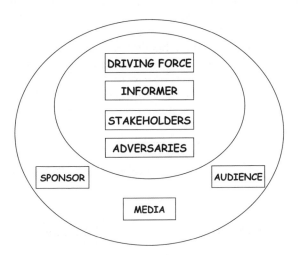

Figure 19 Time for a new model

---

* The assessment of the CEC was not a very useful source of information, because the institution was still an adversary that viewed environmental policy as a boxing match.

With the development of clearer, more objective information, government could concentrate more on driving policy developments. Thus the
'We' role in the old model split into two new roles: the *driving force*, which
pushes for a certain outcome, and the *informer*, which provides objective
information (Figure 19).

From Fighting a War to Managing a Process

By this point, policy can no longer be described as a boxing match, and a
new model is needed. Let's try a hike. Unlike a boxing match, a group
hiking trip does not have clear sides, nor does it have clear winners and
losers. It's not a contest at all, but a process in which everyone works
together to achieve common goals. Some old roles from the boxing match
remain, but they function differently.

There is still a sponsor, for example, but he or she is not the leader who
decides what the group will do. The sponsor encourages people to join the
hike and lets the group decide on its pace and destination. This is a much
better description of what occurs in public policy. Too often, people look
for a clear leader – usually a high-ranking political figure – who will set a
nation (province, city, etc.) on the right path. This is too much to expect
from a sponsor, who must represent many different interests in society and
keep the political process functioning smoothly. A sponsor can put an issue
on the political agenda by saying it is important, but should not become too
involved in the details of the policy debate or take sides.

Hiking is not a spectator sport, but there are people who serve as a kind
of audience. The hikers will tell their friends and family about the trip, for
example, and this 'audience' may also have some impact on the expedition.
The opinions or needs of family members may determine how long
someone can go away on a trip. In the policy process, the audience is the

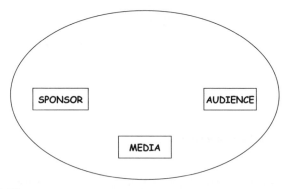

Figure 20 The outer ring

public at large – people who have not yet taken a position on an issue, or whose positions may change depending on how the process develops. Although they are not directly involved in making policy, their opinions can influence the final outcome.

It may be a stretch to say that the media play a role in a hiking trip; they certainly do so in public policy. The audience generally relies on the media as a source of information about the policy process (which is tricky, since the media are not completely objective). The media also transmit ideas from the audience (the public) to those more deeply involved in the policy process, such as elected officials or corporate CEOs.

In our new model of a policy process, we still have an outer ring with a sponsor, audience and media (Figure 20), although they no longer interact in the way they did at the boxing match.

Meanwhile, the centre ring has changed completely. It's no longer a battle, but a process among three actors: the driving force, the stakeholders and the informer (Figure 21). The driving force tries to initiate change. In this case, it is the government, but it may also be an NGO or the private sector. Responding to outside pressure (from the sponsor, audience and media) the government may initiate, for example, a policy to ban a certain harmful pesticide X. Rather than imposing regulations unilaterally, however, it now seeks a dialogue with potential stakeholders. In the case of a pesticide, the stakeholders may include chemical companies that manufacture the product, farmers who use it, and the communities downstream. The informer plays a neutral, intermediary role in the process – providing objective scientific information about the medical and environmental impacts of the pesticide as well as economic information about the impacts of a possible ban. There may still be 'confrontation' in this model. In initiating action by stakeholders, for example, the driving force sets up a kind of confrontation; stakeholders may confront each other, too. The difference here is that the participants try to resolve the confrontation in a more productive way than under the old approach.

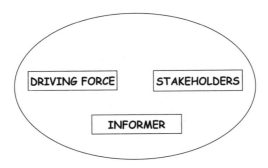

Figure 21 The inner ring

We are still missing some important roles from our model. What happened to the adversaries? They certainly haven't gone away. In fact, they are actively trying to break up the process. As a counterweight, there must also be someone to preserve and facilitate the process. This role, which I call the *process manager*, may be filled by a government official or an independent arbiter. A good process manager will not just block the adversaries but also try to bring them into the process as stakeholders. With such a big task, the process manager may need some help, such as an intermediary to communicate information about the process objectively – both the initiatives of the process manager and the objections of the stakeholders or adversary. I call this person the *right hand*.

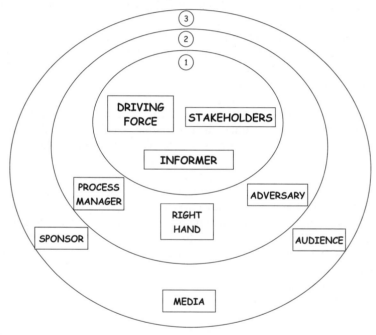

Figure 22 Roles in a policy process

Putting all these roles together, we have the model represented in Figure 22. In this model, specific policy is determined in the first ring by the interactions of the driving force, stakeholder and informer roles. The ability of these roles to enter into and stay in a process, however, depends on the second ring, containing the process manager (who tries to maintain the process), the adversary (who tries to disrupt it) and the right hand (who facilitates communication and interaction). And the second ring is ultimately influenced by the third, containing the sponsor, audience and media. They determine whether an issue is even important enough to be on the public agenda, and they exert various pressures on the ultimate outcome of the process. Thus, each level of the process exerts pressure inward. This pressure is translated from general to specific through the various roles and ultimately has its concrete result in the actual policy resolution.

A Closer Look at Roles

The roles are not necessarily played by individuals. They may also be played by institutions. An NGO, for example, may be a driving force, or even a sponsor, by placing a topic on the political agenda.* A company, or even an association of companies, may be stakeholders or adversaries (or often both). The policy process takes place at many different levels. Sometimes it involves national institutions, such as a government department or an industrial sector. Sometimes it is a process among a few people sitting together in a meeting. To make this model more tangible, let me provide some formal definitions of the roles and examples from the Dutch case.

Driving Force
As the name implies, this role drives the development of policies by initiating discussions and pushing them along. He or she is focused on the *ends* of policy by having a certain goal in mind, but is flexible on the *means* and able to propose different strategies to achieve the goal. The driving force keeps the process fresh by continually reworking theories, revising drafts of documents, and generally providing new input and ideas. Because this role is so focused on the specific content of policies, it cannot simultaneously foster the broader framework of the policy process.

Like all other roles, the driving force may change throughout the policy life cycle. In the recognition phase of policy, environmentalists or scientists may be the driving force by putting a new issue on the public agenda. In the formulation phase, the driving force may be found in the government. I cannot think of any government policies that succeeded without someone who felt personally responsible for the outcome. Gustaaf Biezeveld, for example, was a driving force through his deep commitment in working on *More than the Sum of Its Parts* and the first two IMPs.

I think my personal contribution to the NEPP was as driving force. I introduced notions such as the feedback mechanisms or the 25-year time frame of sustainable development, for example, as starting points to begin discussing the details of policy. Another example was the initiative I took (with coaxing from Anne Alons) in choosing the 100 most important

---

* The environmental NGO Greenpeace, for example, fills the role of sponsor for the protection of seals. Although the organization has a definite preference for the outcome of the process, it also serves the function of simply bringing the issue to the public and keeping it on the political agenda.

concepts from the stakeholder sessions in the autumn of 1988. As project leader of the NEPP, however, I could not always be the driving force. Sometimes I had to play the role of process manager or informer.

Stakeholder
This role does not make policy, but has a strong interest in, and influence on, its outcome. Economic sectors are important stakeholders. They may be affected by policies which regulate a certain substance or production method, or influence the prices of their products. Other government departments may be stakeholders because they are responsible for implementing new policies.

Obviously, the participants at the ten stakeholder sessions in the autumn of 1988 played this role. The local governments, for example, desired better guidance from The Hague in order to implement new policies. The business representatives were perhaps the most critical stakeholders at this stage. The NEPP would make considerable demands on them – to increase energy efficiency, conserve raw materials and clean up their production methods. They wanted to ensure that policies provided enough time and flexibility to avoid the serious disruption of their operations.

Somewhat later, the role of stakeholder was taken up by other government bodies that would have to implement policies, especially the Ministries of Economic Affairs, of Transport and Waterworks, and of Agriculture, Nature Protection and Fisheries. People from the Ministry of Economic Affairs were especially concerned, because they feared the NEPP would be disastrous for their business constituents. Thus Economic Affairs sometimes played the role of adversary.

Perhaps the most concrete example of a stakeholder was the farmer I met on my hike. He wanted to protect the wildlife on his land by cutting down the use of chemicals. But he was concerned about how this would affect his ability to compete in a difficult market.

Informer
This role delivers critical, objective information to the driving force and stakeholders. The person or institution in this role should not have a vested interest in the outcome of the process. The primary interest, instead, should be in the integrity of the information delivered, which may be scientific, economic or legal.

Institutions like RIVM are meant to be informers, and they often play this role quite well. RIVM's economist, Rob Maas, is a good example of a person who acted as informer. He did, of course, have his own personal desires for the outcome of policies (which everyone will have). His primary motivation was providing quality information, however, and he worked with many different parties to collect and analyze it.

I think many environmentalists (or environmental NGOs) see themselves as informers. Given their hefty interest in the process, however, they are usually not accepted in this role by the other participants. In general, their main role is as driving force, taking the initiative to begin a public debate on policy, and pushing for a particular outcome.

Process Manager

People in this role feel responsible for the *process itself*, not necessarily for the particular outcome. This role is not heavily involved in the content of policies but is well informed on the different interests and positions involved. It is generally played by a senior government official, but others may play it as well.

Pieter Winsemius, for example, is an archetypal process manager because of his keen interest in how the policy process functions. His life cycle model shows how policies develop but says nothing about a preferred outcome. His creation of themes and target groups are other good examples. They provided a new framework for people to think about their interactions in the policy process.

Marius Enthoven often served as process manager during the development of the NEPP. As Director General of the Environment Department, he had the authority to chair important meetings and show that maintaining the process was a government priority. Marius was well known and well respected in other government departments and in the private sector, which made him an ideal process manager. This person must be trusted by both the driving force and the parties who will become stakeholders.

Adversary

This role is not simply unenthusiastic about the process, but is determined to stop it. In general, this role fears that any outcome of the process will be harmful to its interests. The adversary's opposition may also be ideological – too steeped in a war mentality to imagine making a deal. Not all processes have adversaries, but they can turn up at any time. Fortunately, adversaries can become stakeholders if the process is well managed and new perspectives are introduced.

Frans Rutten and the other CEC members began as typical adversaries. They felt that their interests were fundamentally threatened by the NEPP, and they saw no advantage in joining a dialogue. Because of their prominent positions in the government, they also thought they were above having to negotiate with other parties.

Right Hand

This role facilitates the process in a very practical way, by relaying information, sending out documents or setting up meetings and workshops. The right hand performs most of the practical organizational functions on which the process manager relies. He or she has a lower profile, and generally a more junior status, than the process manager, but is also very important.

Marie-Therese Lammers was the perfect right hand. She had no previous experience in the environment or public policy, so she did not have a vested interest in the outcome, but she understood the importance of maintaining the process itself. The role of right hand is not a typical job for a secretary, and we were very fortunate to have a secretary who could play this role. After her work on the first NEPP, Marie-Therese continued as a right hand in the Environment Department. It was she who organized the second and third NEPPs.

Sponsor
The sponsor is generally a person in a very high position, such as a political leader, who recognizes the importance of an issue and helps put it on the public agenda. This person maintains a fair distance from the details of policy, and even from the details of process management. The sponsor has an objective, bird's eye view not only of the policy issue at hand, but also of how it fits into other issues in society. People are sometimes frustrated that the sponsor doesn't provide more 'leadership' for a particular policy outcome, but that's a job for the driving force.

Prime Minister Brundtland was a key international sponsor of environmental policy. Her commission introduced sustainable development and placed it on the world agenda, but she did not say much about the details of possible sustainable development policies. Ms Brundtland continued her sponsorship role by joining Prime Ministers Rocard and Lubbers in the *Declaration of the Hague*, which helped create momentum for the UN's 1992 Conference on Environment and Development in Rio.

Ed Nijpels often played the role of sponsor in the Environment Department. He has a keen understanding of how to reach the media and the public; and he helped bring the environment to the top of the public agenda. One of Ed's strengths is his willingness to say unexpected things. He was the former leader of the Liberal Party, which was not known for being concerned about the environment (he himself hadn't been, at first). When the public heard a prominent Liberal talking strongly about the environment, they knew it had become an important political issue.

As the debate intensified with the other government departments, Ed Nijpels became the driving force, and Ruud Lubbers played sponsor. As Prime Minister, Lubbers was certainly in a position to set the agenda for national policy. In the final Cabinet discussions on the NEPP, Lubbers would get even more involved, playing roles as process manager and even driving force.

Her Majesty the Queen became a sponsor for a brief but very critical phase. As monarch, she is considered to be 'above politics'. She cannot take sides in a political struggle, but she can express her concern for an issue and encourage others to take action, which she did in her Christmas speech by drawing attention to *Concern for Tomorrow* and the NEPP process.

Media
This is a very broad term, referring to all the parties that distribute information about policy to the general public, including major television networks and newspapers, but also the local press, and 'alternative' sources which give special attention to a particular area or political perspective. Today the media also include informal but powerful new means of communication such as the Internet. Certainly a lot of people now get information and exchange ideas over computer networks.

Audience
This includes almost everyone. While most people are not directly involved in policy decisions, they are affected by them in some way. The audience is far from a passive observer; its opinions are critical to the outcome of policies. Sometimes the audience is rather small. It may, for example, include the family and friends of people involved in the policy negotiations. Everybody has to confide in someone. In a democratic system, the most important audience is the voting public. They ultimately determine what issues get on the political agenda, and their approval is critical for the legislators or other government officials who make policy.

The Dutch Parliament was an active and critical audience for the NEPP, as for all other government proposals. The Parliament first prompted Ruud Lubbers to become a sponsor through its reaction to the Queen's first speech. While individual parliamentarians or legislators may play other roles in the policy process, such as sponsor or driving force, the body as a whole serves primarily as the original audience for policy makers. It decides whether to approve, amend or reject a government policy proposal.

Environmental NGOs are another audience. They often represent a large constituency of the population (through both their official membership and their general following). Their reactions to government policies, thus, are one important indicator of the opinions held by the general public.

The Evolution of Roles

Policy decisions at the national level are not implemented automatically in a small town or individual factory. Policy must be translated from the general level of government to the specifics of the home, factory or street. A new policy process takes place every time such a translation is made. The same players from an earlier process may still be involved, but they often play different roles. Let's examine this development for the NEPP.

Outside pressures (for example from companies) and inside initiatives (such as the IMPs) placed the discussion of a National Environmental Policy Plan on the Environment Department's agenda. The first generation of the process took place right at the heart of the department. Driving forces like

Gustaaf Biezeveld, Jan Suurland or Koos van der Vaart initially pushed for the development of a plan. Their stakeholders were the other directorates in the department, who had to be convinced that such a plan would help their work (and not threaten their authority).

The first year of work on the NEPP (1987) was difficult because several key roles were missing. Bram Breure had focused on being the process manager, but he was also expected to play the role of driving force. Meanwhile, Bram had lost his traditional sponsor, Frans Evers. We also lacked informers until early 1988, when people like Kees Zoeteman and Fred Langeweg emerged with the preliminary RIVM findings. In early 1988, the project got a driving force (myself), a process manager (Marius Enthoven) and a sponsor (Ed Nijpels). There were still some adversaries in the department (people who were sceptical of the plan), but we eventually turned most of them into stakeholders and reached a basic agreement about the type of NEPP we wanted.*

In the next generation of the process, key people in the other government departments became stakeholders. Prime Minister Lubbers also entered – first as sponsor and later also as process manager. I generally continued as driving force, but this role was also taken by people like Marius Enthoven or Ed Nijpels (especially in their debates with Frans Rutten and the CEC).

We would eventually reach a deal on the NEPP with the other departments, and a third round would begin. Those departments then had to present the deal to their constituencies – farmers in the case of the Ministry of Agriculture, industrial firms for the Ministry of Economic Affairs. Now the other departments, which had previously been stakeholders, would take on roles such as sponsor, process manager or even driving force.

The evolution of roles in the policy process can be rather complicated. Parties generally move through different roles in the different generations of discussions; but roles can also change at other times. A stakeholder who gets angry or feels threatened may suddenly become an adversary. A sponsor who starts getting more interested in policy developments may become a process manager. A stakeholder may even become a driving force if he or she suddenly comes up with an idea for resolving a problem.

I think recognizing the different roles can help one understand the policy process, but it will never be simple. Policy making is a long, complicated affair, and the parties involved must be constantly aware of subtle changes and developments. Recognizing the importance of different roles in the process can certainly help.

---

*This simplifies the process somewhat. There are still elements in the other departments, and even within the Environment Department, which have not bought into the NEPP 'deal'.

CHAPTER 7

The Exercise is Good for You
Economic Benefits of Environmental Policies

There may be many ways to climb a mountain. Even after choosing a destination, there can be a discussion about the trails to take, the places to camp and the pace to keep. After the Cabinet meeting of February 1989, the government had a basic destination in mind for the NEPP. The Queen's speech, *Concern for Tomorrow*, growing media attention and the Prime Minister's personal commitment meant that environmental problems had to be taken seriously. Building on this momentum, Ed Nijpels said that he would not discuss the goals of the NEPP any more, but he was willing to discuss any ideas for how to achieve them. The other departments were most concerned with the cost of environmental measures, and money was the common language in our discussions with them.

Financing and Ecological Tax Shifting

By early February Ruud Lubbers was not only the NEPP's sponsor, but increasingly its process manager. The plan had gained other sponsors by then, such as the Queen and even some business leaders, so Lubbers could concentrate on the difficult financial and political negotiations that followed. His main concern, as always, was balancing the national budget. Next came his 'no nonsense' philosophy of cutting government bureaucracy and reducing regulatory complexity. He insisted that overall taxes could not increase, and that economic burdens be distributed equitably among the target groups.

Lubbers needed clear information to navigate through the Cabinet discussions, and Rob Maas helped provide it. Having worked on *Concern for Tomorrow* and the third economic scenario, Rob understood the costs of new environmental policies better than anyone. He condensed his knowledge into a series of spreadsheets, nicknamed 'Maas tables', that listed measures for achieving the environmental goals in the draft NEPP and cost estimates for the measures. Detailed editions of the tables were sent to the individual

Table 4 Maas table for acidification theme, 11 April 1989
(Costs in millions of guilders/year)

Measure	Total cost	Target group cost	Sector levies	General levies	Tax shift	Means	Budget
1 SO_2 and NO_x from central power stations	75	75					
1a Existing measures	115	115					
2 SO_2 from refineries	20	20					
2a Existing measures	15	15					
3 SO_2 from industry	40	40					
3a Existing measures	20	20					
4 NO_x from households	75	75					
5 NO_x from industry (>20 megawatt)	30	30					
5a Existing measures	40	40					
6 NO_x from industry (<20 megawatt)	40	35		5			VROM/ Economic Affairs
7 NO_x from industry(WKK)	20	15		5			VROM/ Economic Affairs
8 NO_x from traffic (3-way catalytic converters)	550	550					
9 Clean trucks	90		90 (Excise taxes)				VROM
10 Clean buses	30		30 (Excise taxes)				VROM
10a Restoration measures	25			25			WVC
Total for acidification	1185	1030	120	35	0	0	

ministries; and Lubbers used summary versions in the Cabinet discussions.

The Maas tables were broken down according to the environmental themes listed in the draft NEPP. Under each theme was a summary of the measures required to meet environmental quality goals by the year 2010. Next to each measure was its estimated total cost, the required government expenditure, and the costs per target group. In the case of acidification, for example, ten categories of measures were listed, all of which had to be fully implemented by 2010. Based on cost efficiency and equity among target groups, the Cabinet chose the degree to which measures would be implemented in the short term (the next four years); and set a timetable for fully implementing them in the remaining years.*

It was very important that we defined targets based on the level of emissions that would fall within *Concern for Tomorrow's* critical loads. In theoretical terms, it might have seemed better to set targets based on environmental quality, but this would have been impossible in real life. Scientists could have spent years evaluating and arguing about environmental quality, while it continued to deteriorate. Instead, we used *Concern for Tomorrow* to make well-educated guesses about the required emission reductions. Then we had concrete numbers to use in negotiations with target groups.

The Maas tables greatly aided the decision-making process by providing a comprehensive overview of policy measures and their economic impacts.† 'It appeared that consensus was more easily reached,' Rob explains, 'because every party could see that the other parties also had to contribute something.' Previously, the government had looked mostly at individual problems and individual measures to solve them. Reducing nitrogen oxide emissions, for example, could be achieved by various means. Should reductions come from the automobile sector or from agriculture? Which sector is 'at fault'? *Concern for Tomorrow* showed how various sectors were contributing to problems; and the Maas tables described the costs and benefits of addressing these contributions. With this clear information, it was possible to choose a combination that met environmental goals and was equitable in its financial impacts.

Placing the environmental discussion on an economic and financial basis also gave us more credibility in the government. Rather than arguing philosophical points such as 'the environment versus the economy', we could

---

* There had been very different opinions about the time horizon for the NEPP. Rudolf de Korte, the Minister for Economic Affairs, argued for a one-year planning period, since elections would be held in a year. Meanwhile, the NEPP and *Concern for Tomorrow* called for a planning horizon of 20–25 years. Lubbers insisted that 20 years was too far ahead for concrete planning measures but felt that four years was a foreseeable time frame.

† However, the most innovative ideas for the environment were not reflected in the Maas tables. Unlike end-of-pipe measures, systemic changes in technology and production generally didn't cost much. In fact, they often had positive economic impacts.

have very concrete discussions based on the numbers. Cost estimates were especially helpful in dealing with our colleagues from Economic Affairs. For years, they had complained that our information was too vague to base decisions on. Finally, we could present solid numbers.

There were still some cases in which we were not sure how much measures would cost, but we consulted with stakeholders to reduce this uncertainty as much as possible. An interdepartmental group headed by Paul Hofhuis and Rob Maas worked to reach consensus on expected costs, based on the best information we had at the time. To gather the information, government departments had to consult with the different economic sectors they represented. Thus, business stakeholders were involved in the government fact-finding process, and they knew what to expect in terms of future policy measures.

Economic decisions generally followed the 'polluter pays' principle, according to which the sectors responsible for environmental damage should bear the costs of mitigating or preventing it. Thus levies imposed on harmful products or actions could also generate revenue to pay for positive measures that targeted the same environmental concern. For example, Ed Nijpels negotiated a deal on automobiles with Henk Koning, the state secretary for fiscal policies. They decided to reduce the high automobile levy for cars with catalytic converters and raise the levy even higher for those without.

Later, such trade-offs occurred not only between environmental revenues and expenditures, but also in other policy areas. New energy levies, for example, were offset by a cut in the capital gains tax on small business investment. Organizations in many countries are now advocating similar tax shifts to switch economic incentives from 'bads' to 'goods'. We set this ball rolling by the way we framed the discussions. Rather than proposing sweeping reform, we asked simple, practical questions like 'Who should pay for this?' According to Rob Maas, 'It was not explicit. When the Environment Department proposed to increase certain taxes, the Ministry of Finance just decided to reduce others.' In the process, we laid the foundation for developing a true environmental tax system in the future.

Deals with Government Departments

While Lubbers negotiated matters in the Cabinet, the NEPP steering group coordinated work among the government departments. At this stage, the NEPP team played the role of informer for the government. After intense consultations with the different departments, for example, I pulled the results together in a summary for the Cabinet discussions. Meanwhile, Rob Maas led another group which produced macro-economic modelling based on the cost calculations in the Maas tables.

We first reached agreement with our colleagues in the Ministry of Agriculture, Fisheries and Nature Protection. The biggest difficulty was the acidification problem. *Concern for Tomorrow* had shown that manure released large amounts of ammonia, which contributes to acidification in and around forests. The run-off from fields and pig farms had to be reduced by 70 per cent, RIVM concluded, in order to meet the goals for the acidification theme. The Agriculture Ministry strongly disputed these conclusions. It insisted that pollution from manure was much less severe, or that it could be reduced by minor changes in farming practices.

Agriculture Minister Gerrit Braks began as an adversary. He was from the province of Northern Brabant, where many farmers had hauled themselves out of poverty by adopting the same intensive agriculture practices we were questioning (especially in pig farming). Braks couldn't imagine achieving a 70 per cent reduction of ammonia pollution without devastating effects on agriculture, and his opposition threatened to derail the NEPP debates.

Fortunately, we found a good advocate in André Kleinmeulman, who headed a section within the Department of Nature Protection that was charged with coordinating environmental policy in the Ministry of Agriculture. André was the driving force in the Ministry and a stakeholder in the overall NEPP process. 'It was a very difficult position,' he recalls. 'We were to develop nature policies for the whole Ministry. But in the beginning, the Ministry looked a little strangely at these "nature guys" who did environmental protection.'[1] Like Braks, André also came from an agricultural background and knew the value of intensive farming. He sensed, however, that the ammonia problem could not be ignored in the current political environment. It would be better, André realized, for his Ministry to cooperate and have some voice in developing the solution, rather than have one imposed by the Cabinet.

Braks was especially opposed to using 'volume measures' – reducing the number of pigs and cows – in order to meet environmental goals. By shifting the discussion from ends to means, André eventually broke the conflict. In a compromise with the Ministry, language about volume measures was dropped, and Agriculture was given the opportunity to first try all possible technological means for achieving the ammonia targets, such as better design of stables and injecting manure fertilizer into the soil rather than spreading it on the surface.

In the end, technological fixes were not enough (as we had expected).* By the time this became clear, however, Minister Braks himself was starting to see the negative economic impacts from pollution. He eventually introduced an emergency moratorium on the expansion of pig farms. Now, almost ten years later, we are moving to the point where we can actually talk

---

* The Third NEPP, released in February 1998, reported that the Netherlands would not achieve the ammonia objectives for 2005 or 2010.

about volume measures. André Kleinmeulman agrees that the pig-raising business has grown too large to be environmentally *or economically* sustainable. By reducing the number of animals, the prices of pork will rise, taking the pressure off farmers to increase their volume and giving them more money for environmental investments. In 1997, the Ministry of Agriculture and the pig-farming sector reached an historic agreement to trim the sector by 25 per cent.*

We faced a similar challenge with the Ministry of Transport and Waterworks. As Minister Braks had grown up in agriculture, so Minister Neelie Kroes had grown up in the transport industry. She came from Rotterdam, the world's largest port, where her father had owned a freight-hauling company. In 1989, her Ministry had just completed its second 'structural scheme' for road and rail transport. The second scheme was moving in an environmental direction. For example, it contained measures to shift traffic off the road and onto trains. We welcomed these initiatives, but they were not at all sufficient to meet the NEPP's environmental goals.

Despite her inclination to support a large transport sector, Neelie Kroes also had a good sense of the political climate. She gradually saw that her response to the environment would not be perceived as adequate, and that the stand she took on personal car use would be critical. There was no one event or argument which changed her mind; but the steadily accumulating evidence, and the advice of her fellow Liberal Ed Nijpels, proved persuasive. 'Finally, she saw that the problems with the car were going to be so big, that she had to do something.' Nijpels explains. 'Every minister who is facing these problems finally gets convinced.' Of course, Nijpels points out that the NEPP's provisions for transport would also mean additional funding for Kroes's Ministry.

The final discussions on transport were very detailed. Projections at the time indicated that the sector would grow by 70 per cent between 1985 and 2010. After long discussions, we agreed that the growth rate should be cut to 35 per cent. The government found concrete measures to cover most of the reduction in growth rates, and it was agreed to pursue additional measures in the future. Unfortunately, we have yet to identify all these additional measures, but there can be no doubt that the discussion of specific volume targets has accelerated our journey on the road to a solution.

A Positive Economic Forecast

Although the Ministry of Economic Affairs often appeared to be an adversary, it was not monolithic. While some people, like Frans Rutten, tried to block

---

* The agreement was facilitated greatly by a devastating plague of swine fever in summer 1997. This was a perfect opportunity to cap the future growth of an already contracting sector.

the NEPP, others, especially Jan Willem Weck, were working to develop consensus between the two departments. He played a role in Economic Affairs similar to the one André Kleinmeulman had played in Agriculture: stakeholder in the overall process and driving force in his Ministry. As Jan Willem recalls:

> I had to convince our people within the Ministry that all the ecological concerns were not just being pumped up by environmentalists. They were real concerns of a fundamental structural nature which would have enormous economic impacts. The only way we could tackle these problems in an effective, cost-efficient manner was to join this NEPP process, instead of just waiting for a proposal and then trying to mould it to our liking.

In the summer of 1988 Weck asked for an independent review of the NEPP's economic scenarios by the Central Planning Bureau (CPB), the main government advisory body on economic and fiscal matters.* The CPB study was needed to repeat, within the government, the discussions we had already concluded with the private sector stakeholders. The CPB modelled a 'business as usual' scenario and two versions of the RIVM's second and third scenarios. One version of each scenario assumed that other countries would not change their environmental policies, and that the Netherlands would go it alone. The other version assumed that other countries would eventually adopt similar policies to those in the NEPP, thus wiping out any comparative advantage to companies operating abroad under weaker environmental standards.

Most people were very surprised when the CPB's results were released in March 1989. The baseline economic assumption was that, barring any significant new environmental policies, the economy would grow by about 3 per cent annually, essentially doubling in size by the year 2010. The CPB also predicted, however, that similar growth would occur with stricter environmental policies, even those endorsing the most ambitious measures of the third economic scenario. In fact, if other countries also adopted similar environmental policies, the Dutch economy might even grow a bit more under the third scenario than under the baseline assumption! The CPB results are summarized in Table 5.

The differences among the scenarios were truly negligible, since they all fell within the margin of error for the CPB's models. In other words, it appeared that the economy would double by the year 2010, with or without the NEPP. Many people misunderstood this conclusion and assumed that

---

* The bureau was established by the economist and Nobel Laureate Dr Jan Tinbergen after the Second World War. Tinbergen's thinking was in line with other prominent economists of the time, such as the American Lawrence Klein and the Englishman John Maynard Keynes, who believed that careful planning could guide the economy back to health. After the Second World War, Tinbergen worked extensively on international development projects. He was also one of the economists who helped develop the measurement of the gross national product (GNP).

Table 5 Results of the CPB Study

Cumulative effects in year 2010	Baseline assumption	Business as usual Scenario 1	Scenario 2: All end-of-pipe measures		Scenario 3: Structural Changes	
			Scenario 2a (w/o other countries)	Scenario 2b (with other countries)	Scenario 3a (w/o other countries)	Scenario 3b (with other countries)
% GDP growth	+99.4	+98.1	+95.9	+97.5	+95.2	+99.9

the NEPP *advocated* doubling the economy in 25 years. In fact, it didn't say anything about *how much* the economy should develop. The NEPP simply showed that rigorous environmental policies would have no appreciable effect on this development.

The CPB's results were especially surprising because past studies had always predicted dire economic impacts from strong environmental policies. Previous attempts had only examined impacts four years into the future, however, whereas the CPB study made 25-year forecasts. 'If you only calculate your investments for a four-year period and then stop, the cost effect is always severe,' Rob Maas explains. 'So we said, this is a 25-year programme and we should calculate both the cost effects and the *investment* effects at the same time. And they were more or less in balance.' Although the NEPP's policies would cost more, the money spent was also an invest-ment that would lead to future benefits. Economic growth can be strengthened by investments of any sort, be they in environmentally beneficial or harmful technologies and practices. There might be some individual winners and losers from stronger environmental policies, but in the end, they would balance each other out.

The third scenario was not only acceptable for the economy but was considered slightly better than the second scenario, an incremental, end-of-pipe approach favoured by traditional economists. Furthermore, the study only evaluated the *costs* of new environmental measures. It didn't attempt to quantify the *benefits* of a cleaner, healthier environment. We had long suspected that the end-of-pipe approach had run its course, and that structural changes in production and consumption would be more cost-effective. With the CPB report, we had the numbers to prove it, and subse-quent experiences show that the numbers were correct.

Making a Deal with Industry

The CPB results were of more interest to government officials than to businesspeople. We had detailed discussions about cost estimates in the NEPP steering group, especially with Peter Vogtländer, the CEO of Shell

Netherlands, and Hans Blankert, the head of the Federation of Metal and Electric Industries.* To our surprise, the two men didn't take much interest in the CPB report. Smiling, Peter Vogtländer explained: 'We know how these models can lie. We prefer to trust our own knowledge of the economy.'†

Blankert and Vogtländer later joined us for a meeting with colleagues from Economic Affairs, in which we presented our cost calculations for the NEPP. The two businessmen did not challenge our numbers directly, but they explained that their in-house experts had come up with different results. Rather than arguing about which side was 'right', we agreed that no one was certain what the NEPP would really cost. In an impressive show of trust, we decided to pool our experts in a joint fact-finding group.

On 3 March, Marius Enthoven, Rob Maas and I were invited to a dinner at the Federation of Metal and Electric Industries to discuss the cost estimates for industry, especially the figures for the next four years. The fact-finding group predicted that the costs would rise an additional 1.5 billion guilders annually for the main industrial sectors by 1994. 'Suppose we were sure about that figure,' Marius asked. 'Would that be an acceptable cost for the industry?'[2] After exchanging nervous glances, they finally said, yes, it would be acceptable.†† 'So,' Marius continued. 'May we assume that the problem is not the costs, per se, but the uncertainty of the estimates?' Again, the answer was yes.

'OK, perhaps there will always be uncertainty about the costs of implementing environmental policies,' Marius said. 'But is there a way to limit this uncertainty by jointly managing the implementation?' After some thought, Blankert and Vogtländer proposed creating a joint monitoring committee with representatives from industry, Economic Affairs, and the Environment Department (basically a continuation of the fact-finding group we had established).

The group developed a commitment package to manage the economic uncertainties. We began with immediate actions based on the assumptions from our latest economic modelling. Then we agreed to research three types of uncertainties: about NEPP compliance costs, future national economic developments, and the likelihood that other countries would adopt similar environmental policies. If actual conditions turned out very different from those we were expecting, we would consider contingency plans to modify policy. Seeing that even major companies were coming to terms with the NEPP, Economic Affairs softened its objections.

---

* Hans Blankert later became the chairman of VNO/NCW, the umbrella association of nearly all Dutch businesses.
† Peter Vogtländer's statement was reconstructed from the author's memory.
†† We were only able to use such figures because the NEPP targets were expressed in terms of emission reductions, for which costs could be estimated. It would not have been possible to make a deal based only on vague environmental quality targets.

A political agreement was close at hand because the main elements of a policy deal were known. Industry would accept the long-term targets in the NEPP and the medium-term cost of measures to achieve those targets. The government had to accept the contingency plan: if assumptions about technology, economic development or the policies of other countries were wrong, we would reconsider the whole deal with industry.

Driving home that evening, Marius, Rob and I wondered aloud why it had been so easy to reach an agreement. We worked out the reason later: the chemical industry had taken in record profits that year and was quite concerned about how to spend them. Too much money can actually be a problem if businesses are unsure how to invest it and there is no consensus on the areas in which to compete. Without some outside challenge, from either the government or the market, the chemical companies would have been struggling to identify a course for their future research and development budgets.

The ambitious goals in the NEPP provided a common technical challenge for the entire industry and the assurance that the companies were all pursuing worthwhile development strategies. Uncertainty over each other's investment plans, rather than over government environmental policies, may have been the main concern for many companies at the time. Our progress with the chemical industry gave us hope that we could reach an agreement with other sectors of the economy.

The Cabinet Crisis

Lubbers became increasingly interested in the 'polluter pays' principle and developed a hierarchy of sources for funding the NEPP. His first choice was that the responsible economic sectors bear the costs directly. His second choice was that government funds be raised from levies targeted at the responsible sector. The third option was to adjust government financial structures: for example, one could remove subsidies which lowered the cost of environmentally harmful practices. Only when all the previous options were exhausted should the government use general revenue to finance the NEPP.

The Cabinet discussions on funding took place in an increasingly difficult political environment. After almost seven years in office, the governing coalition of the Liberal Party and Lubbers's Christian Democrats was wearing out. I think the root of the problem was that Lubbers and some key members of the Liberal Party had increasingly different philosophies. The Prime Minister often spoke about setting an 'agenda for the future'. He was thinking about big reforms with long-term impacts.

The Liberals, however, seemed preoccupied with rather small, short-term issues, mainly lowering the top personal income tax bracket. Once this measure succeeded, the party leadership didn't appear to be very interested in new policies. Of course, Liberals like Ed Nijpels and Neelie Kroes understood the need for far-reaching environmental reforms, and for creative ways to achieve them. But Nijpels and Kroes did not necessarily represent the sentiments of the party leadership at the time.

Tensions had been rising in the Liberal Party at the end of April 1989 through a series of disputes and controversies such as overspending by the Ministry of Education and tax deduction policies for homeowners. Taken together, these disputes were evidence that a bigger conflict was brewing, not simply between the Liberals and Christian Democrats, but also among different factions in the Liberal Party. A battle was eventually triggered by one of the NEPP financing proposals, a reduction in the tax write-off for people who commuted by car.

On Monday, 1 May, the coalition government forced Prime Minister Lubbers to send a letter to Parliament regarding the NEPP funding dispute. Lubbers's letter simply announced that the Cabinet was preparing a national environmental policy plan and that one of the measures (hardly the most important) would be financed by the 'polluter pays' principle. The text then explained that transport was an important sector affecting the environment and that it would bear its environmental costs by a reduction in the commuter tax credit.

That evening Parliament began debates on the Lubbers letter. This was quite strange, because all Parliament had to go on was a brief document that focused on one funding aspect for a plan that hadn't even been finalized. The draft plan was still sitting on my desk. Thus there was little prospect of having a productive discussion, a result which Lubbers may have intended. The parliamentary session quickly developed into a fight between Lubbers and Joris Voorhoeve, the Liberal parliamentary leader.

By this point, Lubbers had abandoned his roles as sponsor or process manager. Rather than trying to foster a process, the Prime Minister was picking a fight with his coalition partners. After a long debate, Lubbers concluded that Parliament had no confidence in the government and that he would ask the Queen to call new elections. Clearly, he did not want to settle the dispute. He wanted a new Cabinet. This was the first time that a national government had fallen over an environmental issue, and the event attracted international attention.

Gathering Up Our Gear

I assumed that the end of the Cabinet meant the end of the NEPP, but I soon learned otherwise. Gerard Wuisman, the representative of the Prime Minister's office, told us to finish the NEPP on our own and get it to Parliament. Technically, we were no longer producing an official government plan; rather what we had was documentary evidence of why the coalition had fallen apart. In reality, though, public demand and our extensive work with stakeholders had made the environment a critical political issue. We decided simply to publish a full-scale NEPP, as we had always intended.

The Environment Department was authorized to complete the NEPP, but we didn't know how to go about it. There were a number of smaller issues which the Cabinet had not yet resolved, although the different departments had put forward proposals for them. On 9 May the NEPP steering group quickly selected from among these proposals, like children picking out candy. Sometimes we chose the option proposed by the Environment Department, sometimes that from Economic Affairs, sometimes that from another department. These discussions involved a lot of horse trading, especially with Economic Affairs. In one case, I gave in to Jan Willem Weck on some measure and received his blessing to publish the CPB table showing that the NEPP would have virtually no impacts on future economic growth. I think I made a good trade: that table was very influential.

The last challenge was deciding how best to present the NEPP. Until then, the different policy measures were scattered throughout the text, and one had to dig through the document to find them all. We didn't even know how many we were proposing! Marius and I discussed this problem, and we decided to pull all the measures out of the general text and put them into numbered lists of 'A-actions'. There were two advantages to producing these lists. First, it made the NEPP appear more 'action-oriented'. The numbered items always said that the government would *do* something. Second, we had distinct tasks we could assign to those implementing the NEPP. And we had a lot of tasks – 230 in all!

During the week beginning 15 May I spent a few nights in the state publishing house checking over the final text and layout of the NEPP. With illustrations, color photographs throughout and even a few comics, it didn't look like a typical government document. We also thought it should have a catchy name. After many suggestions, Jan Veenman of the VROM's external relations department proposed the title *Kiezen of Verliezen*, which we translate as *To Choose or to Lose*. I wasn't entirely pleased, because this title echoes the old environment versus economy debate: choose one and lose the other. It was, however, the best suggestion we had. Jan Veenman also chose the cover image – the endangered earth cracking in two like an egg. While I first thought this picture was overly dramatic, I realized later that we needed strong images to draw thousands of new stakeholders into the process.

The NEPP was finally sent to Parliament on 25 May 1989, a year and a half later than originally intended. We held press conferences in both Dutch and English that afternoon, and Ed Nijpels handed fresh copies of the NEPP to key stakeholders, including corporate CEOs, the presidents of employers' associations, union leaders and directors of NGOs. Their presence was meant to symbolize broad cooperation on the NEPP, which we would certainly need for its implementation. We had originally intended to produce a 'government plan', bringing together the different national departments, the provinces and the municipalities. Through the writing and later implementation of the NEPP, however, we produced a true social contract, in which companies, for example, came to number among the strongest supporters.

Notes

1 All André Kleinmeulman quotations are from an interview with the author, The Hague, 10 August 1997.
2 Marius Enthoven quotations are reconstructed from the author's memory.

CHAPTER 8

Pretty Shoes or a Beautiful Hike?
The Logic of the NEPP and NEPP Plus

A hiker must have the right shoes. They come in many styles and sizes, and it is unlikely that any two people will be able to wear the same shoes. A similar logic holds for public policy instruments. As with shoes, it is unlikely that one 'size' of policy instruments will fit everyone. Yet governments choose very specific, one-size-fits-all policy instruments to achieve environmental objectives, and they insist that everyone should 'wear' them. In the NEPP, we tried to talk more about the ultimate destination of policies and to leave the choice of shoes up to the stakeholders. This decision proved very controversial.

Four Levels of Reasoning

On the surface, the NEPP mostly retained the structure we had devised at the first RIVM meeting in early 1988. After a preface, summary and introductory chapter came chapters describing the scale levels, feedback mechanisms, long-term goals, economic scenarios, themes and target group requirements. Below the surface, however, was an underlying structure that represented our detailed scientific and economic analyses, and our intensive discussions with stakeholders.

We couldn't just tell people what to do. We had to begin by considering our present situation, analyzing it, and seeing how society could take responsibility for implementing solutions. Only after passing through these three levels of reasoning could we enter the fourth, a discussion of the specific actions to be taken. By this point, however, the actions wouldn't just be decided by the government. Rather, they would be decided by the stakeholders, based on an understanding of everyone's responsibilities.

Level One: the Model

The first level of reasoning – covered in the NEPP's Preface and first three chapters – provides a model for assessing the environment. In terms of a hike, this level is a map showing the terrain the group will cover. The Preface explained the basis of the NEPP and the time frame it would encompass:

> This National Environmental Policy Plan (NEPP) provides a mid-term environmental strategy directed toward sustainable development. This strategy is based on the findings of ... the 1987 report *Our Common Future*. This strategy is also the policy response to the integral environmental survey *Concern for Tomorrow*....[1]

Chapter One, the Introduction, describes the general context in which we had prepared the NEPP. It begins with a discussion of environmental rights and responsibilities, then reviews the history of Dutch environmental policy integration. The Introduction ends by explaining that the present environmental problems pose increasingly severe risks to our society, and that preserving the environment for the future requires a long-term strategic plan. Yet the NEPP will not prescribe exactly what society must do. It will describe the conditions under which environmental quality can be attained, leaving decisions on specific actions to the responsible parties.

Chapters Two ('Environmental Problems: the Trend Extrapolated') and Three ('Premises for Environmental Management') discuss the basic theories behind the NEPP. Chapter Two describes the current problems for each of the five scale levels and the consequences of these problems for future generations. It concludes:

> The environmental problems which we will face in the coming decades are many times more serious than those which have determined the course of environmental policy thus far ....[2]

The three feedback mechanisms appear next. They are defined in Chapter Two, then used in Chapter Three to describe the type of structural changes required for sustainability. Chapter Three also discusses other principles, such as risk management, priority setting, and the division of responsibilities between government and individuals. On this last point, the chapter states:

> The solution is a shared responsibility, in which the government's role is characterized by formulating quality objectives, creating the conditions necessary for environmentally friendly behavior, stimulating, guiding, and investing.[3]

Level Two: Goals

The second level of reasoning begins in Chapter Four, 'Environmental Management for 2010'. Having established a frame of reference, we can now discuss the overall goals for environmental policy. In hiking terms, these goals can be compared to the group's final destination, such as a mountain peak.

Chapter Four begins with a discussion of sustainability. It acknowledges the unavoidable loss of some environmental quality, but also the need to protect what remains by significantly reducing ecological burdens. The goals for reducing these burdens are explained for each scale level. Chapter Four ends by stating environmental goals in terms of the three feedback mechanisms:*

> *Integrated life cycle management:* conserve raw materials by tens of percents in the year 2010 through better use of waste substances [e.g. recycling] and using raw materials more sparingly.

> *Energy extensification:* utilize all possibilities to improve efficiency by tens of percents.

> *Quality improvement:* by the year 2010, double the time that raw materials, capital goods, and products remain in the production and consumption cycle. Make today's products in such a way that they can be easily recycled as raw materials for future products.[4]

Level Three: Strategy

The third level is an analysis of how environmental objectives can be achieved within the broader socio-economic context. What will work, for example, given the present economic system? This discussion must involve the people who ultimately will be responsible for achieving environmental goals. Only by understanding the needs of stakeholders, including local governments, companies and consumers, can we decide on policy instruments which will fit. This argument appealed to many of our colleagues in the other departments, such as Jan Willem Weck in Economic Affairs. 'If we really want to have a quantum leap with regard to effective environmental control,' he explains, 'then we should involve the people who have to do the job. And we should also give them the flexibility and freedom to find their own means.'

Chapter Five, 'Paving the Way to Sustainable Development', discusses the development of a true environmental strategy which considers other social and economic realities. The chapter begins with an economic discussion. It presents the three scenarios and shows that only the third scenario, a structural change in the nature of production and consumption, offers a chance to meet the NEPP's environmental goals.

Chapter Six, 'Main Features of Policy for the Period 1990–1994', explains the NEPP's medium-term strategy with a description of the environmental themes and actions to address them. The original five themes of Minister Winsemius are retained:†

---

* These excerpts are slightly abridged.
† See Chapter 3 for a description of these themes.

- Acidification (*Verzuring*)
- Dispersion of Toxics (*Verspreiding*)
- Waste Production (*Verwijdering*)
- Local Nuisance (*Verstoring*)
- 'Manurefication' or Eutrophication (*Vermesting*)

They are augmented by three new themes:

- Climate change (*Verandering van klimaat*) – this theme deals mainly with problems at the global level of scale, namely the greenhouse effect and damage to the ozone layer.

- Groundwater depletion (*Verdroging*) – a very serious ecological concern in sandy soil regions of the eastern and southern Netherlands. The strategy is to reduce water withdrawals to levels which can be replenished naturally.

- Squandering (*Verspilling*) – addresses the three feedback mechanisms. Strategic response is directed at reducing the waste of energy and resources.

Of all the themes, *squandering* is the least tangible but perhaps the most important. The Cabinet debates were very focused on costs, which worked for most issues. We had good economic estimates for dealing with acidification or waste disposal, for example; but other aspects, such as the three feedback mechanisms, could not be quantified. I could not estimate how much improving quality would cost or exactly what it would contribute to the economy, but I felt it was one of the most critical measures for achieving our environmental aims. Without the feedback mechanisms, the NEPP is a reactive document, discussing how to 'deal with' existing problems. Addressing material cycles, energy use and quality is proactive. It allows for the long-term structural changes that can turn society toward sustainability. Creating this theme brought the topic of structural change into the Cabinet discussions. It was safe from attack, however, because little government money was involved, beyond a small amount for research.

Chapter Seven, 'What is expected of the Target Groups', continues the strategic discussion by explaining the responsibilities of different economic sectors. As with the themes, we also expanded the list of target groups in the NEPP. The original four were:

- *Refineries*
- *Transport*
- *Energy production*
- *Agriculture*.

To these we now added:

- *Industry* – all major manufacturing operations, such as electronics, steel and chemical firms.

- *Construction* – including developers, contractors, the government and building associations. Buildings that efficiently use energy and material are critical to sustainability. The layout of the built environment is also very important, since it affects land use patterns, transport needs, resource use and social cohesion.

- *Water supply* – provided in a way which does not damage vital eco-systems, for example, by maintaining water table levels (groundwater depletion theme).

- *Waste processing* – reducing, recycling and disposing of conventional wastes. It also covers the handling and treatment of toxic byproducts.

- *Retail trade* – this target group can influence consumer choices by providing information on a product's environmental impacts and establishing price incentives for environmentally friendly goods.

- *Consumers* – based on the market demand they create, consumers largely determine what is produced and the manner of its production.

There was some criticism of the sheer inclusiveness – almost all environmental problems and all economic sectors – of the NEPP. What about priority setting? My answer is that sustainable development must be comprehensive. We can only carry the baggage if all economic sectors join the hike. Priority setting should not mean the exclusion of themes or target groups. Rather, it should apply to the pacing of measures by target groups, within the framework of long-term objectives.

As squandering is a rather abstract theme, so consumers are a rather abstract target group. Traditional measures, like licensing and regulation, obviously don't work for this constituency. Instead, information and price incentives are the main routes of influence. In my opinion, we have put too little emphasis on the social element in our relations with consumers – how they change behaviour by watching what their neighbours do. If environmental values are fortified in society, perhaps through education in the schools or outreach to churches and community groups, they will have a powerful influence on behaviour.* People are attuned to social norms; most do not want to be outcasts.

An ongoing international experiment proves that people can change their behaviour. In 1990, I met an American named David Gershon who

---

* The Netherlands now has good environmental education programmes in its schools; but the ability of such programmes to influence the consumer target group (at least in the next generation) has not been fully realized. Too much emphasis is put on the *problems*, and too little attention is paid to the way people can *change their behaviour*.

had recently founded an organization called the Global Action Plan (GAP). Through GAP, David promoted the concept of EcoTeams, groups of citizens who join together and follow a course in limiting local environmental impacts.* He modelled his empowerment programme on the NEPP, as this was the only government plan at the time with official environmental performance targets. There are now about 150,000 EcoTeam participants in 17 countries.†

I secured some funding for David from the Environment Department, and the Dutch EcoTeam programme was officially launched in 1992. There are over 1,000 EcoTeams in the Netherlands today (I joined one with my neighbours). They save about 900,000 kWh of electricity, 30,000 cubic metres of natural gas, and 170,000 kilogrammes of waste each year.[5] Clearly, individuals (working together) can make a difference!

Level Four: Instruments

A fourth level of reasoning, containing specific policy instruments, was only lightly touched upon in the NEPP. Some people considered this a weakness, saying that the NEPP didn't have the teeth to be implemented. Yet I think it was a strength, because we were not too prescriptive. Instead, we chose to negotiate implementation measures later on with the stakeholders. This decision led to a lot of political controversy, especially after the 1989 elections.

Retracing Our Steps: The NEPP Plus

A new government generally promises to do everything quicker and more efficiently than its predecessors. Indeed, this is the fundamental argument of any political campaign. No matter what 'new' ideas a party has, however, it also inherits many ongoing programmes from its predecessor. As with new hikers, the new party needs time to become familiar with the duties it has inherited and to formulate a strategy for continuing or modifying them. This change of roles can be a very awkward transition in the policy process. Without ever becoming a stakeholder, the opposition party may go from being the audience, or even the adversary, to becoming a process manager or driving force.

This jump occurred in the Netherlands after the 1989 elections. After a decade in opposition, the Labour Party (Partij van de Arbeid) replaced the

---

* In recent years the GAP has also contracted with several US cities to provide EcoTeam training for their citizens.
† I joined the GAP international board in 1997.

Liberals in a governing coalition with Lubbers and his Christian Democrats.* As in previous Cabinets, Lubbers awarded the Ministry of VROM to his coalition partner, and Labour chose Hans Alders as the new Environment Minister. The Dutch government 'lost' some time while the Labour Party assumed its new duties. We spent over a year retracing our steps, even issuing a revised plan, before the implementation of the NEPP could begin.

Hans Alders was not experienced in environmental policy. Yet, like his predecessors Nijpels and Winsemius, he was a fast learner with a great readiness to take initiatives. He soon became a powerful driving force, which caused some resentment among stakeholders who felt he pushed them too hard. Today, however, many people acknowledge that Alders had no choice. As Niek Ketting from the NEPP steering group explains: 'Of course, he had the difficult task of having to deliver what his predecessors had only promised to do.'[6]

Political interest in an issue can rise very quickly, and fall just as fast. Environmental concern began to weaken in the autumn of 1989 for two reasons. First, many people felt the 'problem' was being solved. The NEPP had been released and all the political parties had confirmed their commitment to the environment in the recent elections. There were plenty of criticisms of the NEPP, but these were finer points, not nearly as dramatic as the response to *Concern for Tomorrow* or the Queen's Christmas Address. Second, as the policy life cycle had shown, any issue of public concern is eventually eclipsed by new ones.

The public faced major new issues that year beginning on 9 November, when the Berlin Wall opened. Over the next few months, governments fell throughout central and eastern Europe; and forty years of Cold War came to an abrupt end. There were new democratic movements in the east, talks on uniting the two Germanys, and a realization that the European economy was in for major change. Lubbers could no longer devote much energy to environmental policies because he was engrossed in major new political and economic issues. Furthermore, he considered the environmental policy process to have ended with the completion of the NEPP.

The Labour Party, however, had a different view. After years as an outsider, it finally had the chance to put its stamp on Dutch politics. In environmental matters, this meant not simply refining the NEPP, but issuing a revised plan called the NEPP Plus. Labour wanted to change some of the plan's overall philosophies, especially the idea of working with business through cooperative agreements. Furthermore, the Labour Party needed to feel that

---

* Labour had not been in a strong political position since the party had prevented Prime Minister Joop den Uyl from forming a second coalition with the Christian Democrats in 1977. It was part of a coalition with the Democrats and Christian Democrats in 1981/2, but the government collapsed after only fourteen months and failed to introduce significant policies.

it was part of the NEPP 'deal'. This required retracing some of our steps and bringing Labour through the same process that businesses and government departments had just completed.

The mistake, we realized later, was in billing this process as a brand-new plan. Many stakeholders felt that we were attacking them with this new plan. Business leaders had taken great risks by agreeing to the NEPP, as had our colleagues in other government departments. These stakeholders then assumed the roles of sponsors or process managers, as they worked to sell the NEPP deal to their own constituencies. In the midst of this process, they learned that the Environment Department was reconsidering the deal, and they felt betrayed.

Policy Instruments

One main area of contention was the mix of policy instruments to be used for implementing the NEPP, specifically our fourth level of reasoning which emphasized improved relations between business and government. While it maintained traditional regulations to enforce policies, the NEPP tried to shift the government's focus toward more cooperative structures.

The NEPP explored the use of a 'carrot and stick' approach to implementing environmental policies. The 'carrot' would be the offer of covenants, or negotiated implementation agreements, in which companies would be given the certainty of long-term environmental goals and a voice in designing the measures to meet those goals. We had achieved some success with negotiated agreements in the past, such as the Hydrocarbons 2000 programme and another agreement, signed in 1990, to voluntarily reduce SO_2 and NO_x emissions from power plants.* The 'stick' would be the government's recourse to command-and-control regulations if the cooperative approach failed. The NEPP warned all target groups that their willingness to cooperate could spare them from more restrictive (and costly) government policies:

> The more positively ... businesses strive to achieve sustainable development, the more restrained [i.e., less burdensome] the role of government can be. Should environmentally minded behaviour be insufficiently demonstrated, the government will have to adopt a more active attitude to encourage or compel such behaviour ... the basic philosophy remains that those causing environmental problems must find solutions to them.[7]

Achieving sustainability in 20 years, as required by the NEPP, would demand a considerable restructuring of the economy. We doubted that a

---

* *The Covenant to Combat SO_2 and NO_x Emissions*, signed by the Minister of VROM, the Cooperative Association of Electricity Generators, and all 12 Dutch provinces on 12 June 1990.

regulatory approach alone could achieve this restructuring in time. Regulation depends on many slow bureaucratic processes, such as legislation, rule-making, inspection and reporting. Progress is further slowed because companies generally resist coercive regulations. For the sweeping changes prescribed by the NEPP, we needed their cooperation.

The NEPP Plus was far more cautious in discussing covenants. In general, it shifted the emphasis from negotiated agreements back to traditional regulations and financial incentives. It still acknowledged, however, a possible role for covenants:

> There will be procedural safeguards for the drawing up of voluntary agreements [covenants].* Such agreements will in many cases serve to supplement legislation, but they may also be used as an independent instrument if they are more effective and efficient than other instruments.[8]

The NEPP Plus also included provisions to streamline environmental legislation. At Gustaaf Biezeveld's suggestion, we included an outline for combining nearly all of the country's environmental laws into an omnibus Environmental Management Act (EMA) with 22 chapters or modules, one for each area of environmental law.

Other Issues

The NEPP Plus increased funding for almost every theme, most notably for waste disposal, and for enforcement and other implementation measures. Altogether, the NEPP Plus advocated spending over 1 billion guilders (US$500 million) more per year than the original NEPP. The government would supply 450 million guilders of this additional money. Most of the rest would come from industry, while the agriculture and consumer target groups would pay slightly less than under the original plan.†

The NEPP Plus also strengthened the targets for the acidification and climate change themes. *Concern for Tomorrow* specified *critical loads* of acid equivalents which could be absorbed and neutralized in most cases. To protect *all* soils, and thus *all forests* they sustain, RIVM found that pollution could not exceed the critical load of 1,400 acid equivalents /hectare/year. In the interim target for the year 2000, however, we were only able to negotiate a reduction to 2,400 acid equivalents. RIVM estimated that only 20 per

---

* Again, I must point out that only the decision for a covenant (instead of a regulatory approach) is *voluntary*. The requirement to fulfil environmental responsibilities – once the covenant has been signed – is not.

† In general, industry has been asked to pay more for its environmental impacts than other economic sectors. This imbalance may be changing, however. Industry is becoming more resistant to shouldering further costs; and other sectors, like agriculture, are losing some of their political clout.

cent of the country's forests could sustain this level over the long term.

Without recourse to additional measures, I felt obliged to include the following sentence in the NEPP: 'An interim objective of 2400 acid equivalents/ha/yr is being adhered to for the year 2000. This will protect 20 per cent of the Netherlands' forests.'* This statement provoked a public uproar, which gave us support in the NEPP Plus to call for much greater reductions in the sources of acidification.

The original NEPP had rather weak provisions for climate change, the 'greenhouse effect' which is mainly caused by the accumulation of carbon dioxide in the atmosphere. For other environmental issues, we used quality standards to translate *Concern for Tomorrow*'s recommendations into specific targets, thus tracing environmental effects back to their sources. This was not possible for climate change because there was still much scientific uncertainty, and the preliminary evidence we did have indicated that quality standards would require massive cuts in CO_2 emissions – of the order of 70 per cent.† Such a change could not possibly be achieved in one generation, so it would not fit into the time frame of the NEPP.

By the time of the NEPP Plus, public concern and scientific knowledge of climate change had grown, and we were at least able to set the modest goal of reducing CO_2 emissions by 3–5 per cent in the year 2000. Though not especially strong, I must say that our policies on climate change were ambitious in comparison with other countries. While many national governments had expressed 'concern' about the issue at that time, none of them had even mentioned any concrete targets or actions to address it.

The Final Results

Although some important changes were made, the NEPP Plus did not represent the fundamental shift in government philosophy that some people thought it would. In fact, the *content* of this second plan was not so important, it was the *context* that really mattered. In retrospect, I understand that policy is a continual process. Change spreads in a stepwise fashion through society as new constituencies are brought into the policy 'deal'. By the summer of 1990, we had already been through three rounds of the

* I included this statement after the Ministry of Finance made it clear that there would not be any money for costly effect-oriented measures, like putting calcium carbonate in the soils to neutralize the acid. Without recourse to additional source- or effect-oriented measures, we couldn't count on protecting more than 20 per cent of the forests.

† The science of climate change has become more certain in recent years, especially after the September 1995 report of the United Nations Intergovernmental Panel on Climate Change concluded that the observed climate change trend 'is unlikely to be entirely due to natural causes and that a pattern of climatic response to human activities is identifiable in the climatalogical records'.

process. First we won support from key business stakeholders. Then we had very similar discussions with departments in the national government, especially with Economic Affairs, Agriculture and Transport. Following the 1989 elections, we had to repeat the process again for the Labour Party.

After all the drama, we were very relieved when the NEPP and NEPP Plus were presented to Parliament on 28 June 1990. Implementation finally came in the autumn of 1990, and then the real work began.

Notes

1   Ministry of Housing, Land Use Planning and the Environment (VROM), *National Environment Policy Plan*, English translation (The Hague: SDU Publishers, 1989), 5.
2   *Ibid.*, 59.
3   *Ibid.*, 89.
4   *Ibid.*, 105.
5   'Going Dutch: Ecoteams Rule', *Earth Island Journal* (San Francisco), Winter, 1997–8, 10.
6   Ed Nijpels, *Concern for Tomorrow*, English translation (Bilthoven: RIVM, 1989).
7   Ministry of Housing, Land Use Planning and the Environment (VROM), *National Environment Policy Plan*, English translation (The Hague: SDU Publishers, 1989), 123.
8   Ministry of Housing, Land Use Planning and the Environment (VROM), *National Environment Policy Plan Plus*, English translation (The Hague: SDU Publishers, 1990), 12.

CHAPTER 9

Hitting the Trail
Implementation with Target Groups

On Paper and in Practice

Looking at a map, reading trail guides, and making plans with friends over a cup of coffee is very exciting, and very easy. The hike can become an intellectual project, allowing us to travel as far as the mind can reach. So the first few steps on the trail can be surprising. Hoisting our backpacks, we notice how heavy they really are. After half an hour, our feet start burning, and we wonder about blisters. After an hour, we get unusually hungry and wonder if we have packed enough food.

The first stages of implementing public policy are like the first kilometres of a hike. Beforehand, we looked over scientific data and reports, as hikers do with a map and trail guide. We wrote policy plans over a cup of coffee (or Marjolijn Burggraaff's hot chocolate), just as hikers commit themselves to days of work with the sweep of a finger. On paper, the NEPP had already been implemented, but nothing had changed in the real world.

Translating policy into action is a very slow process because of the countless transactions that must occur from the level of decision makers to the level of people whose small, everyday activities actually implement those decisions. A civil servant, or even a Prime Minister, cannot *directly* affect society. He or she can only set in motion a long, slow process – a series of deals – that finally may result in concrete actions on the street, on the factory floor or in people's homes.

Sugar Cubes

The pressure to begin implementation came largely from the private sector. Business leaders had been through a long, difficult process developing the NEPP. They did not want to repeat the process with the NEPP Plus, so they argued for just moving on with implementing the original plan. By late October 1989, we knew that implementation had to begin very soon.

Although the NEPP had not been approved formally in Parliament, the societal 'deal' had been closed with key stakeholders and we could begin some NEPP-related actions under existing programmes and budgets.

The implementation effort was lead by Arie Deelen, who had previously served as chief of staff for the Director General and then replaced me as Deputy Director for Radiation Protection. Turning implementation over to Arie was a good idea, because formulating and implementing policies are very different tasks. 'I can't imagine those things together. You have to separate these responsibilities,' Arie explains. 'Let the people who are making the policy product go to the finish; and let other people ask themselves how to implement it.'[1] With a fresh perspective, Arie began by identifying three challenges.

The first was developing a sense of ownership for the plan within the Environment Department. According to Arie, 'there was not a widespread feeling in the organization that the primary mission was implementing the NEPP.' Our colleagues had followed the NEPP as an audience. They thought it was interesting, but didn't see any connection with their 'normal work'. Arie thus made an effort *not* to portray the NEPP as a special project, he says, but as 'normal work, *new* normal work'.

The second challenge was getting people to think strategically about the NEPP's end results and the steps needed to get there. 'We did not think like

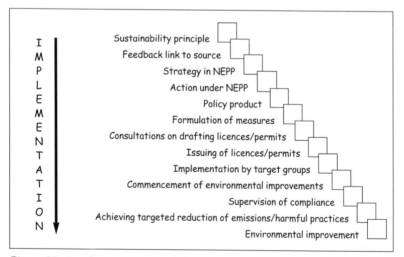

Figure 23 Sample sugar cube model*

---

* This model is based on an example from the NEPP. It is not meant to be a definitive model of implementation, just an indication of possible steps. The point is that the implementation of any policy has many steps, each really a complete policy in itself, which prepare the ground for deals with the next group of stakeholders.

good planners – from now to the future, from the future back, and about the steps in between.' Arie recalls. He devised the 'sugar cube model' as an amusing way to illustrate strategic thinking. 'Here we are now,' he said, placing a sugar cube at one end of the desk. 'And here is the end result of our policies,' he continued, placing another cube at the opposite end. Then he laid a trail of cubes between the first and last and asked 'Now, what are the steps we have to take to get from today to the end result?' It was a very basic and somewhat silly exercise; but it helped us visualize what previously had been a rather abstract idea.

Our third challenge was to repackage the NEPP's action items into a more manageable form. 'Some of the actions were very small,' Arie points out. 'Others were very broad.' In addition, there were simply too many actions – 230 in the original NEPP, and another 80 in the NEPP Plus! To manage that many diverse actions, we decided to group similar ones into programmes which would be handled by special teams. Some teams inherited many small related actions; others were kept busy with just a few of the larger ones. The programmes generally corresponded to the NEPP's themes and target groups, but there were a few which didn't fit into the framework. One of the most important was the programme for region-specific strategies.

Deals with Provincial and Local Governments

Region-specific strategies allow several government institutions to work together on geographical areas that require special attention. The regions may be highly polluted, as in large industrial developments, or pristine and fragile, as in many nature reserves. Managing such regions requires combining the disciplines of land use planning and environmental protection, abbreviated ROM in Dutch (*Ruimtelijke Ordening en Milieubeheer*).* The key players include the municipal and provincial governments, as well as national government departments such as Environment, Land Use Planning, and Transport and Waterworks.

The first NEPP identified ten ROM areas, including the seaport of Rotterdam and Schiphol Airport near Amsterdam. The intergovernmental steering groups for each project were charged with both stimulating economic growth *and* improving environmental quality, the first time both objectives were given equal weight. Generally the ROM programmes have been successful because the people involved were able to define their goals and attack them efficiently. They have overcome the tendency of govern-

---

* The ROMs were the link between the NEPP and the fourth White Paper on Land Use Planning, issued in draft form in 1988 and then reissued after the 1989 elections to incorporate the new environmental policies of the NEPP.

ment bodies to confine their attention to each other's bureaucratic responsibilities, without much integrated effort to focus on real-life problems and solutions.

The project at Rotterdam concerned the Rijnmond area, a once-infamous contaminated site that had been thoroughly rehabilitated in the 1980s. The Rijnmond ROM decided to pursue a green redevelopment which incorporated protected natural areas and conserved energy through co-generation.* The different governmental bodies in the ROM steering group also established mechanisms for the coordinated development of transport infrastructure and for joint monitoring of environmental developments.

The Schiphol ROM dealt with the region's problems of growing air traffic, especially noise pollution. In fact, air traffic had not been touched upon as a specific problem in the NEPP, because road traffic was then seen as the overriding transportation problem. The ROM group developed a common system to use the standards for aircraft noise in relation to zoning and finally proposed a cap on the total number of passengers who could pass through the airport annually. The growth of Schiphol remains one of the most challenging and contentious issues in Dutch environmental policy.

The NEPP inspired many parties, such as business sectors, to develop their own plans – rather like mini-NEPPs – to elaborate aspects of environmental policy. Some of the most important contributions came from provinces and municipalities, the authorities ultimately responsible for implementing environmental policies. As Arie was beginning his work on implementation, the Interprovincial Council (IPO) and the Association of Dutch Municipalities (VNG) approached the Environment Department with their own plans. They had read through the NEPP's action items and identified several that seemed best suited to the provincial or local level. Some individual municipalities were also taking action. In 1990 the city of Amsterdam released a directive that echoed many theoretical points from the NEPP, such as taking an integrated, multi-media approach to environmental problems. Meanwhile, the city of Rotterdam was probably the first municipality to produce a fully integrated environmental plan with concrete targets.

An important advocate of greater local involvement was Jan Cleij, the Director of Amsterdam's Department of Environmental Affairs and the head of VNG's environmental commission. Cleij was enthusiastic about the theories in the NEPP, but he didn't feel the document gave much practical guidance to the municipalities. Jan's main criticism then, and today, is that national policies are often too rigid to accommodate the special needs of cities. One of his best examples is the policy for soil pollution and the

---

* Co-generation 'recycles' energy by using the heat released from one operation, such as electricity generation, for some other purpose, such as heating a building.

principle of 'multi-functionality' that requires contaminated properties to be cleaned up to pristine conditions. 'Soil pollution is a big problem in a town like this,' he explains.[2] For centuries, the city dumped trash into the marshlands to reclaim more land. The centre of Amsterdam now sits atop six to seven metres of trash. 'If we wanted to meet VROM's ecological criteria for soil, we would have to demolish the entire historical city.'

The Environment Department has gradually improved its coordination with local governments in policy implementation. We worked out common strategies and programmes to spend new funding in a series of conferences (in 1990, 1992 and 1994) involving provincial environment ministers, mayors, city council members and representatives of the water boards. One product of these meetings was a strengthened consultative structure for key environmental areas, chaired by the Director General of the Environment Department, which is still used to discuss new environmental legislation with local governments.* The meetings also led to formal agreements on sharing implementation responsibilities. In 1990, VROM and IPO nego-tiated an Inter-Provincial Programme recognizing about 75 NEPP A-actions to be implemented by the provinces. VROM also signed an agreement with VNG called the Framework Plan for Municipal Environmental Policy. The plan provides technical and financial assistance to municipalities for the development and implementation of local policies. In 1991, VROM and the Association of Water Boards produced a cooperation plan they called 'Working on Quality'.

Hans van der Vlist, the former Environment Minister for the Province of South Holland, lists three reasons why provincial governments were enthusiastic about the NEPP: RIVM's levels of scale, new funding, and the provinces' own recognition of their poor environmental performance. All three illustrate that the provinces were overtaxed by their current duties and welcomed assistance from the national government.

The scale levels, according to Hans, demonstrated that purely local approaches were inadequate for modern problems. RIVM's model clearly showed what problems should be addressed at the municipal or provincial level and what problems required national (or international) action. Thus, provincial leaders saw the need to accept responsibility for problems in their jurisdictions, but also to work with each other and the national government on bigger issues.

The NEPP promised substantial funding for the provinces and muni-cipalities to implement new policies. An additional sum of 65 million guilders (US$32.5 million) per year was allocated specifically for environmental activities, and another 80 million guilders (US$40 million) per year for the police and courts to enforce environmental laws. In total, the extra funding

---

* A peculiar structure developed here, in which a civil servant chaired meetings that included politicians, among them elected provincial environment ministers and city council members.

would pay for 1,000 new people working on environmental matters at the local level.

The new money and personnel were certainly needed, as seen in the backlog for inspection and licensing at the time. The provinces are responsible for about 3,000 large industrial installations and the municipalities for about 400,000 smaller ones. In 1990, an astonishing 78 per cent of all industrial operations were conducted without the proper licences.[3] The solution was not to punish the provinces and municipalities, but to strengthen them through new funding and a more workable framework for environmental policies. The poor licensing situation was partly the fault of the provincial and municipal authorities, but it was also the result of complex national guidelines. Even with the greatest diligence, it is doubtful that local governments could have kept up with the bureaucratic demands of the confusing, sector-specific environmental policies.

Hans van der Vlist feels the provinces have won a level of freedom because they chose to have a closer relationship with the national government. Provinces are no longer overwhelmed by trying to determine environmental targets, which are now set at the national level. This frees them to concentrate on their real work – implementing environmental policies in the licensing of individual facilities.* In terms of hiking, they are not able to decide the ultimate destination, but they are given more opportunity to choose their equipment and set their own pace.

Deals with Business Target Groups

We spent much of Minister Alders's first year discussing how best to implement the NEPP. The conventional method was to use a strict command-and-control regulatory approach. This approach had worked in the past but, for several reasons, the senior staff of the department felt it would not be adequate for the new challenges of the NEPP. For example:

- At best, regulations can set emission limits for particular substances by using *existing* equipment or methods (mostly based on end-of-pipe technologies). Many of the NEPP targets, however, could only be achieved by stimulating business to invest in process-integrated solutions, to develop new technologies and to eliminate many harmful substances and practices.

- The transition to sustainable development cannot simply be a *reaction* to government initiatives. It requires that stakeholders *proactively* assume

---

* In some cases, however, we realized that strict national standards are not needed, and can even hinder the work of local governments. I had a discussion, for example, with Jan Cleij about standards for noise pollution in Amsterdam. There are many neighbourhoods in the city which are especially known for their night life. Strict measures to keep these areas quiet are silly. People go there for the noise! Chapter 10 offers further discussion of this point.

responsibility for integrating environmental concerns into their core business.

- A standard regulatory approach would have placed licensing authority with the individual provinces and municipalities – possibly leading to a crazy quilt of different environmental requirements throughout the country.

- The Netherlands' ability to impose new regulations on its own was limited. Many would have to be enacted through the European Union, which would have been a very long process (if it were possible at all).

Building upon the experience of agreements Minister Nijpels had made with industry sectors, we proposed negotiating legal contracts, called covenants, to set the terms for implementation in place of the standard regulatory approach. Covenants would be set with industrial sectors and negotiated with their trade associations. We felt the covenants would allow better communication with the target groups, including the opportunity to consult with them on the most cost-effective strategies for achieving the NEPP's goals.

Minister Alders, however, was wary of the covenant approach. As a Member of Parliament before the elections, he had been working to strengthen the regulatory framework for enforcement. Alders wanted assurance that a covenant would not preclude or amend existing laws. He also wanted a mechanism to monitor a company's performance under a covenant, and the ability to impose stricter regulatory measures if the company failed to meet its obligations. Finally, he did not want to limit parliamentary involvement by switching from legislative instruments to negotiations handled by a government department. Alders insisted that Parliament have final authority to review all covenants.

The first overture by business came from Peter van Duursen, then CEO of Shell Netherlands, who met with the Environment Department in the summer of 1989. Van Duursen said that industry probably could meet the NEPP targets, provided the government pursued a consistent policy, allowed sufficient lead time, and gave industry the freedom to choose the means of implementation. The covenants showed promise of offering this freedom.

There was also a mechanism for discussions with industry via the joint monitoring group we had established in the spring of 1989. The group was headed by Marius Enthoven and Hans Blankert, Chairman of the Federation of Metal and Electric Industries. One of the members was Cees Moons, the newly appointed target group manager for industry. In the summer of 1990, shortly after the approval of the NEPP and NEPP Plus, Cees sent a memo to Minister Alders explaining that the group had chosen covenants as the best means of implementing environmental policy.

The key to eventually winning Alders's support, according to Cees, was convincing him that the cooperative approach would not weaken his powers as Minister. The covenants would not replace environmental laws, Cees explained. They would simply set a planning cycle and framework for companies to implement the NEPP. 'A covenant is an agreement about this planning cycle,' Cees explains. 'It is not a covenant *instead* of legislation. It is used as a management tool for implementing NEPP targets *within the existing legal framework.*'[4]

A History of Cooperation

Cees Moons already had a good record in negotiating with businesses on environmental matters. He had worked with many large industrial sectors, for example, while developing a plan for the transport of liquefied petroleum gas (LPG), a valuable fuel and 'feedstock' for the chemical industry. LPG posed considerable safety risks, especially the chance of explosions. To manage these risks, Cees convened a steering group including representatives from the ministries of Economic Affairs and Transport and Waterworks, plus the petroleum and chemical sectors, many industries, filling stations and transport companies. With help from Allen Hickling, the steering group developed a commitment package of present actions, research, and future actions for developing an LPG distribution system and a contingency plan for accidents. The package formed the basis of the 1984 *nota* that still guides LPG policy. To date, there have been no major accidents.

Cees also drew lessons from the Hydrocarbons 2000 agreement, signed in 1989, which called for reducing hydrocarbon pollution by 50 per cent. This goal, which industry once considered impossible, was achieved by the mid-1990s – well before the year 2000 deadline. Moreover, the working group negotiated an enhanced target of 69 per cent reductions after the first implementation evaluation. The Hydrocarbons 2000 agreement is now recognized as a success story even by tough critics like Greenpeace Netherlands, which is generally quite sceptical of the 'cooperative approach'.[5]

By the summer of 1990, Minister Alders had also become more enthusiastic about covenants, perhaps due to his successful conclusion of an agreement with the electricity sector. Niek Ketting, the director of the Dutch Electricity Generating Board (Samenwerkende elektriciteits-produktie-bedrijven, or SEP), had been trying for years to negotiate an agreement on acidification with the Environment Department. Ketting first went to the Air Directorate in 1980 to propose, among other things, the use of a 'bubble concept' for regulating emissions. In essence, this approach placed an imaginary 'bubble' over an entire industrial facility and measured the *total* emissions coming from it. Under the bubble metaphor, some individual sources could exceed their legal emission limits, as long as these instances were compensated for by above-average reductions from other sources within the same plant. In the end, the same level of emissions would come from the facility; but its owners would have freedom in choosing the most economical combination of measures to achieve that level of emissions. According to Ketting, his overtures were not well received for almost a decade.

In 1988 Niek challenged the Environment Department's requirement that he fully upgrade the controls on a power plant which was already scheduled for decommissioning. Instead, Ketting proposed that SEP put its money into desulphurization technology for a few rather dirty power plants in Poland. This proposal is an early example of the 'joint implementation' concept, which advocates distributing environmental investments internationally for the most cost-effective solutions to regional, continental and global problems. The same investment money that produces marginal benefits in a highly developed country with advanced environmental technology might have significantly greater effects in its less-developed neighbours. Variations of this concept have since been proposed as the most cost-effective strategy to reduce global carbon dioxide emissions.

Ketting approached the Environment Department again after the 1989 elections and found that Minister Hans Alders, despite his scepticism, was willing to try the covenant approach.* Although they were on different 'sides' of the environmental debate (in the traditional, adversarial sense), Alders and Ketting were both interested in making a deal. Alders wanted a binding agreement that would prevent the electricity producers from backpedalling on their environmental commitments. Ketting wanted a deal that would prevent the Environment Department from arbitrarily tightening emissions requirements without sufficient warning and consultation. According to Ketting, 'Minister Alders was open-minded and constructive. He was a tough negotiator, but that's all in the game. And he did stick to his guns.' Alders's firm environmental stance and scepticism about negotiated agreements were probably assets to the covenant. Sceptical negotiators ensure that many safeguards are built into agreements, and they never promise what they aren't prepared to deliver.

On 12 June 1990 (two weeks before the Cabinet approved the NEPP Plus) Alders and Ketting signed the *Covenant to Combat SO_2 and NO_x Pollution*. The agreement focused on the two most troublesome acidification pollutants and set a ten-year time frame for reducing emissions closer to acceptable levels. By the year 2000, SEP pledged to cap its SO_2 emissions at 18 kilotons per year and its NO_x emissions at 30–35 kilotons.† The

---

* Alders was also familiar with this sector because he had been on the board of the provincial energy firm while serving as a council member in the province of Gelderland.

† The range for NO_x had to do with the development of co-generation. If a sufficient portion of the 'waste' energy from SEP's operations could be re-used for heating, it would be allowed to release an extra 5 kilotons of NO_x annually.

agreement also allowed SEP to invest in two desulphurization installations in Poland, in lieu of upgrading the Dutch power plant that was scheduled for closure.

The covenant sets up interim goals and a monitoring system to verify that the agreement is on track. In 1995, SEP had already outperformed its year 2000 goal for SO_2, and its interim target for NO_x. In 1997, SEP also reported financing four desulphurization operations in Poland. Like Hydrocarbons 2000, the electricity covenant is recognized as a success by even the most sceptical observers. In a 1995 report, for example, the covenant was endorsed by the Dutch NGO Stichting Natuur en Milieu (Society for Nature and Environment), which has been very critical of most negotiated agreements.[6]

Niek Ketting's personal commitment was crucial to the success of the electricity covenant. His very active leadership role – as sponsor and driving force – showed that the initiative for new policies need not always come from the government; it can also come from the business community. Ketting's role demonstrates the continuity of the policy process, in which former sceptics become advocates of reform within their own constituencies.

The First NEPP Covenants

Cees Moons had some good experiences to build on, but he was still facing many new challenges. The 'pre-NEPP' environmental agreements had covered fairly distinct problems – like hydrocarbons or acidification. In implementing the NEPP, Cees had to craft comprehensive agreements that would cover several environmental themes for huge industrial sectors.

Cees first found receptive negotiating partners in the primary metals (steel and aluminium) industry. His most important contact was Rob de Brouwer, the head of environmental affairs for the sector's dominant player, Hoogovens Steel Group. De Brouwer was enthusiastic about covenants, which he believed would provide more long-term security than just waiting for new regulations from the Environment Department. Rob was also the eyes and ears for the entire metals sector. He reported directly to the CEO of Hoogovens, Oliver van Rooyen, and frequently consulted Hans Blankert.

As in the electricity agreement, both sides had similar visions of how a covenant might function. 'I think we agreed on the basic picture after an hour,' Cees recalls. Individual companies should take greater responsibility for their environmental performance. The larger Dutch industrial firms were already beginning to develop environmental management systems,* and

---

* An example of such systems was the 'Responsible Care' programme initiated by the Chemical Manufacturers Association in response to the catastrophic 1987 leak of poison gas from a Union Carbide facility in Bhopal, India. Responsible Care set up an environmental and safety management structure to ensure that such accidents would not happen in the future.

the negotiators realized that such systems could be used to translate environmental goals into a company's regular planning cycle. After overall targets had been agreed at the sectoral level, the covenant would require individual facilities to prepare four-year environmental plans and yearly progress reports for approval by the permitting authorities. Given the sectoral goals, the plans would then state the specific measures each facility would take to achieve them. The starting point was always the emission reduction targets in the NEPP, which were framed in a way that could be meaningful for the stakeholders.

Nevertheless, teams from the Environment Department and industry spent two years working out the details of the primary metals covenant and the subsequent chemical industry covenant. In the process, they answered key questions about the structure of future agreements in other sectors. The Dutch covenant guidelines were also adopted by the European Union in 1997 for its policy on environmental agreements. After several years of debate, the Union agreed that covenants can be used by member states to implement Union-wide regulations.

Anatomy of a Covenant

The primary metals covenant begins by naming the parties to the agreement: the authorities and industry. The authorities include the ministries of VROM, Economic Affairs, and Transport and Waterworks. They were joined by local governments, as represented by the Interprovincial Consultation Committee, the Union of Netherlands Municipalities, and the Federation of Water Management Boards. Most major subsequent covenants have similar government representation, although some smaller covenants have also been negotiated between individual firms and local governments or NGOs. Industry was represented by the Foundation for the Primary Metals Industry, an association of all steel and aluminum companies formed specifically to negotiate the covenant.

Next come a preamble and introduction, which describe the general structure of the agreement and its legal basis. The preamble introduces the Integral Environmental Target Plan (IETP), a direct translation of the NEPP for the industrial sector. The IETP addresses each of the relevant environmental themes and explains how targets will be met for the years 1995, 2000 and 2010.* The contributions of individual facilities are to be described in company environmental plans (CEPs) prepared for each facility every four years.[7] The introduction then describes the covenant as an 'agreement in civil law' – in other words, a business contract.

---

* The NEPP had not yet set any targets for depletion of groundwater or *verspilling* (squandering). Thus the first IETP could not address these themes.

The fourth section of the covenant provides for an industry consultation committee with members from the authorities and the primary metals industry. An appendix to the covenant lists the specific duties of the committee, which include:

- Coordinating and harmonizing industry's implementation of the covenant.

- Monitoring implementation of the IETP by evaluating the CEPs.

- Discussing general problem areas, and providing guidance on how to address them in the next generation of CEPs.*

The committee prepares an annual report of its activities for submission to the Environment Minister and Parliament. As with all covenant documents, the annual report is available to the public.

The next two sections detail the development and use of CEPs. Each facility must prepare a detailed plan describing its present situation and the specific measures to be taken in the next four-year period (as well as a rough strategy for an additional four years). The company then submits a draft plan to the licensing authorities, who may, after careful examination, return it to the company with requirements for revisions or amendments.

If an acceptable plan is finally produced, the authorities will use it as the basis for the company's environmental licence. The CEPs allow facilities to set the terms of their own permits, rather than having them imposed by outside regulators. This is the 'carrot' of cooperation, as described in the primary metals covenant: 'The relevant authorities will, insofar as their powers allow, adapt the licensing machinery available to them so that it harmonizes with the anticipated initiatives [of the facilities].' If the company fails to make the required adjustments, the authorities can mandate them via coercive regulations. This is the 'stick' of covenants, which the document also explains:

> If, however, the relevant authorities are of the opinion that a company does not make sufficient effort to implement the Declaration of Intent, they will, inasmuch as their powers allow, unilaterally impose stricter conditions on the licences relating to the companies....[8]

The approach generally succeeds because it offers substantial advantages to both business and government. Companies gain because they can choose the environmental technologies, processes, or investment strategies which are best suited to their particular situations. This choice may include some

---

* For example, although the chemical industry achieved its 1995 covenant targets for nitrogen oxide (NO_x) emissions, the participants foresaw difficulty in achieving the targets for the year 2000. As part of the next generation of plans, the chemical companies agreed to research all possible strategies for further reducing NO_x emissions, so that a cost-effective strategy could be implemented in time for the year 2000.

freedom in setting environmental priorities for each facility. In the first four-year planning cycle, for example, a facility may decide to focus its efforts on reducing air emissions. In the next four-year cycle, it may put more emphasis on reducing waste production. Such decisions by individual facilities are permissible, as long as the sector as a whole meets its objectives on time. A covenant thus exhibits something like the 'bubble' concept – not simply for a singe facility, but for an entire sector.

The ability to prepare CEPs has proved to have an additional benefit. In 1991 the International Standards Organization (ISO) in Geneva, Switzerland began developing guidelines for company environmental management. The ISO had already developed a series for general business management called ISO 9000. Although it has no legal status, ISO 9000 certification is really a prerequisite for doing business among many companies. The new environmental management series, called ISO 14000, will have similar importance. One element of the series, ISO 14001, requires the preparation of company environmental management programmes, and the experience with CEPs has given many Dutch firms an edge in meeting the new ISO requirements.

Cees Moons described the relationship between CEPs and ISO 14000 in a 1996 speech:

> For the implementation of the CEP within the company, a valid and operational environmental management system [tuned to the covenant's 4-year planning cycle] is crucial.... A management system in accordance with ISO 14001 is in fact a planning cycle too, functioning within the company itself. What we are really trying to do in the Netherlands is to combine these two planning cycles.[9]

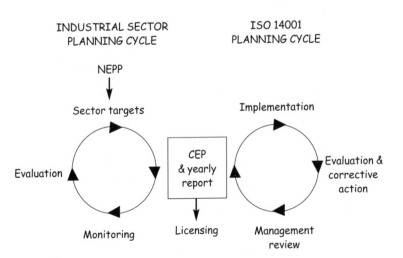

Figure 24 Covenant and ISO 14001 planning cycles

THE GROUND RULES OF COVENANTS

The experience negotiating the primary metals covenant (and the chemical industry covenant of April 1993) led to a *provisional code of conduct* for future environmental agreements. The code was later used by the Ministry of Justice to establish guidelines for all covenants, not just environmental agreements. It was also adopted by the European Union for its environmental agreements.

According to the provisional code, each covenant should include:

1 The definitions of key terminology.
2 The subject area: the relevant companies and environmental problems must be clearly described.
3 The parties to the covenant: it is preferred that the parties grant the power of attorney to a few authorities that negotiate on their behalf.
4 Provisions under which new signatories may join the agreement.
5 The objectives, including the overall deadline for implementation, as well as any interim objectives and their deadlines.
6 The obligations of the covenant, including:
   • The exact responsibilities of each party.
   • The means of enforcement. Covenants have the status of civil contracts, unless otherwise stated.
7 The contract's period of validity.
8 The arrangements for consultation among the parties, such as the creation of a steering group.
9 The means of evaluating progress towards implementation: the covenant should specify who is responsible for evaluation and what criteria will be used.
10 A mechanism for dealing with uncertainty – the economic, technological or environmental changes which fundamentally affect the implementation of the covenant.
11 A means for resolving disputes among the parties, such as an arbitration committee.
12 The measures to be taken if any parties violate the agreement.
13 The rules for accessing information provided by the parties: in general, all information is made public, except material considered crucial to a company's competitive advantage, such as trade secrets.
14 An explanation of whether, and to what extent, consultations are held with 'third parties', such as environmental NGOs.
15 A pledge to avoid provisions which conflict with the laws of the European Union.
16 The relationship between the covenants and public laws: the provisions of the covenant may not supersede or contravene any environmental legislation.

Licensing authorities also benefit from cooperation because their workload is reduced to more manageable levels. Under the cooperative approach, individual companies do the legwork of evaluating their operations, calculating the benefits of different measures, and devising specific policies to achieve environmental requirements. Thus, local governments can spend less time studying the details of a facility's operations and more time evaluating whether it meets overall environmental performance requirements.

CEPs are evaluated both locally and nationally, as the next section of the covenant explains. The industry consultation committee monitors the implementation of the IETP by collecting and assessing all CEPs. If the aggregate effect of the plans does not fulfil the terms of the IETP, the committee will propose additional measures to be taken in the next planning cycle. The committee will not propose changes to a current IETP, because this would violate the promise not to impose new requirements without sufficient notification.

While the covenant is considered a legally binding agreement, Cees Moons can't imagine the parties actually going to court over it. As long as the parties to the agreement believe that everyone is negotiating in good faith, they will continue to use the covenant. If they feel that trust has broken down, however, the parties can simply terminate the covenant and go back to the adversarial approach. 'If trust is no longer the basis of the relationship, then you should end it,' Cees explains. 'It's like in a marriage. If there is no longer any love, you get divorced.' As in marriage, however, the parties have invested a lot of effort in the relationship, and they are unlikely to end it lightly.

Establishing Trust

The industry covenants were crucial to ensuring the continuity of the NEPP process. Until that point, businesses had been sceptics, playing the roles of stakeholder, audience or even adversary. They had given input during the development of the plan, but the advocates for change had mostly been the government or NGOs (Niek Ketting and Peter Vogtländer being notable exceptions). To continue the process, businesses had to evolve from sceptics to advocates of reform in their constituencies. CEOs had to become sponsors or process managers, and they had to find driving forces to win over the sceptics in their own companies. By 1990, some key people foresaw the changing role of business in environmental affairs. One of them was Jan Jaap de Graeff, who headed the joint VNO/NCW Environment and Land Use Planning Office (BMRO).

De Graeff believes that business has no inherent concern for the environment but will react to outside pressures. 'Industry moves when the market moves and when government moves, in that order,' he explains. 'There's nothing idealistic about the whole thing. Why should there be?' The primary reason for cooperation, he thinks, is not because companies want to improve the environment, but because they want to improve the terms under which they are required to improve the environment. 'If you, as the government, approach industries – be it in the Netherlands, the US, or any other country – you can only ask them to do things in their own interest.'

De Graeff believes that the corporate environmental officers were the first people – ahead of the CEOs – to recognize the benefits of giving business a voice in the licensing procedure. Because they had not been involved in the negotiations, many CEOs and board members of the primary metals companies were instinctively suspicious. 'The top people didn't know the details,' de Graeff explains. 'They didn't know the field of booby-traps and mines … so they began seeing them everywhere.'[10]

These concerns were not limited to the metals sector. Leen Koster, Manager of Environmental Affairs for Shell Netherlands, remembers that his company was very concerned about the legal implications of a primary metals covenant for the whole of industry. For example, what about the role of an individual party to a covenant? If a company, such as Shell, were to sign an agreement, would it also assume responsibility for the success or failure of other companies that had signed? Furthermore, was it wise to make a private contract with a public entity? No matter what the covenants said, the government still had the power to change the rules through public law.

Legal ambiguities seriously jeopardized the process. 'Big trouble started with the covenant at the last minute, when legal people from industry started getting involved,' de Graeff recalls. The attorneys had two demands. First, the covenant should preclude the government's recourse to other legal measures, such as regulation; and second, the licences issued by local governments should perfectly reflect the CEPs.

De Graeff advised the attorneys against making such demands. He explained that the covenants were contracts in private law between two parties – the government and business. Environmental protection, however, is a matter of public law: any agreement between the government and business could still be challenged by Parliament, citizens, or NGOs. Although the Environment Department might sign the covenant, it could not guarantee that Parliament would also agree to the terms. Furthermore, even if the covenant were not challenged, there was no guarantee that licences would match the CEPs. Licensing authorities are responsible for ensuring that companies fulfil environmental requirements. If they judge a CEP to be inadequate or feel it is not properly implemented, the authorities must take other measures to enforce policies.

Still, why would attempting a cooperative approach be any worse than continuing with the coercive system? According to de Graeff, the covenants represented two new risks. First, companies could no longer stall environmental measures. As he explains:

Before, they were in the following position, 'You are government, I am business. You want something from me, and I always tell you what I *cannot* do.' You keep fighting forever. You don't buy a solution, but you buy time.

Under a covenant, business leaders cannot claim that government is setting unreasonable terms, because they have signed an agreement accepting those terms.

Second, the covenants require company executives to put their own credibility on the line. Regulations never involved a real commitment. Companies just followed regulations to stay out of trouble with the government. In the business world, real commitment is signified by a contract. 'When companies do business with each other, it is all about trust,' explains de Graeff. The failure of a company, and its chief executives, to fulfil *any* contract, even one with the government, would damage their credibility in the business community.

Given these risks, and the advice of their attorneys, some CEOs of the metals industry considered breaking off negotiations. However, both de Graeff and the new chairman of the VNO, Dr Alexander Rinnooy Kan, strongly felt that the companies should proceed. De Graeff presented three arguments in favour of covenants. First, he said, the government was likely to honour the agreement, because it was in the government's best interest for industry to do the technical legwork of designing its own implementation measures. Second, the metal companies would pay a high political price if they pulled out, because they had no legitimate excuse. They couldn't criticize the environmental goals in the NEPP, which the business community claimed to support. They also could not demand that the government give up its recourse to regulatory measures. The public and many Parliamentarians were very sceptical of covenants. If they didn't work, the public would *demand* that government resort to coercive measures. Third, and most important, covenants allow companies the opportunity to work with government in devising the best strategy to implement environmental policy.

De Graeff's arguments were persuasive, and the CEOs signed the primary metals covenant on 10 March 1992. In the years since the signing, industry's position has changed dramatically on a main area of contention: government's use of traditional regulatory means to enforce some aspects of covenants. While originally opposed to regulations, some signatories have since asked that the covenant terms be set in traditional legislation in order to eliminate 'free riders', companies that do not join the agreement and could thus gain an economic advantage by maintaining lower environmental standards.

The primary metals covenant has been a large, complex experiment with mixed results. The NGO Stichting Natuur en Milieu, for example, has tracked progress on the covenant and pointed out some important shortcomings in implementation. Stichting Natuur en Milieu's work demonstrates the very important role of NGOs as independent critics who monitor the covenant and pressure the signatories to fulfil their commitments.

The organization's 1994 report on the sector showed that many of the interim targets for 1995 would not be met, and it questioned whether the targets for 2000 would be achieved either.[11] In 1995, for example, the sector failed to meet its goals for many substances such as SO_2 and NO_x; air emissions of cadmium, chrome, copper, lead and zinc; and water emissions of cadmium, chrome, nickel and mercury. It also, however, outperformed its goals for two-thirds of all substances, such as air emissions of arsenic and mercury, water emissions of copper, iron and zinc, and emissions of nitrogen.

A 1997 article by Stichting Natuur en Milieu was still critical, but more optimistic. It noted considerable progress for several environmental themes, concluding that 'On the positive side, most goals for air and water pollution, while not initially achieved [for the 1995 interim targets], are likely to be reached by the year 2000.'[12] The article then concluded that combating acidification would be the biggest challenge for the sector. On one hand, most companies are unlikely to meet their targets for the year 2000. On the other hand, important process changes after 2000 promise considerable, sometimes revolutionary, improvements.

We cannot yet rank the primary metals agreement with success stories like Hydrocarbons 2000 and the electricity covenant, but it *is* progressing in a positive direction. Perhaps some disappointments were unavoidable in the beginning, as the actors grew accustomed to a very new management approach. More recent developments show that the sector is on its way to meeting the ultimate goals, even if they are not achieved exactly on time.

The Chemical Sector Covenant

The successful negotiations with the primary metals industry gave us the momentum to pursue a covenant with the major chemical companies. 'If we had started with the chemical industry, I don't think the covenants would have been possible,' Cees Moons explains, 'because the companies were too divided amongst themselves.... We more or less used the primary metals agreement as an example for the chemical industry.'

Although Dutch chemical firms were reassured by the primary metals covenant, the industry also had an international component: approximately 20 per cent of the facilities are American-owned.* 'There, not only the Dutch legal people came in, but also the legal people from the USA,' Jan Jaap de Graeff recalls, 'the same sort of people, but even worse....' The Americans were 'worse', according to de Graeff, because of their cultural differences. Environmental policy is much more confrontational in the US; so the

---

* Some of the major US firms include: Dow (the fourth largest chemical concern in the Netherlands), Du Pont, Exxon, GE Plastics and Archer Daniels Midland.

Americans were all the more wary of a 'cooperative' approach. They also had anti-trust concerns. Would a contract between several firms and the government be considered a 'sweetheart deal' which limited competition in the industry? While the Dutch chemical firms chose to sign the covenant, some American firms did not. 'But they act as if they have,' says Cees Moons, explaining that all companies have honoured the terms of the agreement.

The chemical industry covenant, concluded on 2 April 1993, has a very similar structure to its counterpart in the primary metals industry. The covenant allowed the Environment Department to aim for pollution reductions that would have been unthinkable five years earlier, under a command-and-control approach.

Table 6 Acidification targets (partial list)[13]

(reductions as a percentage of 1985 emissions)

	1995	2000	2010
Sulphur dioxide	35%	75-80%	90%
Nitrogen oxide	25-65%	55-65%	90%
Ammonia		50%	83%

Table 7 Air diffusion targets (partial list)

(reductions as a percentage of 1985 emissions)

	1995	2000	2010
Formaldehyde		50%	90%
Vinyl chloride		90%	90%
Particulates		75%	90%
Lead	70%	70%	70%

Table 8 *Vermesting* (eutrophication) targets (partial list)

(reductions as a percentage of 1985 emissions)

	1995	2000	2010
Nitrogen	50%	70%	75%
Phosphorus	50%	75%	90%

Table 9 Waste disposal (partial list)

(quantities in thousands of tons)

	1986	2000	2010
Volume of waste for disposal (not re-used or recycled)	2,421	571	648*

* Although waste for disposal increases from the years 2000 to 2010, it is still 73 per cent less than the 1986 level (despite the fact that the level of total waste, before recyling, was forecast to grow by 66 per cent).

Most observers have been fairly positive about the chemical sector covenant. In a 1996 assessment, for example, Stichting Natuur en Milieu's expert on covenants, Jan Willem Biekart, concluded that 'The best example of (relative) success has been the negotiated agreement with the chemical industry.'[14] There have also been some positive reports from industry. The companies Hoechst and DSM, for example, estimate that the covenant has led to a saving of time (and therefore money) of at least 10 per cent in their environmental compliance work.[15]

A current list of industry covenants in this and other sectors is presented in the Appendix.

The Right Shoes

Clearly, cooperation must be different in each sector. In those which are highly organized, a covenant may serve as a 'business contract' for implementing far-reaching environmental goals. But what about the more diffuse sectors with many more firms and small businesses that don't have in-house environmental experts? We may need to make greater use of regulations and economic incentives in these cases, but a cooperative approach may still be possible. Rather than being imposed from above, regulations may serve to codify the terms of negotiations between government and businesses, in the same way that a business contract does.

A good example is the 1991 Working Programme of Environmental Measures for Gasoline Filling Stations, which covers soil and groundwater pollution and air emissions of volatile organic compounds. The filling stations make up a diverse economic sector. Some are owned by the large petroleum companies, while others are small, independent businesses. The participants understood from the outset that their sector was too complex for a business contract approach. Instead, they decided to codify the terms of their agreement in traditional law. The legal backing of the agreement, among other things, has eliminated the problem of 'free riders' who might realize an economic gain by not joining or not adhering to the agreement. Like the electricity covenant, the filling station agreement was endorsed by Stichting Natuur en Milieu as a success story.[16]

Over the years, we have realized that there can be different types of covenants for different business sectors. As a hiker needs the right kind of shoes, an economic sector needs the approach which best fits its circumstances. Cees Moons thinks that the business contract covenant works best for target groups which are well organized, and which understand that environmental issues will ultimately affect their operations. He feels this is generally the situation for industry, refineries, electricity generation, mining and (to some extent) construction and environmental services.

I think that economic incentives and regulatory instruments might be more appropriate for the transport and small business sectors, which do not have the cohesion and resources to undertake detailed negotiations with the government. If it seems more appropriate to make deals and prepare contracts like covenants, we should realize that the internal organization of the stakeholders is a crucial factor for success. It might be necessary first to invest in these organizational issues before starting a process of negotiation: a well-organized counterpart in a negotiating process turns out to be a precondition for making progress. Without such a counterpart, it's like dealing with fellow hikers who don't have good shoes. They can talk only about the blisters, not about the target of the hike.

These views are roughly shared by Teo Wams, who directs Vereniging Milieudefensie (VMD), the Dutch affiliate to Friends of the Earth. Teo points, for example, to the relative success of covenants with industry. This success is mainly due to the target group's inherent structure. It is highly organized, usually into sectoral groupings such as the Association of Dutch Chemical Industries. The entire target group is also closely tied through the united umbrella organization VNO/NCW. In these cases, it was fairly easy for the Environment Department to find negotiating partners. 'There's a limited number of big actors that you can address on an individual basis,' Wams explains.[17] 'You can really sit down with them and make agreements.' Furthermore, the industry target group comprises large companies with considerable in-house technical expertise (and financial assets). Large companies have the resources to evaluate their operations and prepare detailed implementation plans, as well as to experiment with new technologies or process innovations.

Dutch environmentalists rightly point out that transport and agriculture have made much less progress than the industry target group. The different structure of these sectors and the government's different approach to them indicate why progress has been so poor:

- For both transport and agriculture, there used to be government authorities that felt responsible for all aspects of the sector. That has not been the case for industry. The Ministry of Economic Affairs feels responsible for general economic progress, but not for individual firms. The philosophy is to let the free market do its work in picking winners and losers. The ministries for transport and agriculture were more concerned with shielding their constituencies from market forces and regulatory requirements.

- There was no clear message for these target groups. The 70 per cent ammonia reduction target, for example, was not endorsed by the Ministry of Agriculture at the time. The same held for the transport targets. They were kept in the bureaucrats' desks and not put on the table for the stakeholders. The government was also unable to agree on a common picture of causes and effects, so the target groups didn't have a clear idea of where the hike was going.

- There was less of a basis for deal making with agriculture and transport. First, the ties between the Environment Department and these target groups were not as strong as the ties with industry. Second, environmental licensing procedures were only recently applied seriously to agriculture, and they are still lacking for transport. A target group is unlikely to come to the negotiating table unless it feels strong pressure from the government, society, or both. Our colleagues in the Ministry of Agriculture, for instance, were very reluctant to provide final standards for environmental performance. They preferred only to specify intermediate steps, which had to be adapted again and again.

Developments in recent years have moved towards fulfilling some of the preconditions for a negotiated approach. In transport, for example, systems like road pricing, which help capture the costs of the sector, may develop as a means for negotiation. In addition to environmental concerns, the transport sector is also under increasing pressure due to negative impacts of congestion. Meanwhile, some sectors of agriculture, most notably the dairy industry, are under political pressure over their environmental impacts. They are reorganizing themselves on a local or regional basis into 'environmental cooperatives', which might be a good vehicle for integrating the responsibility for environment and nature into the farmers' core business.

New Hikers: The Role of 'Third Parties'

Environmental organizations were not involved in the early covenant negotiations. Some of them, like Greenpeace, did not (and still do not) want to be parties to the agreements. They feel that covenants require compromises they are not always prepared to make. As the late Ton Tukker,* executive director of Greenpeace Netherlands, explained: 'We are not greatly in favour of covenants, in general, so I think we would have a principled answer of "Sorry, not us."'[18] Its disapproval of covenants, however, does not mean that Greenpeace is opposed to any dialogue with other parties. 'I think we are always prepared to talk about certain subjects, and perhaps we can reach an agreement,' said Tukker, 'But we are not willing to look for a compromise. If we disagree, we simply disagree.'

Instead of being a negotiating partner, Greenpeace prefers to judge the final results of negotiations and to influence the public debate, often via protest actions. I believe this is a legitimate strategy, because the organization does not have to compromise any of its core beliefs. Instead, it can play the role of a critical and vocal audience, keeping the environment on the public agenda and applying pressure to the government and business. As

* Sadly, the young Ton Tukker died unexpectedly in 1998.

Shell's Leen Koster acknowledges 'We are a part of society. If environment drops off the social agenda, it drops off our agenda.'[19]

Organizations which do want to play an active role in negotiations have often criticized their exclusion from the early covenants. A common critique among such organizations is that the covenants do not go far enough – neither in their planning horizon nor in their stimulation of new technologies or practices. Many NGO leaders feel that their organizations can play a valuable role as 'third parties' that push government and business towards better solutions.

Among the major environmental organizations, Milieudefensie, especially, is committed to playing a more active role in negotiations. Teo Wams rejects the idea that his organization can be more effective as an 'outside' critic. In fact, if anyone is to be excluded, Wams thinks it should be the government. He feels that covenants should be agreements between the environmental movement, business and, possibly, trade unions. According to Wams, the government should be on the outside saying, 'Go ahead, make your deal, but these and these are the criteria that we apply when deciding whether to respect your deal.'

The Wams model isn't just theoretical. It is based on the traditional negotiations between employers and unions, as well as their experience with growers of potatoes, or *piepers* as they are called in Dutch slang. The so-called '*Pieper* Covenant' was a temporary truce in which potato growers agreed to greatly reduce pesticide use and Milieudefensie agreed to suspend their work organizing a consumer boycott. The covenant may have been weak, but it helped raise awareness among large retailers who now try to sell more environmentally friendly potatoes.

What Covenants Can Achieve

I believe covenants have led to greater progress than we could have expected using only traditional regulatory means. By that measure alone, I consider covenants a success. In addition to the 'numerical' benefits of promptly meeting many ambitious targets, covenants have also improved our working relationship with many companies. Even strong critics see the benefits of better communication. According to Jan Willem Biekart of Stichting Natuur en Milieu, 'We think there is value in the concept of shared responsibility between government and industry, because we do not see that sustainability can be reached through command-and-control only.'[20]

Notes

1 All Arie Deelen quotations are from an interview with the author, The Hague, 3 March 1997.
2 All Jan Cleij quotations are from an interview with the author, Amsterdam, 28 July 1997.
3 Organization for Economic Cooperation and Development, *Environmental Performance Review: the Netherlands* (Paris: OECD, 1995), 122.
4 All Cees Moons quotations are from interviews with the author, The Hague, 4 and 15 March 1997 and 20 August 1997.
5 From a discussion with the late Ton Tukker, Executive Director, and Jan Bijlsma, Campaign Director, Greenpeace Netherlands, Amsterdam, 8 August 1997.
6 Jan Willem Biekart, 'Environmental Covenants between Government and Industry: a Dutch NGO's Experience', *Review of European Union and International Environment Law* (Oxford: Blackwell, 1995).
7 Ministry of Housing, Land Use Planning and the Environment (VROM), *Declaration of Intent on the Implementation of Environment Policy for the Primary Metals Industry*, English translation (VROM, 2 April 1993), 2.
8 *Ibid.*, 4.
9 Cees Moons, 'Experiences with the Dutch Approach', paper presented at the conference on 'The Significance of ISO 14,000 for Government's Policies towards Sustainable Industrial Development', Beijing, 6 November 1996, 14–15.
10 All Jan Jaap de Graeff quotations are from an interview with the author, Rotterdam, 3 March 1997.
11 Jan Willem Biekart, *De basismetaalindustrie en het doelgroepenbeleid industry: Analyse van proces en resultaten op weg naar 2000* (Utrecht: Stichting Natuur en Milieu, 1994).
12 Nanette Hagedoorn, 'Verzuring blijft heet hangijzer in basismetaalindustrie', Natuur en Milieu (July/August 1997), 8–11.
13 Ministry of Housing, Land Use Planning and the Environment (VROM), *Declaration of Intent on the Implementation of Environment Policy for the Primary Metals Industry*, English translation (VROM, 2 April 1993), 6–14.
14 Jan Willem Biekart, 'Negotiated Agreements in EU Environmental Policy', in Jonathan Golub, ed., *New Instruments for Environmental Policy in the EU* (London: Routledge, 1998), 165–90.
15 *Ibid.*
16 Jan Willem Biekart, 'Environmental Covenants between Government and Industry: a Dutch NGO's Experience', *Review of European Union and International Environment Law* (Oxford: Blackwell, 1995).
17 All Teo Wams quotations are from interviews with the author, Amsterdam, 10 March 1997 and 28 July 1997.
18 From a discussion with the late Ton Tukker, Executive Director, and Jan Bijlsma, Campaign Director, Greenpeace Netherlands, Amsterdam, 8 August 1997.
19 All Leen Koster quotations are from an interview with the author, Rotterdam, 29 July 1997.
20 Jan Willem Biekart, 'Negotiated Agreements in EU Environmental Policy', in Jonathan Golub, ed., *New Instruments for Environmental Policy in the EU* (London: Routledge, 1998), 165–90.

Making A Deal
Framing the Policy Discussion

If you take a 'military' approach and force people to go along on a hike, they will not move very quickly, and you will not reach your destination on time. People perform much better when they are motivated to do something than when they are forced. The traditional adversarial approach drags people down the path of environmental policy. They move slowly, reluctantly. Companies, for example, can simply stonewall by using political and legal pressure to delay government action. As Pieter Winsemius noted, business makes its money by solving problems and will find a way to meet any challenge. If the challenge is fighting regulation, business will get quite good at it, and a stalemate will result. If the challenge is devising creative solutions to environmental problems, business may, in fact, make real progress towards sustainable development.

In Interchapter 3, we examined policy as a process, rather than a battle, by recognizing the different roles and their interactions. In this Interchapter, I would like to describe what actually happens in the inner circle or roles, where a deal is made between the driving force and stakeholders.

The Boxing Match/Win–Lose Game

Both a process and a battle may begin with pressure and conflict. The environment would not be an issue in the Netherlands, or elsewhere, if it weren't for public concern. The policy process begins when the public demands a change by government and business. Under the adversarial approach, business ignores the demands, and government responds with punitive measures designed to force a change by business (although citizens, as consumers, also have a role in environmental problems).

Naturally, business fights back. By this point, all the parties have assumed that their interests are mutually exclusive. The 'environment vs the economy' debate is such an assumption. According to the thinking, more environmental quality equals less economic prosperity; or more economic prosperity equals less environmental quality, as shown by the graph in Figure 25.

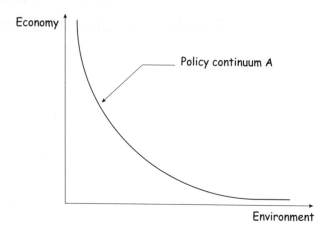

Figure 25 The win-lose continuum

This is the win–lose mentality, as typified by a boxing match. Repeated battles are fought to shift policy along this either/or continuum. Sometimes the environment wins, and policies move toward environmental quality (and away from the economy). Sometimes the economy wins, and policies move away from environmental quality. The result of each battle is some kind of compromise or, more accurately, stalemate.

Three Steps to Framing a Deal

An integrated, cooperative approach does not frame policy in win–lose, either/or terms. *Concern for Tomorrow* showed, for example, that the environment can absorb and neutralize certain critical loads of pollutants. Manure, for example, is not 'bad' in itself. If used sustainably, it can provide economic benefits to agriculture without harming the environment.

In some ways, the adversarial approach is too easy for everyone. When government simply prescribes what to do, business doesn't have to pursue its own creative solutions. When business opposes government regulations, politicians have a chance to gain political attention. Stalemate provides opportunities to make strong political statements about problems without the risks of having to implement solutions. While business and government are locked in stalemate, NGOs only have to say what others are doing wrong; they needn't propose how to do things right.

A cooperative approach forces everyone to address environmental problems seriously. They cannot frame discussions in absolutes by saying what is wrong, or what is impossible. Rather, they have to negotiate real solutions and take responsibility for implementing them. This cooperative approach has three steps.

Step One: Finding Points of Agreement

The adversarial approach begins with the differences among parties, which is a good way to start a fight. The cooperative approach, in contrast, begins with the points of agreement and common interest. I believe it's much better to start framing things positively, with a common vision, than to start with an argument. A critical part of this vision is recognizing and respecting everyone's legitimate concerns. Let's try this with the 'environment vs economy' debate.

Many citizens, NGO representatives, and government officials sincerely care about the environment. But is it really true that their opponents, such as company CEOs or other government officials, do not? Anyone who believes that corporate CEOs, for example, are against the environment should look at where these people live. Like anyone else, they prefer to live in the best environments, with the cleanest air, the quietest neighbourhoods and the prettiest gardens. They at least care about the environment in their private lives, which provides an entry point for discussing their business decisions. It's a matter of tactics. If you treat people like enemies, they will be enemies. If you treat them like potential allies, you may be able to work with them. I generally begin discussions with stakeholders by saying something like, 'I know you care about the environment as much as I do. So how can we work together to protect it?'

The same logic holds for people who are mainly concerned with the environment. Is it really true that environmentalists or government regulators are 'druids' who want to sabotage the economy and return to a primitive, medieval condition? Anyone who believes this should look at where the 'druids' live. They may not live in castles, but they don't choose to live in medieval hovels, either. These people also earn money and buy consumer goods. They criticize the structure of the economy, but they are not against all economic progress and opportunity.

After fighting for quite a while, the parties may discover another point of agreement – none of them are pleased with the stalemate of the adversarial approach. Governments, for example, can only demonstrate success under command-and-control policies for so long before they reach a point of diminishing returns. NGOs are also seeing diminishing returns, as environmental problems have grown from local or regional issues to more and more global challenges. NGOs begin seeing that winning individual battles does not mean they will ever win the war. Meanwhile, companies may realize that the adversarial approach is simply too expensive and disruptive to their operations. Progressive companies eventually accept that they can't get rid of environmental requirements – and the associated costs – but they can take initiatives to improve efficiency and reduce the expense of compliance.

Step Two: Looking for Mutual Benefits

The next step is for the parties to agree on objectives that benefit everyone. It's quite a leap to acknowledge that such objectives exist. In the adversarial approach, every issue was win–lose (Figure 25). In the cooperative approach, the parties look for ways to combine their interests. Such a framework is illustrated in Figure 26. In this view, economic prosperity and environmental quality are still not the same thing. Environmental measures will not *necessarily* lead to a stronger economy; and economic prosperity will not *necessarily* lead to a better environment. There are scenarios (such as line B), however, that combine environmental and economic goals. One of the simplest examples is energy efficiency. By better insulating a home, for example, a family can save some money on heating bills and also 'save' some environmental quality by causing less pollution.

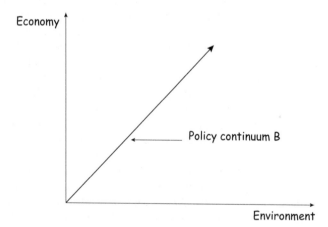

Figure 26 The mutual benefits continuum

In the NEPP, continuum B was the new theory of sustainable development. It covers economic security by 'meeting the needs of the present generation', but also covers long-term environmental survival by not 'compromising the ability of future generations to meet their own needs'.[1] The appeal of sustainable development is hard to deny. People can argue neither for depriving the present generation nor for stealing from their children and grandchildren.

For me, the most important word in the Brundtland Report was 'generation'. My colleagues and I had long worked on cleaning up the environment, but we never knew when, or if, our work would end. After Brundtland, we firmly stated that we should try to resolve environmental problems within one generation. With this perspective, we could no longer make piecemeal, incremental reforms. We had to think about the fundamental, systemic changes that really would solve problems. Environmentalists were naturally pleased with this approach, but so were companies, because they finally had sufficient warning of where policy was headed and what it would require.

Concern for Tomorrow provided scientific and economic arguments to support the sustainable development principles. Because the report enjoyed such widespread scientific consensus and political sponsorship, its targets were generally accepted. It took us beyond the 'economy vs environment' or 'jobs vs nature' debates, in which people argue about whether the environment should be 'traded' for economic growth. The report made a strong case that all human activities, including economic growth, depend on a healthy environment. After *Concern for Tomorrow*, and the third economic scenario, we could show that a clean environment is an asset, not simply a cost.

Step Three: Negotiating Towards a Deal

Of course, implementing new policies required more than an agreement on philosophical goals or ambitious targets. It required agreement on concrete strategies. The Environment Department missed this step in its summer, 1988 draft of the NEPP by announcing policy recommendations without first getting input from stakeholders. The NEPP steering group noted this flaw, and we responded by initiating the ten stakeholder sessions in the autumn of the same year. On the surface, drafts of the NEPP from before and after the stakeholder sessions don't appear to be very different, since most of the policy recommendations were retained. The difference, however, is that the later recommendations represent the consensus view of the stakeholders, not merely the view from the Environment Department.

Agreeing on recommendations required a discussion of both specific measures and their costs. On its own, the Environment Department might only propose measures which are best for achieving environmental targets but are not necessarily cost-efficient. Therefore, input from stakeholders was critical, since they are mainly concerned with the efficiency of measures. The work on details continued and intensified after the publication of the first NEPP through a series of negotiations with local governments and other target groups in the early 1990s.

In the covenant negotiations with business, the fundamental goal was fostering greater environmental responsibility for individual companies. The numerical task was to translate targets from the NEPP into guidelines for each sector. The administrative task was to restructure licensing procedures to give companies more input. Working out the details of covenants and company plans is an involved process that continues today. A covenant, furthermore, is only one means for working out details, and it may not be the best in all situations. For several target groups, we are still searching for the best means.

THE EIGHT ELEMENTS OF A POLICY PACKAGE

A complete deal is a policy package with the following elements:

Vision – the values or concepts that the parties readily agree on, such as the need for working toward a clean environment in one generation.

Analysis – parties evaluate information about causes and effects, guided by common visions such as: the third scenario in the NEPP, increased energy efficiency, integrated life-cycle management, and improved quality.

Objectives – general goals geared to environmental *effects,* the baseline for normative statements on environmental quality.

Targets – address environmental *causes,* such as emission reductions, but do not necessarily specify how they will be achieved.

Measures – specific proposals for achieving the policy targets through physical changes in environmental performance and/or production and consumption patterns.

Costs – an evaluation of economic efficiency that helps in choosing the best environmental measures.

Implementation provisions – ground rules for maintaining the deal. They may include organizational questions (How often and with whom do we meet? Who will set the agenda? Who will provide information?) They also include the use of policy instruments, be they classical regulations, financial mechanisms, social and educational tools, or international diplomacy.

Feedback mechanisms – timing and evaluation for the policy deal. How will we measure progress? What monitoring programmes are needed? What are the parameters for discussing next steps?

Maintaining the Deal

Negotiations on many deals in the Netherlands continue to this day. There are still important issues of shared responsibility and regional autonomy to be resolved with local governments. There are also many more issues to be worked out with target groups, especially hard-to-reach ones such as agriculture, transport and consumers.

It is uncertain what role NGOs should play in deal making. Should they be parties to agreements? Or should they keep their hands free as outside critics? Some people in the private sector argue that NGOs have nothing at stake in entering a covenant and therefore no incentive in seeing that it works. If the covenant fails, the argument goes, NGOs can simply say 'See, I told you so.' NGOs that have chosen to support the cooperative approach counter that they *are* taking a considerable risk. It is safer to criticize the policy process from the outside than to join and take responsibility for a possible failure.

In fact, all parties take considerable risk in joining this process. Having set long-term policy goals, the government is now under pressure to deliver. Companies also take great risk. By agreeing to cooperate, they give up the argument that environmental protection measures are universally bad for the economy, and they lose a possible excuse for failing to meet environmental targets. Furthermore, abandoning the highly prescriptive nature of regulation gives them more freedom, but also more responsibility. Companies have often argued that they could find cheaper ways to meet environmental standards; now they have to prove it. Risk strengthens the cooperative approach because everyone has a stake in the deal's success.

Deal making is an ongoing process. Getting an agreement on paper is not a guarantee that it will be honoured. Documents are simply a record of the political and societal processes that produced them. In their excitement about reaching an agreement, parties sometimes forget that implementation is a long process that will never go exactly as planned. To keep on the path, the parties must design mechanisms to evaluate feedback and develop contingency plans together. Continuity is difficult in the adversarial approach, because the implementation agenda is set by pre-existing policy instruments, which become ends in themselves. In cooperative environmental management, parties agree on goals and procedural rules but are free to experiment and modify, using the mix of policy instruments that works best. I will say more about continuity in Interchapter 5.

Notes

1   World Commission on Environment and Development, *Our Common Future* (1987), 43.

CHAPTER 10

Marching On
Continuity in NEPP 2 and NEPP 3

Hiking is not something you do once, but rather over and over again. Though individual outings end, the sport doesn't. You will continue to learn by trying new routes or by taking the same trails under different conditions. The seasons change. You may be in a different frame of mind or in different (hopefully improving) physical condition. Furthermore, the process does not stop with yourself. New people may join in, and you must remember your own learning process in order to help them find their way.

Continuity in Government

After completing the first NEPP in the summer of 1989, I was asked to head a new section for strategic planning in the Environment Department, basically an extension of the NEPP project group. We were responsible for producing yearly environmental plans, as well as subsequent generations of the NEPP every four years. We would also work on refining the new concepts that the NEPP had introduced, such as the definition of sustainable development and the *verspilling* (squandering) theme. By institutionalizing our group, the Environment Department made it clear that the NEPP would be the vehicle for formulating and coordinating all future policies.

That summer Rob Maas returned to RIVM to coordinate its *National Environmental Outlook* reports, annual updates of *Concern for Tomorrow*. Rob's successor was Gerard Keijzers, who previously had worked on long-term economic forecasts for the National Scientific Council. 'I still wonder why Paul took me on for the job,' Gerard explains, 'because I didn't know anything about the environment.'[1] That was fine by me. I often prefer to work with people who are not traditional environmentalists. Achieving sustainable development requires involving everyone and helping them see that, whatever their core business, the environment should be part of it.

I decided to hire a deputy who could manage the next National Environmental Policy Plan. I had already done that job twice (counting the NEPP

Plus); and I thought it was a good idea to turn the task over to someone new. Otherwise, I might have continued covering the same ground, instead of leading new journeys. I had wanted to bring in someone from the private sector, and I came very close to hiring an executive from Shell Netherlands. But we couldn't match their salaries. Meanwhile, I had developed a good working relationship with Gerard; and I decided to make him my deputy. Thus, in a few months, he went from knowing very little about the environment to being the NEPP project leader. Odd as that transition may seem, it worked out perfectly.

I brought many other new people into the group. There was Annette van Schreven, a consultant who had worked with Arie Deelen on the implementation of the first NEPP, and Erik Brandsma, who had been working in Canada with the consulting firm Environmental Resources Management. I picked up a bright academic named Lodewijk Lacroix, who was loaned to us from the University of Nijmegen; and I filled the economist position, vacated by Gerard, with Herman Sips from the Centre for Energy Saving and Clean Technology in Delft. Marie-Therese Lammers also continued with us. No longer a secretary, she had become the coordinator of the inter-departmental group that would consult on the second NEPP. In other words, she continued playing the role of right hand. The new NEPP team was nicknamed the *Jonge Honden*, the 'young dogs', which referred not only to their age, but to their energy and enthusiasm. Most of them were around 30 years old, which is pretty young for European civil servants.

Though we had a team for the next NEPP, it still wasn't clear when the plan would be produced, or even *if* it would be produced. The New Environmental Management Act* required us to prepare a new NEPP every four years, meaning that another plan would be due in 1993 or 1994. It was always understood, however, that we could send a report to Parliament explaining that we would just continue implementing the original NEPP.

We had many discussions, starting in 1990, about the wisdom of pre-paring another plan, and there were arguments against it. The NEPP/NEPP Plus had just been approved, and we were only starting to negotiate the first covenants with industry target groups. The next NEPP was to have been a response to our experiences with the first plan, a process that had yet to run its course. Moreover, a NEPP 2 would have to be completed and approved within a very tight political time frame – really no later than the end of 1993. Otherwise, it would spill into the next campaign season, which would start in January 1994. (The elections were scheduled for May 1994.) If the elections resulted in a new coalition government (as, in fact, they did), we would need at least a year to break in the new minister before he or she could oversee another NEPP process.

---

* *Wet Milieubeheer*, first proposed by the Cabinet in 1989. The act was approved by Parliament in 1992 and implemented in 1993.

Minister Alders, however, thought the political timing was fine. Although finishing a plan in 1993 was too early, waiting until 1995 or 1996 might be too late. There was no legal mechanism to continue the NEPP process. It was essentially a political decision. We couldn't assume that a new government would have a similar commitment to the NEPP. If we didn't establish the continuity of the plan under Minister Alders, the next government might simply drop the whole process.

In the spring of 1992 Alders was the only Cabinet member in favour of a new plan, though the others later agreed to support it under two conditions. First, the NEPP 2 should not introduce major new policies or targets, but rather concentrate on implementing measures from the first plan. Second, the implementation should be guided by a thorough evaluation of the first NEPP, involving the other government departments, outside consultants and university experts.

Our enthusiasm for a second plan grew in the autumn of 1992, after a staff workshop called 'the implementation challenge' and led by Larry Susskind, a professor of urban and environmental planning from the Massachusetts Institute of Technology (MIT). Larry explained that many countries had produced national environmental plans, or 'green plans' as they were often called, but none of them had continued the process. For instance, many plans were written in conjunction with the UN Conference on Environment and Development (UNCED) in the spring of 1992 and then forgotten.* From an international perspective, Larry explained, it would be an important statement to produce a *second generation* green plan.

Larry assured us that the plan needn't be earth-shattering. It would be sufficient to simply *confirm* that the implementation process was continuing. We didn't have to reinvent the wheel every four years, but rather make sure that the existing wheels of policy were still turning, and to apply a little grease to them as needed. 'We found it rather important to have a second NEPP to show that this was a strong process to be reconfirmed,' Gerard Keijzers explains. 'This was not just a one-time document for 1989, but a very serious process dealing with many target groups in society.'

The NEPP 2 was published on 20 December 1993, just three days before the Christmas holiday. At the last moment, Hans Alders gave it the name *The Environment as a Yardstick* (*Milieu als Maatstaf*).† As with the first NEPP, I was not happy with the title of this plan, because the integration of environmental, economic and societal concerns didn't seem possible if the environment were to be the measure of all things. No one else, however, seemed too troubled by the name.

---

* I will discuss UNCED in detail in Chapter 13.
† The official translation was *The Environment: Today's Touchstone*, but I think 'yardstick' is a better translation of the word *maatstaf*.

Continuity of the Roles

The NEPP 2 process was successful because we continued to fulfil the roles in the policy process, although often with different people. I had played the role of driving force in the past, but I didn't want to play it again. Instead, I was moving into a sponsoring role, working to bring people together and get them enthusiastic about the new plan. As a veteran of the NEPP process, I had the credibility with stakeholders that a sponsor needs.

Perhaps my new title also helped. By 1990, the leadership of the department was overtaxed by maintaining all the external relations with stakeholders. As a solution, Kees Zoeteman, who was then Deputy Director General, proposed creating more top positions and dividing the department's portfolio among them. Kees continued in his position, but he was augmented by two additional Deputy Director Generals – Gerard Wolters and myself. Together with the Chief Inspector, Pieter Verkerk, we divided the direct oversight duties and freed Marius Enthoven to take more of a coordinating position for the whole department. This team was rounded out by Jan Altenburg, the head of the Environment Department staff group, who played a perfect right hand.*

Meanwhile, the strategic planning group became a full directorate under my colleague Joke Waller. She had previously been the Deputy Director for International Environmental Affairs in our department and had drafted both the government response to the Brundtland report and the *Declaration of the Hague*. Joke and Gerard Keijzers took turns in the roles of driving force and process manager.† Though very interested in the content of the NEPP, Gerard increasingly took on the role of process manager. He organized numerous workshops with stakeholders and other government departments and built up a good relationship with Kees Kruyt, who was the representative from the Ministry of Economic Affairs. Though Joke began as a process manager, she became more and more of a driving force, pushing negotiation items such as whether or not environmental targets should be readjusted. Her driving force role was eventually taken over by Environment Minister Alders in the final stages of developing the plan.

The NEPP 2 process shows that there is no direct relationship between people's roles and their official titles. We might expect the sponsor to be the most senior person, like the Environment Minister, but that wasn't the case. Although I clearly had much less authority than Alders, I mostly played the role of sponsor, while he took the role of driving force. One might also expect that Joke, as the Director for Strategic Planning, would be the process manager; but often her deputy Gerard played this role. People take certain

---

* Jan is now deputy director for External Relations in the current Prime Minister's cabinet.
† This is reminiscent of the interplay between Marius Enthoven and myself while working on the first NEPP.

roles because of their individual personalities, talents and experiences, not because of their official titles, and no one role is 'more important' than another.

Continuity for Stakeholders

Confirming the continuity of policies in the Environment Department only met the needs of a few 'hikers'. We might have been ready to continue on our trip, or start a new one; but it wasn't clear that the others would join us. We had to improve the integration of environmental responsibilities for the target groups (as well as provinces and municipalities); and we had to show stakeholders how the NEPP would function in the international context.

Evaluations of the original NEPP were conducted for 17 different sectors. Some were coordinated by our staff, but many were led by the other departments. Gerard thinks this broad involvement increased the sense of ownership in the other ministries: 'They were also taking up their own responsibility to make sure that what was going into the NEPP 2 had some basis in the other ministries, and in the target groups.'

The evaluations concluded that some target groups are much easier to reach than others. The NEPP 2 explains that there had been better results with well-organized groups, such as industry and refineries. In the construction target group, developments grew from the very enthusiastic implementation of the NEPP's programme for sustainable building. Although much effort was put into a stakeholder approach with agriculture, there was still an emphasis on command-and-control because implementation went through the traditional policy-making bureaucracy in the Ministry of Agriculture. There had been little progress with less accessible groups, such as consumers and small or medium-sized companies. In these cases, it is often very difficult, or even impossible, to establish negotiating or regulatory permitting systems.

The NEPP 2 introduces the concept of customized implementation to recognize that different solutions will be needed for different groups:

> Customized implementation requires that the instruments should be chosen according to the characteristics of each target group. The instruments currently being used for the more easily accessible sectors – including covenants, long-term agreements, and direct regulatory instruments – will continue to be used.... The target groups which are more difficult to reach will be encouraged to modify their behaviour mainly by means of financial and social instruments. Financial incentives and reliable information [such as product labelling and consumer education] will be important in this regard.[2]

The NEPP 2 advocates greater flexibility and cooperation with the target groups that are more accessible. As Gerard explains, 'One of the major issues of the second plan was to have not only a top-down but also a bottom-up process.' The mechanism for this 'bottom-up' approach was called *self-regulation within limits*. The limits are the environmental goals. Self-regulation is the commitment to give target groups freedom to find their own ways to meet the goals, as we were doing in the covenants.

On international issues, Gerard explains that it was most important 'to show the avant garde of the enterprise sector that it did not walk alone'. We would consider our demands on Dutch companies in view of the international possibilities; and we would also work to harmonize the requirements of environmental policy internationally, especially in the European Union. The NEPP explains that 'the Netherlands must take account of the international competitiveness of its industry.' And it adds that 'the Netherlands will work for the inclusion, as far as possible, of the costs of environmental damage in prices at the international level'.[3]

The NEPP 2 dedicates a chapter to international aspects of policy. It lays out a strategy for cooperation at all levels of the global community – from forging agreements with neighbouring countries to strengthening the 1992 UNCED treaties. The text describes an ambitious plan for environmental diplomacy, working not only through existing organizations such as the EU, OECD and UN, but also through the creation of new networks for environmental policy makers (I will discuss these networks in Chapters 11 and 12). The international chapter ends with a discussion of the 'certain tension between the interests of trade and the environment'.[4] The plan does not rule out unilateral measures to counteract environmentally harmful trade practices. It expresses a clear preference, however, for integrating environmental capacities into existing institutions, such as the General Agreement on Tariffs and Trade (GATT) and the World Trade Organization (WTO).

City and Environment

The NEPP 2 recognized the need for greater flexibility with local governments. Because many national officials are removed from the real, everyday conditions at the local level, their new policies may have unintended consequences when implemented. Municipal leaders are the experts on local issues, and they often have valuable insights on how to improve the implementation process. In approaching the Environment Department with these ideas, local officials took the role of driving force, and national officials became stakeholders (or sometimes even adversaries).

This change of roles is taking place in our efforts to create sustainable urban environments. Dutch cities, like their counterparts throughout Europe, were originally very densely populated. Leyden, for example, had about as many inhabitants in the seventeenth century as it does today. Yet the modern city, with all its suburban neighbourhoods, covers a much larger area. Starting in the 1950s, people left crowded downtown areas for the open space of the suburbs, spreading themselves more thinly over a broader area. People moved outward for many reasons. They may have wanted more space or a quieter neighbourhood. They may have considered the city dirty or unsafe.

This demographic shift was further encouraged by environmental laws that seek to limit harm by increasing the distance between the sources of environmental damage and the affected communities. From an individual perspective, this makes perfect sense. Who would want to live next to a noisy street or a polluting factory? On a macro level, however, this segregation of activities has unfortunate consequences. Moving houses back from freeways, for example, does reduce noise pollution on that spot; but it also creates a no man's land suitable for neither development nor recreation. Greater distance between houses, or between home and work, means that public transport is no longer cost-effective. Forced to travel by car, people consume more energy and produce more pollution. Regulations which were meant to improve one aspect of the environment may damage other aspects, having an overall negative effect. This problem is certainly not unique to the Netherlands. Nearly every country is experiencing urban sprawl, encouraged by old-fashioned zoning and environmental laws.

The challenge is to devise consistent policies that preserve the positive aspects of high standards and strict laws yet allow common sense exceptions. I confronted this challenge at the end of 1992 when Jan Cleij, the Director of Amsterdam's Department of Environmental Affairs, told me about problems he was having with the country's noise pollution laws. Jan explained that strict application of the standards would be disastrous for Amsterdam, which has many neighbourhoods that are popular *because of their noise* (that is, their liveliness). One of these areas is Rembrandt Square (Rembrandtsplein), a busy neighbourhood of open-air cafés which are often crowded and noisy until late at night. The only way to fulfil the national noise standards, Jan told me, would be to close the café terraces and move everyone inside, thereby destroying the character of the square.

In the summer of 1993, I brought the relevant directors of the Environment Department to observe this dilemma first-hand. In this case, people like Jan Cleij were driving forces; and the sectoral directors were stakeholders or adversaries. Meanwhile, I played the role of process manager, trying to broker a deal among the parties. We began on the Rembrandt Square meeting with the café owners. Later we held a series of workshops with the Association of Dutch Municipalities (VNG) to study urban problems and propose solutions. I inserted a discussion of these urban dilemmas in the NEPP 2 under the title of 'City and Environment' (*Stad en Milieu*).

The people from the sectoral directorates were concerned that our discussions would lead to a weakening of environmental standards – a settlement on the lowest common denominator. They feared that we would have to set minimal standards nationally, with a provision that local governments *could* set stricter standards on their own. This policy would put the burden on advocates of tougher standards, and they would have a hard time convincing their constituencies to go *beyond* compliance with the national laws.

In the summer of 1994, I proposed that we do the opposite. National standards should remain very strict, but we would consider granting exceptions if local officials could demonstrate that they were warranted. If possible, we might then ask for some compensation to offset the additional environmental burdens – for example, allowing a neighbourhood to be noisier if city planners compensated with more green space. The Rembrandt Square became one of the first City and Environment pilot projects in 1994. We defined a strict border around the square. The level of noise could exceed the national standards within the border, but it could not spill into surrounding neighbourhoods.

After additional study and negotiations, an official City and Environment programme was launched in 1997. Twenty-five pilot projects were set up to experiment with the kind of environmental trade-offs that might lead to more sustainable and viable communities. In Utrecht, for example, new housing will be built in the no man's land along the rail corridor by shielding the residences with a 'wall' of office buildings, which can be exposed to higher noise levels.

The largest City and Environment programme is the renovation of the Bijlmer in Amsterdam, a 1960s-style public housing project of ten-storey concrete apartment blocks surrounded by park land. The Bijlmer failed for many reasons. Rents were too expensive for the low-income people it was meant to serve. Residents found the concrete towers sterile and monotonous. The parks fell into disrepair and became centres for crime.

The City and Environment project for the Bijlmer calls for ending the isolated feeling by linking parts of the neighbourhood with new homes and commercial corridors of shops and restaurants. Because a number of major roads already cross the neighbourhood, strict adherence to noise standards would prevent much of this new development. The city plans to remedy this by building sound barriers and putting extra insulation in the houses near the roads. The increased density of development will also reduce the amount of open space, but this will be compensated for by improving the quality of streams and canals so that they are clean enough to swim in.

I believe the logic of the City and Environment programme can also be applied at an international level. In the European Union, for example, some people fear that bringing in new members with lower environmental performance will result in a weakening of standards to the 'lowest common denominator' for the entire Union. I say that standards should remain high (and can be even higher) but that we can allow for exceptions and compensation by member states. Some eastern European candidates, for example, have badly polluted freshwater resources that don't meet EU standards.

These countries are often less densely developed, however, and therefore better endowed with wilderness. Perhaps these areas could be booked as a trade-off until the new members are able to improve their water quality adequately. I will discuss other applications of the Dutch approach to the EU, and other international settings, in Chapters 11 and 12.

The Third National Environmental Policy Plan

In February 1998 a team led by Felix Luitwieler of the Environment Department completed work on the NEPP 3. I have a very different experience of the third NEPP because I was no longer working in the Environment Department. In 1997, I became the Director of Nature Protection in the Ministry of Agriculture, Nature Protection and Fisheries, which gives me a new perspective on integrating the environment into the work of other departments.

At first glance, the NEPP 3 is discouraging because it reports that many environmental problems are difficult to resolve and that several targets are unlikely to be met in the year 2010, the NEPP's sustainability deadline. In other respects, the plan is very encouraging. First, it does not abandon the objectives of the NEPP and NEPP 2, but simply makes an honest statement of the difficulties in attaining them. Second, the most difficult problems, such as ever-growing transportation or rampant consumerism, are common to almost all societies, so the Netherlands' experience may be instructive for other countries. Third, the NEPP 3 introduces a whole new class of policy measures based on economic incentives which may revolutionize environmental policy.

The NEPP 3 takes an important step toward integration by relating environmental concepts to broader economic and social concerns. For example, it describes the *decoupling* of economic growth and environmental pressure. The NEPP 3 acknowledges that the Netherlands has achieved a *relative* decoupling, in that environmental pressure is not increasing as swiftly as economic growth (Figure 27). New manufacturing processes, for example, consume less material and energy per unit of production, and new vehicles produce less pollution per kilometre. It would be a mistake, however, to conclude that the overall environment is improving. In many cases, the advantages from greater efficiency are wiped out by increases in the volume of goods produced or the number of kilometres driven. We will only achieve sustainable development through *absolute* decoupling, when environmental pressures drop in absolute terms and not merely in relation to economic growth (Figure 28). The notion of decoupling had been in the first NEPP, which stated that environmental targets can and should be met regardless of the pace of economic growth. But the word 'decoupling' made this point clear for a new group of stakeholders.

Economists and businesspeople very often concentrate on marginal

Figure 27 The relationship between CO_2 emissions and gross domestic product (relative decoupling)
Source: NEPP 3

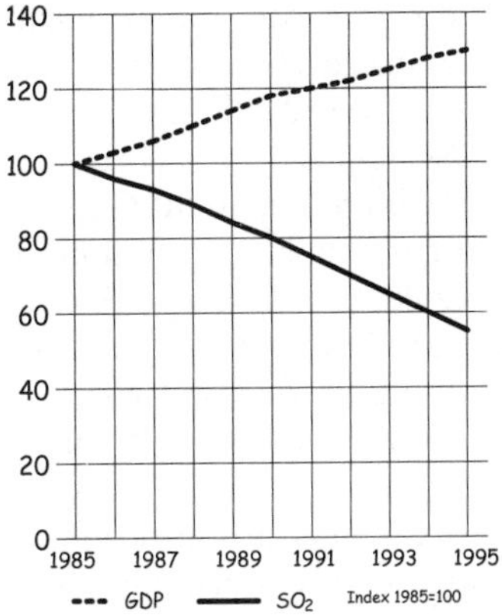

Figure 28 The relationship between SO_2 emissions and gross domestic product (absolute decoupling)
Source: NEPP 3

improvements. The marginal efficiency of making an additional product, for example, determines its price and the quantity produced. Business profits result from incomes which are marginally higher than expenses. For the economic and business constituencies, relative decoupling was a sign of success, since it was built on continual marginal improvements. The concept of absolute decoupling helped them understand that continuous improvement is not necessarily enough, if the *rate* of improvement cannot keep pace with the rate of environmental pressure.

The decoupling paradigm is one of several economic concepts to emerge from the *nota* 'Environment and Economy' released in the summer of 1997 by the Ministries of VROM, Economic Affairs, Transport and Waterworks, and Agriculture, Nature Protection and Fisheries. The Environment and Economy *nota* and the NEPP 3 place more emphasis on the economy, as the first chapter of the NEPP 3 states: 'The public authorities in the Netherlands are charged with enhancing the well-being and living standards of all its inhabitants, both now and in the future. This requires economic growth.'[5] Until this time, the NEPP had been neutral on economic growth, neither endorsing nor condemning it, but simply demonstrating that environmental policy should have no appreciable impact on the economy.

The NEPP 3 also recognizes the juncture of environment, economic development and urban renewal through the creation of a ninth theme – *contaminated land*. In a crowded country like the Netherlands, every bit of land is valuable, yet we have 175,000 sites that are unusable because of severe soil contamination.[6] Contaminated sediments in major waterways also have economic consequences, because we cannot dredge the waterways for fear of stirring up pollutants. In the NEPP 2, the clean-up of all contaminated sites had been estimated to take 80 years and cost 100 billion guilders (US$50 billion).

The NEPP 3 provides extra funding and new measures intended to halve the clean-up time to 40 years. An important policy change is ending the retroactive application of multi-functionality for properties contaminated before the Soil Protection Act of 1987. Thus a site targeted for redevelopment as a factory, for example, need not meet the same clean-up standards as for a nature reserve. Pieter Winsemius's vision of restoring all properties to pristine conditions will only apply to those sites contaminated after his 'Guests on Our Own Soil' speech. The government is also considering preferential tax treatment for investments in contaminated sites and the creation of a not-for-profit corporation to negotiate clean-up agreements with companies.

I fear that the ninth theme may be a step back to the sectoral policies that preceded the NEPP. Unlike the other themes, contaminated land is not an overarching, cross-media issue, and it duplicates much of the work already covered by the dispersion and waste-disposal themes. Moreover, we are straying ever further from Pieter Winsemius's rule that people cannot remember more than five subject areas at a time. It was already difficult to keep track of eight themes, and a ninth further complicates our overview of environmental policy. Nevertheless, I recognize that the NEPP is a political statement of government priorities, and soil contamination is an increasingly important issue that demands a political response.

The contaminated land theme reflects the government's new emphasis on the 'living environment', a concept championed by the last Environment Minister, Margaretha de Boer, which combines environment, economic development and quality of life considerations. The concept also promotes better integration of environment and land-use planning, a constant challenge within VROM. The living environment encourages integration of several key policy sectors, including many that had not been considered to be 'environmental'. Indeed, 'the living environment' might have been a better choice for a new theme, covering both disturbance and contaminated land as well as the accompanying economic and social concerns.

A Survey of Progress

Progress in addressing different themes and reaching different target groups varies considerably. Some problems are approaching the phase of control, and they may not require a separate theme to be managed in the future. Other problems are growing worse, and the government concedes that as yet it does not know how to solve them. Many of the seemingly intractable problems are not unique to the Netherlands, but are faced by most other

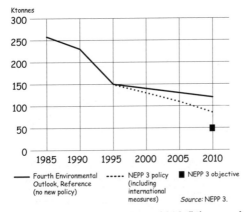

Figure 29 NH₃ emissions, 1985–2010 (kilotonnes)

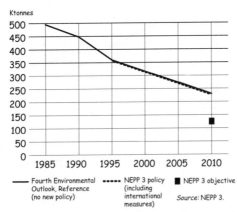

Figure 30 VOC emissions, 1985–2010 (kilotonnes)

industrialized countries, and quite a few developing nations. In an exchange programme with Costa Rica, for example, our potato farmers and their banana farmers found that they were facing essentially the same environmental difficulties. While I will discuss a few issues in the Dutch context, I think they offer lessons of international significance.

Acidification was really the first theme, and unfortunately, it may be one of the last to go away. Although there has been tremendous progress since 1985, it has been inadequate to achieve most targets for the year 2010. The one bright spot is sulphur dioxide (SO_2) emissions, which have fallen considerably in the past decade. The Netherlands surpassed its 1994 SO_2 objective and may well meet the objective for 2010. Unfortunately, there has been much less progress for emissions of ammonia (NH_3), nitrogen oxides (NO_x) and volatile organic compounds (VOC). While their

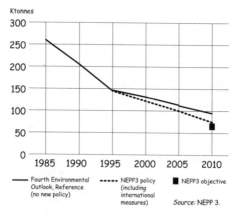

Figure 31 SO$_2$ emissions, 1985–2010 (kilotonnes)

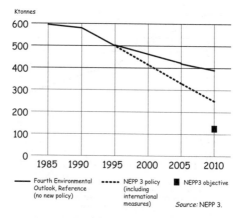

Figure 32 NO$_x$ emissions, 1985–2010 (kilotonnes)

emissions are also declining, they are not expected to drop below critical loads by 2010.

Agriculture is still the main cause of ammonia emissions. After a decade of trying technological fixes to control manure pollution, there is a growing consensus that volume-oriented measures will also be needed. The recent agreement to cut the pig farming sector by 25 per cent is an encouraging sign that we finally have the political will to make the necessary changes.

Nitrogen oxides are a more vexing problem because, regardless of political will, we don't have the tools to control the problem yet. The NO$_x$ situation is also a good indicator for several other environmental issues, such as climate change. Both problems stem from the same causes – our continuing dependence on hydrocarbon fuels, especially in an ever-growing transport sector. Since 1986, the number of kilometres driven for private cars in the Netherlands has grown by 24 per cent and overall freight traffic has risen by 40 per cent, including a 50 per cent growth in road traffic.[7] Moreover, NO_x and CO_2 emissions for air transport are rising in absolute terms.

The NO_x problem is a prime example of cases in which end-of-pipe measures have run their course. Emissions per kilometre have been falling for years, but further improvements will be much smaller, and much more expensive. Furthermore, these reductions only represent a relative decoupling and will not be adequate to compensate for the steady increase in traffic volume.

Managing acidification and the transport sector will require process changes that restructure the way people and materials move. First, the gasoline and diesel-powered internal combustion engines will have to be replaced with new technologies, such as fuel cells, batteries, or hydrogen and biomass fuels. Second, we have to rethink the way we structure the physical environment. The Dutch government is now trying to revise its land-use planning methods by designing developments that minimize the distances people must travel to work or to the store. The information age may provide some benefits by allowing people to work from their home computers via 'teleworking' or 'telecommuting'.

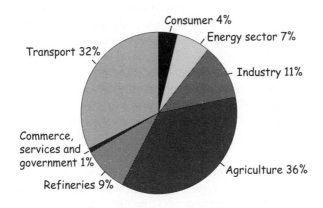

Figure 33 Acidification breakdown, NEPP 3
Source: NEPP 3.

We can also rethink the transportation of goods. Some researchers, for example, are looking into underground pipeline networks that would shuttle canisters of material around the country. There is a danger, however, that technological daydreams may keep us from recognizing the need to fundamentally rethink the role of transport in global consumerism.

The Netherlands can do only so much on its own, however. As a small country with no domestic automobile companies, for example, we cannot have a significant impact on the industry – though we are working through the European Union on regional agreements with the automobile manufacturers. Reforms of the airline industry are equally dependent on international consensus. The Netherlands favours economic measures to discourage air travel, such as an end to the value-added tax exemption for kerosene and airline tickets. We cannot change a global industry, however, without global support. In this respect, the local and regional debates on airport expansion around the world should lead to an international effort to manage and reduce transport needs.

A Measure of Progress

I don't think it's necessary to give a detailed assessment of the remaining themes, but I would like to give a quick summary of progress to show how issues move through the policy life cycle and eventually approach the control phase.

- *Squandering* – is still in the recognition phase because there is generally no acceptance that resources are finite and that consumption has to be limited. Also, we don't yet have a sufficiently accurate way to measure squandering and so are unable to formulate concrete goals or policies. The emerging concept of eco-efficiency could be a key tool for understanding this theme.

- *Climate change* – the world is definitely reaching the control phase for ozone depletion, but we are only in the early stages of formulating policies for controlling greenhouse gases. At least, however, we have recognized the problem. (I will say more about both these issues in Chapter 13).

- *Contaminated land* – was recognized as a problem long ago, but its full impact was underestimated. By realizing that this environmental problem also has economic and social consequences (for example, stunted development in urban areas), political attention has risen to the point of formulating stronger policies. Due to the very specific nature of the issue, contaminated property is more of a single problem area than a true theme.

- *Acidification* – we have long recognized the issue and have done a great deal to address it. But we will not solve the problem until we accept the need for process changes: restructuring the agricultural industry to solve the NH_3 problem, switching from emission controls on power plants to true clean power (solar, wind, biomass), switching to clean power sources for automobiles and air transport, and rethinking land-use planning and transport needs.

- *Disturbance* – even with all the available end-of-pipe measures, like noise insulation, we are still far from the target because process changes in transport and land-use planning are needed (see *acidification*).

- *Vermesting (eutrophication)* – there has been a lot of progress, but we are just starting the process changes of reducing agricultural intensity and promoting a shift to organic farming. Encouraging steps are the 1997 agreement to reduce the pig farming industry by 25 per cent and the 1998 government proposal to cap the growth of poultry farming.

- *Waste* – a lot has been done through recycling and composting to reduce the volume of waste, but these measures have nearly run their course. Further progress can only come from process changes and eliminating the behaviours that encourage people to produce waste (see *squandering*).

- *Groundwater depletion* – is still a serious problem, especially for nature areas, but farmers now realize that continually pumping water will threaten their viability. Also, Dutch society is reaching a consensus that we cannot continue to keep the entire country dry. In the future, we may decide to flood some of the *polders* near rivers and lakes, which will provide a safety valve for flood waters and help recharge groundwater reserves.

- *Dispersion* – is approaching the control phase. There are strong policies to limit pollution, and we are beginning to make process changes such as using soyabean ink in printing, ending chlorine bleaching of paper, and using soap and water solutions in place of CFC cleaning agents. A huge volume of toxic substances remains in legal commercial use, however, and there may always be some illegal production and smuggling of banned substances (such as the black market in CFCs).

The nine NEPP themes run the spectrum of the policy life cycle. Figure 34 notes the progress of the various themes and adds a new element showing the barriers that separate the different policy phases.

- The *denial barrier* separates the recognition and formulation phases. People deny the existence of a problem when they cannot foresee a way to solve it. This border is crossed either when a long-denied problem surfaces in a catastrophe, such as Chernobyl, or when new ideas or technologies point to ways of solving the problem.

- The *consensus barrier* separates formulation and implementation. Even when a problem is recognized, there is a long process of forging political consensus on the measures to address it.

- The *process change barrier* separates implementation and control. The first implementation measures are mostly end-of-pipe changes that minimize the effects of the business-as-usual approach, without changing the nature of that business. In many cases, end-of-pipe measures can produce very impressive results, but they almost never succeed in fully resolving a problem.

Most of the themes are still waiting for process changes, which require a longer time period than the decade that has elapsed since the NEPP 1. That's why we set 25-year, generational goals for the plan. That's also why we will retain the generational goals, even if they are not all met by the year 2010. By keeping the goals, we will continue encouraging the shift to process changes that will solve environmental problems in the long run.

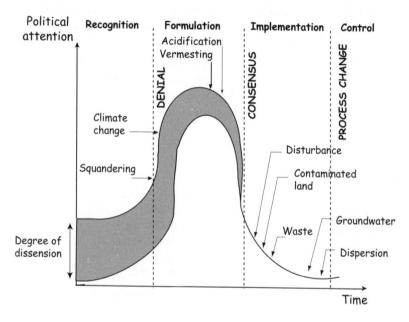

Figure 34 The NEPP 3 policy life cycle

Economic Incentives

Along with the transport sector, consumers are a very difficult target group (in fact, there is considerable overlap between the two). Consumers cannot be regulated as can other economic sectors, nor can they enter covenant negotiations as industry does. Although this group is very difficult to reach, we can hardly ignore it. Consumers drive all economic processes by their demand for goods and services, and their impact is increasing. The latest *National Environmental Balance* report by RIVM shows that consumption is growing rapidly, especially in energy use, consumer durables, and the demand for new housing and transport infrastructure.

In the past, the government has approached consumers mainly through educational campaigns. In some ways, the campaigns have been a great success, because they have raised overall environmental awareness and motivated positive behaviour. The percentage of waste recycled, for example, rose from 61 per cent in 1990 to 72 per cent in 1996, and the government is targeting even higher rates for the future.[8] But recycling is fairly easy, as the NEPP 3 acknowledges: 'Behaviour has been successfully changed, for example, in getting residents to separate waste [for recycling], but little progress has been made in regard to car-use and energy consumption because there is such a perceived penalty for making changes.'[9]

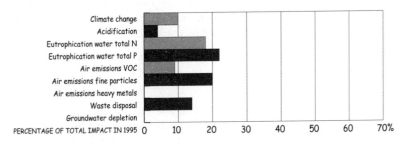

Figure 35 Consumers target group: contribution to environmental themes
Source: RIVM.

NEPP 3 concludes that the only way to change behaviour is to change the price structure so that there is a greater penalty for actions which harm the environment. Building on the Environment and Economy *nota*, the NEPP 3 proposes a number of tax reforms that shift the balance of incentives for both consumers and many other target groups. Some proposed measures include:

- Increasing annual energy taxes by 3.4 billion guilders (US$1.7 billion) and applying part of the money to incentive programmes for promoting conservation and renewable energy.

- Raising taxes on water and groundwater use.

- Introducing or increasing tax concessions for environmental investments or sustainable business practices.

- Differentiating taxes on vehicles based on their environmental impacts.

The NEPP 3 proposes that money raised from new environmental taxes be recycled into reductions of other taxes, such as the payroll tax. These reforms could mark the fruition of tax-shift proposals that surfaced when the Lubbers Cabinet was debating the first NEPP in 1989. Think tanks and NGOs in many countries are advocating the benefits of a revenue-neutral ecological tax shift, but the Netherlands may be the first country to incorporate this idea into government policy.*

Despite the inherent difficulty of introducing broad-based national tax reform, the prospects look very good in the Netherlands because the Environment Department has already made deals with the key parties. In addition to working with Economic Affairs on the Environment and Economy *nota*, the Environment Department also coordinated policy with a working group in the Ministry of Finance led by Koos van der Vaart. Koos, who helped link scientific and policy concerns for the RIVM and the Environment Department ten years ago, has done the same with fiscal and environmental concerns for the Ministry of Finance and the Environment Department. The new cooperation of former adversaries is clear in the NEPP 3, which for the first time is endorsed by the Ministry of Finance.

Long-Term Continuity

Although the first NEPP was written a decade ago, I think now is the best time to tell the story. In the early years, we had a very ambitious piece of paper, but no proof that it would lead to real changes in the Dutch or international environment. In 1999 the NEPP has an implementation record which demonstrates the elements of the plan that were successful and the areas in which new ideas are needed. I don't consider the difficulties outlined in NEPP 3 an argument against the Dutch approach, because it is a process, not a piece of paper. After ten years, we can confidently say that the NEPP did lead to a change in Dutch policy and, more importantly, that the NEPP process will continue to be the vehicle for change in the future.†

---

* Similar reforms may be coming in Germany. The coalition of Social Democrats and Greens in the state of Niedersachsen has been advocating ecological tax reform for the past few years. Now the new Social Democrat–Green federal government is advocating an ecological tax shift.
† One of the first decisions taken by the new Environment Minister, Jan Pronk, was to prepare an NEPP 4 during his term (1998–2002).

Notes

1   All Gerard Keijzers quotations are from an interview with the author, The Hague, 5 March 1997.
2   Ministry of Housing, Land Use Planning and the Environment (VROM), *National Environment Policy Plan 2*, English translation (The Hague: SDU Publishers, 1993), 10.
3   *Ibid.*, 57.   4 *Ibid.*, 68.
5   Ministry of Housing, Land Use Planning and the Environment (VROM), *National Environment Policy Plan 3*, English translation (The Hague: SDU Publishers, 1998), 3, 11.
6   *Ibid.*, 21.   7 *Ibid.*, 101, 106.   8 *Ibid.*, 19.   9 *Ibid.*, 55.

Many Steps
Continuity

Paper vs Process

It takes a lot of work to reach an initial deal on environmental policy, but the process certainly does not end there. In hiking, a lot of time and effort may go into getting a group together, studying maps and choosing a route that suits everyone. Up to this point, however, the 'real' hike hasn't even started. The team may have a goal in mind, but they have countless steps ahead of them before they reach it.

While it is true that ideas can change the world, there is a lot of 'legwork' between the original idea and actual changes in real life. I'm troubled when people put too much emphasis on developing an environmental law or plan, because a good piece of paper cannot automatically produce changes in society. Policy is a long, continuous process. Those who start the process must hand it over to others who will finish (or at least continue) it. The NEPP, for example, was first conceived during the tenure of Pieter Winsemius in 1984. Work on the plan began under Ed Nijpels in 1986. The first NEPP had just been completed by the end of Ed's term; and his successor, Hans Alders, spent the next four years setting up the mechanisms to implement it. Finally, over a decade after the NEPP process began, the last two ministers have been able to announce some results, but also the need for additional measures.

As the NEPP has grown, absorbing new ideas from new people, many adjustments and refinements have been made. The NEPP 2, for example, addressed the difficulties of implementing the first plan and offered greater flexibility to local governments (in this it was influenced by the City and Environment project). The NEPP 3 recognizes that the original policy measures from 1989 are not sufficient for achieving sustainable development and proposes a greater role for fiscal and economic measures. These new issues were not covered in the original plan (or at least not adequately), and their subsequent inclusion provides a critical lesson about continuity.

I think the NEPP was a good policy response for 1989, but it would not be adequate for 1999.*

A Series of Deals

In Interchapter 3, I explained how the roles in a process evolve as agreements are translated from the general to the specific level. The original deal on overall policy (as described in Interchapter 4) is only a general agreement. It sets in motion a series of subsequent deals which translate that agreement into specific changes.

Throughout the process, roles may change dramatically. The biggest and most surprising change is the conversion of *sceptics* from the original deal into *advocates* who initiate subsequent deals. In the case of a covenant, for example, corporate CEOs (playing the role of stakeholders) make a deal with the environmental authorities (who play the role of driving force, and perhaps also process manager). Next, the CEOs have to take the agreement home and make a deal in their own companies.

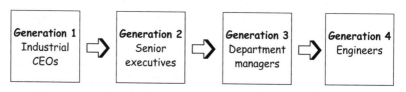

Figure 36 Generations of deals

In this second generation of deal making, the CEOs may typically play the role of sponsor, or sometimes even process manager. The CEO has agreed to some environmental targets, but he or she must make a deal on achieving them with the company's own senior executives, the new stakeholders. Throughout the process, shareholders and the board of directors may act as a critical audience, just as Parliament does for the development of government policies.

After making a deal with the CEO, the senior executives become advocates and go on to make deals with the managers in their departments. Then the managers have to make deals with their chemists, engineers or

---

* For the same reasons, I am now critical of the regulations for environmental impact assessments (EIAs), which I feel have become too bureaucratic. People may be surprised to hear me criticizing my own 'baby', as it were, but I recognize that circumstances have changed. The EIA regulations were developed 20 years ago, and no longer fit current conditions.

other employees on how to implement changes in actual daily operations. These final deals are where environmental goals are really achieved (or not achieved).

A schema for the generations of deals is presented in Figure 36. A similar process is followed by the other stakeholders, such as local governments, unions and business associations. In each case, those who were sceptics towards the original deal become advocates of subsequent deals in their own constituencies. The process continues until the general policy document has effected real-life changes on the street, in the home or on the factory floor. The evolution of roles is summarized in Figure 37.

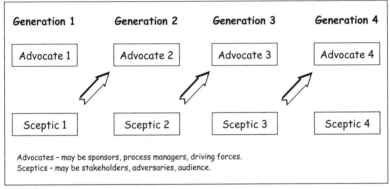

Figure 37 Sceptic to advocate

The Four Stages of Stakeholder Concern

There is an important transition for stakeholders as they move from sceptics, who perceive the deal as a threat, to advocates, who perceive benefits in subsequent deals. Our colleague, Annelies Kakebeeke, helped us understand this transition during our discussions about a second NEPP in 1991. Annelies proposed a model with four phases of 'concern' that stakeholders must complete before becoming advocates. She called these phases: (1) *credible story;* (2) *tell them what to do;* (3) *continuity of business;* and (4) *joint earnings* (Figure 38). I would like to describe them in terms of a hike.

Stakeholders first need a *credible story* for why they should take any action at all. Why should you carry a heavy backpack, walk all day long, perspire, and probably get blisters on your feet? There may be several convincing arguments. Hiking is good for you, the exercise will keep you in shape. All your friends are going, and you don't want to be left behind. Or perhaps the weather is changing; if you don't move, you're going to get rained on. In policy terms, the health argument might be citizen concern about the dangers of pollution or chemical additives in food. When enough individuals are motivated to action, this creates a social pressure for changes in society; people don't want to get left behind. As the movement grows, it creates political and market pressures on businesses to modify their operations. In other words, they'll be 'all wet' financially if they don't get moving. In the Netherlands, the original five themes and *Concern for Tomorrow* provided the credible story to bring in the original stakeholders.

Even when they accept a credible story, stakeholders prefer that you *tell them what to do*. When they first start walking, they may just follow at the end of the group, not carrying any of the baggage or making suggestions for how the hike should proceed. In policy terms, citizens perceive a problem and then expect the government to 'fix it'. They may not realize that they are partly responsible for environmental problems – through the products they buy and the lifestyles they choose to live. Meanwhile, businesses realize that the government will force them to behave in a more environmentally responsible way, and they put their faith in prescriptive regulations to stay out of legal trouble.

If we don't get bogged down in the *tell them what to do* stage (as often happens in the adversarial approach) we move on to the *continuity of business* stage, in which the hikers start wondering how this trip will affect their other plans. Are they really in shape for this hike? Will it take up too much time, not allowing them to do other things they had planned? In policy, this is a phase in which regulatory measures may create unnecessary bureaucratic burdens, and uncertainty, for companies. Existing regulations are often ineffective because they prescribe add-on measures that don't address the sources of problems, and the government has to keep preparing additional measures. Meanwhile, business is never sure what new requirements will be imposed; and local governments can feel trapped by national standards that don't consider the particular needs of their region. There is an urgent need to develop more flexible and cost-effective policy instruments, so that environmental objectives can be achieved without thwarting other economic or societal goals.

If the continuity of normal activities can be preserved, stakeholders may reach the last stage of concern, *joint earnings*. At this stage, our 'hikers' understand how to integrate the new activity into everything else they do, by fitting the trips into their holiday plans or into their established exercise routine. Rather than a potential cause of injury, hiking is perceived as good exercise. In policy terms, this is the stage in which citizens, for example, see that the 'sacrifices' they have made to protect the environment are rewarded with cleaner air and water, safer food, and more opportunities to enjoy nature.

The stakeholders may also see benefits. Conserving energy, for example, saves them money. Eliminating toxic chemicals saves the hassle and expense of their disposal; and meeting consumer demand for 'green' products can be quite profitable. *Joint earnings* may mean saving money through greater resource efficiency, or it may mean saving through greater regulatory efficiency. Environmental protection will often cost a business more money, since it can no longer rely on 'subsidies' from nature. Integrated policies, however, with less bureaucracy and more predictability, may be less expensive than the sectoral command-and-control regimes they replace.

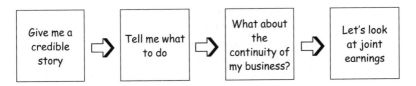

Figure 38 The four concerns of stakeholders

There is some relation between the four concerns of stakeholders and the four phases of the policy life cycle, but they are not interchangeable. The life cycle is used to describe issues, while the stakeholder cycle describes how people perceive those issues. Some groups, for example, may have reached the fourth stage of joint earnings for an issue; but the issue may not be one that arises in the fourth phase of the policy life cycle. If a majority of people are still looking for a credible story, the issue itself remains in the policy life cycle's first phase of 'recognition'. Furthermore, the stage of concern is dependent on the problem, not on the stakeholder group. Stakeholders with an advanced understanding of some issues may just be coming to terms with others.

Feedback and Contingency

Assuring continuity depends on recognizing that things may *not* turn out as planned. Uncertainty is inherent in every process, be it public policy or hiking. In the latter, the group may gather the best information before starting, but their information may not prepare them for everything they will encounter. The trail map shows what the route *should* look like, but things can change at any time. A bridge may have been washed out in a rainstorm, or a section of the trail blocked by a landslide. These uncertainties needn't ruin the hike, however. The party should look for ways to circumvent the bad section of trail but keep to the basic route they have agreed upon.

The same philosophy applies to public policy. Despite the best scientific and economic research, parties cannot anticipate everything that will happen during implementation. But they can monitor uncertainties closely, so as to minimize disruptions and stay on the policy trail. Monitoring and adjusting policy deals involves a consideration of *implementation provisions* and *feedback*, which are both derived from the commitment package described in Interchapter 2.

Implementation provisions are either the package's 'immediate actions' based on current assumptions or the 'future actions' based on research into uncertainties. In an integrated policy approach, implementation provisions should largely be the responsibility of stakeholders. In a covenant, for example, the government and companies agree on the objectives to be met and the time frame for meeting them. How companies meet these objectives, however, is left to them. Stakeholders must make a sincere effort to keep their part of the deal; but sincerity is not a guarantee of success. In examining the commitment package, we see that even the most carefully designed policies are based on *assumptions* which may or may not hold in reality.

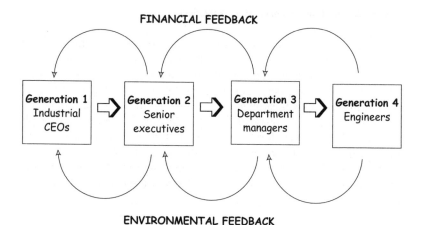

Figure 39 Generations of feedback

Feedback is the information component of the commitment package that we use to check our assumptions. A policy does not produce direct changes in society but sets in motion a series of deals which *may* produce these changes. Each 'deal' provides feedback on whether policy is having the desired effects or whether refinements are needed. There are many different kinds of feedback – providing information on social, environmental, economic, financial or other effects. Many deals on environmental policy are most sensitive to financial and environmental feedback.*

* Please note that I did not mention economic feedback in this context. Since the economy ultimately depends on a strong environment, good environmental policy should also be good economic policy. There may still be financial difficulties for individual firms implementing environmental policies, but a good deal on policy should not involve the 'environment vs economy' debate.

A deal is threatened not so much by technical difficulties as by poor communication. A company, for example, may receive feedback at some level that indicates it cannot meet environmental goals on time. This feedback is not a problem, as long as the company carefully explains its difficulties to the government and negotiates a (still ambitious) extension for meeting the goals. The government is equally responsible for maintaining good communications. It may well receive new environmental feedback indicating that a problem is worse than originally believed and that more ambitious goals or accelerated timetables are needed. If it consults with business stakeholders, explains the need for new actions, and welcomes their input on how to achieve new targets, continuity may be preserved.

Each generation of the policy deal has its own set of financial and environmental feedbacks. The feedback from one generation may call for some adjustments to the previous generation. As long as the parties share their information on feedback and discuss it promptly, they should be able to retain the basic structure of the original deal. Returning to the example of deal making in the business sector, we can picture the effects of financial and environmental feedback as in Figure 39.

It is not enough for stakeholders to make a promise; they must make a full effort to deliver. In a covenant, for example, much of the day-to-day evaluation of a facility's operations is turned over to the company itself. Environmental authorities, however, still must ensure that overall goals are being met. Without constant public involvement, and pressure, strong environmental policies may not have the political support to succeed. The public is the ultimate audience for all policies, and it must have access to clear, open information on environmental quality and the environmental performance of businesses.* Collecting and analyzing this information can be an important role for NGOs, which may act as a check on the thoroughness and integrity of both companies and government authorities.

Measuring Real Success

Continuity is a crucial element in a long and complicated process. It requires negotiating new deals, monitoring feedback and maintaining dialogue among the parties. Environmental policy cannot be judged a success simply on the basis of paper agreements. Nor can it be judged a failure due to some

---

* In the United States, for example, the 1986 Emergency Planning and Community Right-to-Know Act called for the creation of a Toxics Release Inventory (TRI). The TRI currently requires large companies to report their annual emissions of about 650 chemicals. Later, the Netherlands introduced a regulation requiring all major companies to produce yearly reports of emissions, as well as waste production, transport-related pollution, and other aspects of their environmental performance.

difficulty or delay in meeting the goals on that paper. Ultimately it must be judged by the conversion of sceptics into advocates and the continuity of efforts to translate general policy goals into specific, real-world changes.

Joining Others on the Trail
International Partners

The Netherlands is only one small country in a very big world – one member of a global hiking party. For the Dutch approach to work, we have to coordinate it with policies in other countries. In this chapter, I'd like to describe a few of the Netherlands' exchanges with other countries and international institutions. Through such exchanges, we found that the Dutch reforms are part of a larger international process for rethinking environmental polices. We also began learning what the Dutch approach can contribute to this process.

The Need to be International

The Dutch spirit of internationalism goes back to the beginning. The Netherlands is a small, crowded country with scant natural resources, so foreign trade has always been an essential part of our economy. The country is also surrounded by much larger and more powerful neighbours. Geographically speaking, these are France, Germany and the United Kingdom. In economic and cultural terms, we are also strongly influenced by the United States. We are increasingly tied to many of our neighbours through the European Union, which now has a major impact on our own domestic policies, as well as our international trade relations. Finally, the Netherlands was once an important colonial power; and this experience broadened our view to countries outside Europe. Though the former Dutch colonial attitude influenced foreign policies for a long time, we have worked to achieve a more productive relationship through development assistance and support of international organizations, such as the United Nations.

As I explained earlier (Chapter 7), the NEPP had to be developed with the international community in mind. If the Netherlands were to go too far in creating new laws and regulations, we would run into difficulties with the European Union, which seeks to harmonize laws and standards among its members.* Furthermore, we might jeopardize the position of Dutch companies vis-à-vis their competitors from nations which have less stringent (thus presumably less costly) environmental standards. As part of the covenant deals, the government promised Dutch businesses that it would promote the harmonization of high environmental standards with our major trading partners, especially those in the EU.

The European Union

In 1957, the Netherlands joined Belgium, France, Germany, Italy and Luxembourg in signing the Treaty of Rome, which established a trade association called the European Economic Community (EEC). In 1965, the EEC merged with two other communities in the fields of atomic energy and coal and steel production to form the European Community (EC). The 1965 treaty established the EC as a purely economic association, but it soon grew into a forum for cooperation on other issues, such as social policy and the environment. Interest in the environment was especially strengthened after the Stockholm Conference of 1972. In that year, the Community released a declaration stating that 'Economic expansion is not an end in itself ... it should result in an improvement in the quality of life as well as the standard of living.'[1]

The term 'quality of life' provided an initial justification for the Community's executive branch, the European Commission, to prepare five-year action programmes for harmonizing environmental standards. The first programme was a statement of general principles, such as the 'polluter pays' requirement, which should guide policies in the member states. It was followed by three other plans that essentially provided 'shopping lists' of measures to be taken by the member states. The European Commission had no authority to devise environmental policy at this time. It could only propose Community legislation, which then required unanimous approval by the member states. This led to a large number of laws, some of them quite effective. It was not possible, however, to begin integrating the laws into a coherent policy until amendments to the Treaty of Rome added environmental policy to the Community's competencies.

At the time, the Commission's Environmental Directorate (DG XI) was headed by the Dutchman Laurens-Jan Brinkhorst. With Brundtland and the NEPP in mind, Brinkhorst decided to use the EC's Fifth Action Programme (1993–2000) as an opportunity to articulate a more strategic, integrated environmental policy for the European Community. To set the tone for this integration, Brinkhorst invited two people from outside his directorate to be

---

* The covenant approach, in fact, was partly an effort to take new policy initiatives without proposing new national regulations that have to be approved in Brussels.

project leaders for the plan. He chose the former Irish attaché to the Community, Philip Ryan, and the Dutch attaché at the time, Robert Donkers.

I had first met Donkers in 1980 when we both joined the Environment Department's new directorate for *Bestuurszaken*. Before entering the department, Robert had worked as an economist and attorney with the Ministry of Economic Affairs. From 1984 to 1988, he worked as Deputy Director for International Affairs under Willem Kakebeeke, who had led the Department's international section since its inception in 1973. In general, Kakebeeke has concentrated his efforts in areas such as international treaties on air and water pollution, the Montreal protocol negotiations, and cooperation with eastern Europe. He left the European Community to Robert Donkers, who already had ties with the institution because he had worked for the Commission in the early 1980s. In 1988, he returned to Brussels as the attaché for VROM. Because Donkers was experienced not only in environmental issues, but also in economics and diplomacy, he was in a good position to help integrate the environment with other EC concerns, especially economic matters.

Donkers wished to employ aspects of the Dutch approach, but he knew they would require significant adaptation to suit the needs of many European countries. The Netherlands was quickly approaching an environmental crisis in the late 1980s, and no one could deny that important measures had to be taken. The situation was (and still is) different in other parts of Europe, such as the so-called 'cohesion countries' of Spain, Portugal, Greece and Ireland, which received economic aid from the Union's cohesion fund. Spain or Portugal, for example, are not as densely populated or as developed as the Netherlands, and many of their environmental problems are less severe. In these countries, economic development is the main concern, and must be addressed clearly in environmental initiatives. 'The arguments in the Netherlands were environment-driven. They were not economy-driven,' explains Donkers. 'Now, we [in the EU] are still in an economic community. I can't tell people to accept less profit today or tomorrow with the message that they will have benefits after the year 2010.'[2]

According to Robert, the NEPP was designed for the particular situation and concerns of the Netherlands: it would not have been possible to 'copy' the plan for the European Community. It was possible, however, to translate many of the NEPP's ideas by framing the discussion to address the concerns of the member states.

In designing the Fifth Action Plan, entitled *Towards Sustainability*, Donkers put special emphasis on the economic benefits of environmental protection. He also pointed out the economic drawbacks of environmental deterioration. 'You can't have a flourishing agricultural sector if your soil, water and air are polluted,' says Donkers. 'You can't have a flourishing tourism sector without the capital on which tourism is based, such as bathing water, dunes, forests, lakes and birds. I mean, you're not going to a landfill for your vacation!'

In overall structure, *Towards Sustainability* bears considerable resemblance to the Dutch NEPP. A key emphasis of the plan, for example, is the importance of clear information in policy making. In its executive summary, the plan states that 'the range of options which can be brought into play will rely heavily on the success in identifying cause and effect relationships and in finding appropriate scientific and technical solutions.'[3]

To address environmental causes, *Towards Sustainability* designates five target sectors, analogous to the target groups of the NEPP. The plan states that these sectors – industry, energy, transport, agriculture and tourism – are not an exhaustive list of environmental causes. Rather, they represent the sectors which have the biggest impacts and are most suitable to actions at the European level.

The selection of target sectors says a lot about the power structure of the EU. As a general rule, political authority remains with the member states, unless they specifically recognize the value of vesting that authority in the Community. This principle, called *subsidiarity*, was a key provision of the 1992 Maastricht Treaty which transformed the Community into the European Union. Some member states, especially the UK, would only agree to the treaty if it specified that primary authority would remain with the individual nations, not the institutions in Brussels.

Following the subsidiarity principle, *Towards Sustainability* is more of a framework plan than the NEPP. It recommends the type of actions that member states should take, but it cannot prescribe details. To reduce automobile traffic, for example, the plan recommends the use of road pricing and high parking fees. These reforms are not the task of Brussels, but of national, and often local, governments in the member states. As a framework plan, *Towards Sustainability* may be a valuable model for other large federations, such as the United States.

Like the NEPP, the European plan also recognizes environmental effects through the designation of themes.* The seven themes of *Towards Sustainability* are:

- Climate change

- Acidification and air quality

- Nature and biodiversity

- Water resources

- The urban environment

- Coastal zones

- Waste management.

---

* *Towards Sustainability* also gives high priority to the issue of risk management.

Again, the themes are not meant to be an inclusive list of all environmental effects in Europe. Instead, they represent the most critical matters, which must be handled at a Union-wide level.

Like the NEPP, *Towards Sustainability* was also released in conjunction with a state of the environment report. The EU plan also calls for consolidating future research under the authority of a new European Environmental Agency (EEA), set up in Copenhagen, Denmark in 1994:

> The success of this approach will rely heavily on the flow and quality of information....The role of the European Environment Agency is seen as crucial in relation to the evaluation and dissemination of information, distinction between real and perceived risks and provision for a scientific and rational basis for decisions and actions affecting the environment and natural resources.[4]

The EEA released its first report at the end of 1995. The document was part scientific study and part policy evaluation. It detailed the empirical progress (or lack thereof) for the seven themes of the EU plan; and it also made recommendations for EU policies to address each theme. The report has a structure similar to RIVM's biannual *National Environmental Outlook,* which is more than a coincidence. RIVM is one of the main contractors responsible for preparing the report.* Its influence is especially clear in the assessment of acidification, which is mapped out in terms of critical loads. The report also uses three of RIVM's five environmental scales – global, continental and regional.

In terms of roles, the process in the European Union developed differently from its counterpart in the Netherlands. Robert Donkers certainly played the the role of driving force, but he worked without a true process manager or sponsor. Ripa de Meana, the Commissioner for the Environment at the time, could have been a sponsor; but he didn't take much interest in the plan. None of the ministers from the member states took a sponsoring role, either (although people like Hans Alders and German Environment Minister Klaus Töpfer had been very active in other areas, like global warming). *Towards Sustainability* did have Laurens-Jan Brinkhorst as a sponsor, but his official position as Director General was better suited to the role of process manager. Indeed, he was to make an important contribution to process management by convening an implementation group for *Towards Sustainability* consisting of environmental director generals from the 12 member states at the time. This organization closely resembled the steering group we had convened to implement the Dutch NEPP.

Brinkhorst's work was continued in 1994 when Marius Enthoven became the Commission's new Director General for the environment. As in the Netherlands, Marius worked hard at improving the directorate's

---

* Other contractors include the Dutch consultants DHV Milieu en Infrastructuur, as well as the British consultant Environmental Resources Management, which also assisted in the preparation of the NEPP 2.

managerial competencies and strengthening its relations with the other departments. I believe that Marius did a great deal to advance the continuity of *Towards Sustainability* by building up trust among the member countries and bringing more of them into the environmental deal.*

After Marius took up his Brussels appointment, his old position as Director General of the Environment Department was filled by Hans Pont, who had a decided preference for domestic affairs. As a result, I generally represented the Netherlands at meetings of the EU implementation group. As with its Dutch counterpart, the EU group was valuable as an informal network in which we could get to know our colleagues and hear their concerns. Being civil servants, we could not make political decisions ourselves, but we could share information and guide the policy process that would help frame those decisions. Another example of such process management is the recent joint meetings of the Union's environment and transport ministers in 1998.

Towards Sustainability did not have enough stakeholder involvement for a true deal on environmental policy, though the European Commission did take important steps towards framing a future deal. The most important element was recognizing the different concerns of less-developed countries within the Union and eastern neighbours which aspire to join one day. Economic improvement is the priority for many of these countries, and they need to see that economic matters can be compatible with a forward-looking environmental policy. I believe that *Towards Sustainability* has been influential, for example, in promoting the gradual reform of the Union's Common Agricultural Policy (CAP).

CAP was originally designed to maximize farm production for an impoverished post-war Europe, but it has more than overshot its mark. The EU has been producing far more agricultural goods than it can consume, or even profitably export. Yet price supports have encouraged farmers to produce ever more intensively, which involves over-working marginal land, wasting energy and using exorbitant amounts of fertilizer and pesticides. Policies have essentially paid farmers to pollute the land, ultimately threatening the agricultural base for future generations.

In recent years, CAP has begun to change. Farmers are now receiving compensation to preserve fragile lands. In addition, the whole concept of agricultural aid has changed. Payments are now being seen as a means to maintain the farmers' economic security rather than as a measure to encourage more production. The reform of CAP still has a long way to go, but progress has been made. *Towards Sustainability* also seeks to provide

---

* Unfortunately, Marius had to leave his position in August 1997 when another Dutchman, Carlo Trojan, was named Secretary General of the European Commission. There was a general feeling that the Dutch were occupying too many high-level offices in Europe, and Marius decided to step down.

new opportunities for farmers. While Europe has a surplus of agricultural resources, for example, it has a dearth of timber and must import about half the wood resources it consumes. By making farmers into foresters, the Union may address several problems at once. Sustainable forestry provides revenue to maintain traditional rural communities. It also preserves habitat and open spaces which might otherwise be swallowed up by urban sprawl, and it provides a 'sink' to absorb CO_2 emissions.

The Union has considerable influence over economic development, especially in poorer regions, through its control of 'structural' funds such as the cohesion fund, the European Social Fund and the European Regional Development Fund. The EU has begun to encourage more sustainable infrastructure investments by building stronger environmental provisions into its funding criteria. In addition to the existing programmes, *Towards Sustainability* also created a new fund called LIFE, or the Community Financial Instrument for the Environment. LIFE helps advance sustainable development by funding research, technical demonstrations and pilot projects in sustainability.

Like the Dutch NEPP, *Towards Sustainability* also has a mechanism for review and revisions. In 1996, the Commission published an assessment of the plan, showing where it was succeeding and where it needed more effort. The reviewers found, for example, that industry attitudes toward the environment have improved. More firms are realizing that they are not threatened by environmental policies. In coming to terms with environmental responsibilities, firms are more interested in pursuing process changes, rather than being forced into end-of-pipe measures after protracted legal battles. After initial reluctance, the EU is now taking steps towards a covenant approach with business. The Union's first environmental covenants were signed in September 1997, when industry associations agreed to 20 per cent efficiency improvements for the next generation of televisions, VCRs and washing machines. Though relatively small in the grand scheme of things, the covenants were significant as the first occasion on which the EU agreed to voluntary measures in place of strict regulations. And the momentum for cooperative approaches is growing, as the Union now pursues a covenant with automobile manufacturers on reductions in carbon dioxide emissions.

The Commission has also been advocating greater integration of policies through changes in the tax policies of member states. The Commission's 1997 annual report on employment noted that taxes on labour have risen considerable since 1980, presumably hampering job creation. As a remedy, the Commission recommended shifting the tax burden from labour to environmentally harmful practices, thus encouraging job creation and discouraging environmental damage. The concept of an 'ecological tax shift' has received support from the new governments in Britain and France, but a European employment policy still faces strong opposition from some countries, such as Spain.* It will certainly be a long hike, but I believe that, step by step, such a tax shift will be introduced.

Austria

The Dutch approach has had some influence on the European Union, but it is difficult to compare the NEPP and *Towards Sustainability*. The NEPP is a national policy for a small, fairly homogeneous country with about 15 million inhabitants. *Towards Sustainability* is a framework plan for a multi-national union encompassing over 300 million people with different languages, histories and cultural traditions. In the remainder of this chapter, I will compare the Dutch approach to the policies of a few national govern-ments (in Chapter 12, I present a more detailed analysis for the United States). My first example of how something resembling the Dutch approach can be implemented in other countries is Austria. I must stress, however, that similar approaches are being developed in many other places: essentially, I present Austria as a case study.

The Austrian process was initiated and driven by Wolfram Tertschnig, who held a similar position in his country's environment ministry to mine in the Netherlands. Tertschnig's involvement began in the summer of 1991 when he first read a copy of the National Environmental Policy Plan. According to Wolfram, he was most impressed with the NEPP's emphasis on planning. Although Austria has very thorough laws on individual problems, it does not have a tradition of defining long-term, overall goals for policy development. In addition, Wolfram was impressed with the NEPP's broad stakeholder involvement in decision making.[5]

Traditionally, Austria has had a thorough, very institutional legal structure for environmental policy. Though rather compartmentalized and heavily oriented to command-and-control methods, the Austrian environmental laws have been quite effective in the past. They were reviewed in 1995 by the Organization for Economic Cooperation and Development (OECD):

> Austria has been *very successful* in dealing with all major environmental issues of the late 1970s.... Austria has enacted elaborate environmental legislation, developed detailed regulations and enforced its policies very strictly. The main emphasis has been on the use of end-of-pipe technology with a strong regulatory

---

* Germany had also opposed, but this may change with the new Social Democrat–Green coalition, which has already shown interest in an ecological tax shift.

system.[6]

Yet recently, especially with its entry into the European Union, Austria has discovered the limits of a traditional approach to the environment. Considerable pressure for change has come from the country's business community, which is concerned that high administrative costs could affect their ability to compete in new European and global markets. As a recent survey by the Austrian Industrialists' Association found:

> The administrative expense in the environmental sector, such as record-keeping, reporting, and inspections, was listed as the number one burden. Thus a *de-bureaucratization* and simplification of the Austrian environmental laws is the highest priority [emphasis added].[7]

Tertschnig appreciated the growing dissatisfaction with the traditional approach, and he asked the Dutch Environment Department for advice on working with stakeholders to develop a long-term vision for new policies. In the early spring of 1992, we went to Vienna for a one-day workshop on environmental policy planning. I put together a team consisting of my assistant Ronald Flipphi, Jan Jaap de Graeff from VNO and Huib de Bliek from the environmental section in the Ministry of Economic Affairs.

In the course of the workshop, I noticed two things which surprised both our Austrian colleagues and ourselves. First of all, the Austrians were certainly not accustomed to the informal structure of a brainstorming session. I saw, for example, that our Austrian colleagues sat according to a strict hierarchy. When we asked to them join a brainstorming exercise, we noticed that both Director General Heinz Schreiber and the young people at the far end of the table started enthusiastically writing down their ideas. But the middle management officials were paralyzed, because this exercise seemed to go against the traditional hierarchical structure of decision making. I even noticed one of the deputy directors peeking over to see what Heinz Schreiber had written, before deciding what he himself should put down.

The second surprise, for us as well as the Austrians, was the level of consensus among the Dutch delegates. After the meeting, the Austrians told us that they saw no difference among the positions taken by Huib de Bliek, J. J. de Graeff and myself. Although we represented different interests and had differing opinions, we all had the same objective assessment of how the NEPP process had worked.

The Austrians took several lessons from the Dutch approach in developing their own national environmental plan (*Nationaler Umweltplan* or NUP, in German). Like the NEPP and *Towards Sustainability*, the NUP recognized a number of target sectors for environmental policy, and the government asked representatives of these sectors to form working groups to help develop the plan. The seven working groups were:

- Industry
- Energy and petroleum
- Traffic and transportation
- Agriculture, forestry and water resources
- Tourism and recreation
- Natural resource management
- Consumers.

The groups spent almost three years developing the plan, which the Austrian Parliament approved.

The NUP appears to have a strong information component. The various working groups put together assessments of their sectors which are extremely detailed. In many ways, the NUP bears a closer resemblance to *Concern for Tomorrow* than it does to the NEPP. It contains extensive environmental data for the various sectors, as well as multiple scenarios for future developments. The energy section, for example, contains four different growth scenarios which are a bit reminiscent of Rob Maas's economic scenarios for the NEPP. According to Wolfram, the NUP could be described as a cross between *Concern for Tomorrow* and the NEPP.

In addition to scientific findings, the NUP seeks to clarify policy-making information. For each economic sector, and a number of specific areas, the plan provides detailed matrixes stating the problems, goals of policies, measures to be taken, and the parties that are responsible for those actions. These matrixes are generally more qualitative than quantitative. They describe the *type* of actions to be taken, but do not specify the policy instruments.

The NUP made a good start at managing the policy roles. The recognition of stakeholders has been quite good. Indeed, Austria already had a strong tradition of stakeholder involvement. Through its 'social partners' system, government, chambers of commerce and labour unions work together to resolve difficult policy issues such as wage rates for workers. Dr Oliver Dworak, who heads up industrial policy for the Austrian Chamber of Commerce, likens the social partners system to the Dutch *polder* model.[8] One weakness in the Austrian consultations, however, is that the NUP didn't contain any detailed economic analysis of what policy reforms would cost, or save. Without this information, the parties could only talk in theoretical terms, instead of having concrete negotiations.

Perhaps the most innovative aspect of the Austrian stakeholder outreach has been its efforts to involve the next generation in decision making. Alongside the NUP, the government decided to prepare a Youth Environmental Plan (*Jugendliche Umweltplan* or JUP, in German) for young people between the ages of 15 and 25. The JUP did not have any official power to influence the national plan, but the views and concerns of its participants were reported to the working groups that developed the national environmental plan. In addition to being a vehicle for youth to express its concerns, the JUP process also launched an outreach programme to improve environmental education in the country's schools.

I think the NUP process may have established a rough framework for future deal making, as well as a continuity mechanism to ensure that there will be future deals. The text itself acknowledges that the NUP is only the beginning of a long-term reform process. As the last paragraph of the plan concludes:

> Developing a National Environmental Plan for Austria was a necessary first step designed to intensify the discussion on sustainable development. The next step will be to implement the measures and strategies listed here and show that sustainable development is a viable opportunity to secure Austria's future.[9]

Like the Dutch NEPP, the Austrian plan can be renewed every four years. These revisions will be informed by assessments of the previous plan and state of the environment evaluations conducted by the Federal Environmental Agency, an independent body. Future versions of the NUP are also intended to elaborate how environmental protection and other government policies can be integrated.

The Austrian process shows that cooperative environmental management can be applied in other countries, but also that a policy system cannot be copied. One can recognize many elements of the Dutch approach in the Austrian policy, but they are not identical. We have made similar observations from other exchanges. For example, Valts Vilnitis of the Latvian Environmental Department also invited the Dutch to conduct a seminar on environmental planning, which was facilitated by Allen Hickling. The Latvians were impressively focused on what they wanted from us. They essentially used the Dutch as consultants to help resolve certain issues for their environmental plan, which was very much a home-grown project. In addition to Austria and Latvia, we have also worked closely on some aspects of sustainable development planning with the governments of China, Costa Rica, Benin, Bhutan, Hungary and the Netherlands Antilles.

Canada and Green Planning

We originally perceived the Netherlands' international role as that of a teacher, bringing the Dutch approach to other countries and shaping the development of their environmental planning. We soon realized, however, that several countries were already developing strategies similar to the Dutch approach, although they hadn't even heard of what we were doing in the Netherlands. We first discovered these partner nations in the spring of 1990, when we met a delegation led by Fern Hurtubise, Director General of

International Affairs for the Canadian environmental ministry, Environment Canada.

In meetings with the Canadians, Kees Zoeteman and I learned for the first time that they had been pursuing a policy reform very similar to our own. As in the Netherlands, public concern for the environment in Canada had been growing tremendously in the late 1980s and early 1990s. This concern crystallized in 1985 around a series of public meetings on sustainable development convened by the Brundtland Commission in Canada.

As a follow-up to the Brundtland visits, the Canadians decided to establish a set of permanent forums, called round tables, in which government officials and stakeholders could discuss the interface of environmental and economic issues. One duty of the round tables was to produce 'blueprints for sustainable economic development' for provincial, national and international environmental policy.[10] Within three years, round tables had been established at the national level, in all the provinces, and in many communities. These forums received strong support from Dr Robert Slater, the Assistant Deputy Minister of policy at Environment Canada. As one of the ministry's highest-ranking civil servants, Slater occupied a similar position to that of Marius Enthoven in the Netherlands.

In the elections of 1988, the environment emerged as the top public concern in Canada. The Progressive Conservative government of Prime Minister Brian Mulroney had not received high marks in the past for its environmental policy, and it had to do a much better job in order to win a second mandate. Before the elections, Mulroney announced that his government would henceforth give the same weight to environmental issues as it had previously given to economic concerns. Furthermore, this new approach would be set out in a comprehensive 'Green Plan' for environmental policy.* Mulroney's promise may have been a decisive factor in his coalition's victory that year.

After the election, Mulroney appointed a new environment minister, Lucien Bouchard, who then brought in a new crop of civil servants. They included a new Deputy Minister in Len Goode; a new director general for policy and project leader for the Green Plan in Brian Emmett; and a new director general of policy and coordination in Rick Smith. All three were economists.

The original drafts of the Green Plan were very close to the Dutch NEPP. They began with a philosophical discussion and then described a comprehensive, five-year programme for environmental policy, involving new government spending of C$3 billion (approximately US$2 billion). The programme contained over 100 items, grouped into eight policy categories which specified the amount of new government funding they would entail.

---

* The official name of the plan, released in 1990, was *Canada's Green Plan for a Healthy Environment*.

In its final form, however, the Green Plan led with the announcement of new funding and the list of action items. The overriding economic philosophy was buried deep inside the document, and the public mostly perceived the Green Plan as a political commitment by the conservative government to spend more money on the environment. This became a fatal weakness of the plan during Canada's serious economic slump of the early 1990s.

Under the pressure of political demands, Environment Canada was given only a year to prepare the plan, which was not long enough to lead a true policy process. The government released a draft in the spring of 1990 and then held a frenetic series of public meetings – 60 in a ten-week period. These meetings did solicit a large number of suggestions – five hundred recommendations were collected, and four hundred of them were incorporated into the final plan. But stakeholders were not given enough time to respond carefully to the plan, and there was not enough effort to frame a policy deal or win over adversaries. The final draft of the plan, released in December 1990, was immediately attacked by several environmental organizations. Perceived as a political document, the Green Plan was also targeted by Mulroney's rival parties.

In 1990, however, it still looked as if the Green Plan could lead to a genuine reform of environmental policy, and we were very excited to see that other countries were dealing with the same issues as we in the Netherlands were. We met more partner nations in the autumn of 1991 when the Canadians held an informal meeting on 'green planning' in Ottawa. We learned that there had been similar policy reforms in the United Kingdom and France. The British plan, *This Common Inheritance*, was co-ordinated by John Stevens, who also chaired an OECD working group reviewing the environmental performance of member states. The French *Plan Vert* (green plan) had been coordinated by Lucien Chabasson.

We also learned that there was a strong interest in green planning in the United States. The US Environmental Protection Agency was represented in Ottawa by Robert Currie, the Director of Strategic Planning in the Office of Policy, Planning and Evaluation. Building on the EPA's excellent work in comparative risk analysis, Currie led a project to identify future priorities for federal policy by conducting a series of risk assessment exercises with the US states. He intended to use these priorities as the foundation of a comprehensive, integrated environmental strategy that would transcend the fragmented policies caused by America's numerous environmental laws.

We also met Huey Johnson and Peggy Lauer of the San Francisco-based Resource Renewal Institute (RRI). Huey had been Secretary of Natural Resources for California under Governor Jerry Brown in the late 1970s and early 1980s. In 1982, he founded RRI as a think-tank for promoting integrated environmental planning, then spent the next few years investigating polices throughout the US and in other countries. Huey was so excited by the Ottawa meeting that he offered to host another green plan conference near San Francisco the following year.* I liked the idea and secured some funding for the conference from the Dutch government.

New Zealand

The California meeting, held in the spring of 1992, was an important opportunity to meet colleagues from other countries which were pursuing cooperative environmental management. Perhaps the most important meeting was with our colleagues from New Zealand's Environment Ministry, Secretary General Dr Roger Blakeley and Deputy Secretary Lindsay Gow. At the time, they had just completed a sweeping reform of their environmental laws, in which 59 acts of Parliament were replaced by a single Resource Management Act (RMA) of 1991.

New Zealand is a very different place from the Netherlands. Although it is nearly seven times the size, it has only a quarter as many people (who are vastly outnumbered by sheep). While the Netherlands is crammed among other European countries, New Zealand consists of three islands which are almost 2,000 kilometres away from Australia, its closest neighbour. While the Netherlands has a substantial industrial economy, New Zealand's is based mostly on forest, agricultural and mineral exports. Finally, New Zealand's environment, though not pristine, could be considered a green paradise compared with the Netherlands. Serious pollution is mostly limited to a few industrial sites, and 30 per cent of the indigenous forests are still intact. However, intensive agriculture has led to serious water pollution, as in the Netherlands.

For much of its post-war history, New Zealand had a high level of bureaucratic complexity. The national government played a major role in the economy, controlling such basic industries as forestry, energy, transport and communications. Taxes were high, and the public sector accounted for over half of the county's gross domestic product (GDP). Local government administration was also extremely complex – with over 800 units of local government 'right down to the local dog catcher,' as Roger Blakeley described it.[11]

New Zealand's economic performance had been sluggish since about 1950. It then began a severe downturn in the 1970s after the oil shock and the entry of Britain, its main trading partner, into the European Community. By 1984, the country was running a substantial budget deficit and had excessive foreign debts, high unemployment and stagnant wages.

---

* For more information about Huey and his work, I recommend his book, *Green Plans: Greenprint for Sustainability*, University of Nebraska Press, 1995.

In 1984 a new government promised to revive the economy by dismantling much of the country's bureaucracy. This bears some resemblance to the promises of the new Dutch government in 1982; but the magnitude of New Zealand's problems, and the sweeping nature of its reforms, were much greater. The reforms called for privatizing government industries, removing controls on foreign exchange, reducing income taxes and requiring a balanced budget by 1993/4 (the country actually ran its first budget *surplus* that year). In environmental terms, the most radical economic reform was the abolition of all agricultural and many consumer subsidies.

By 1987 the reform efforts had spread to environmental policy and an equally dramatic restructuring took place. The New Zealand reform process took three years and involved a thorough framing of discussions and outreach to stakeholders. Hundreds of meetings were held throughout the country, and the government established a toll-free hotline that was sometimes staffed by the environment minister himself.

Government planners logged about 10,000 comments into a database which they could reference while drafting the Resource Management Act. 'It's a very time-consuming and costly process,' Roger Blakeley admits, 'but you get the benefit of people's ideas, and if people have been involved, they're far more likely to have the commitment to the product at the end.'[12] As in the Netherlands, this public commitment was even strong enough to survive an election and a change of government during the development of the RMA.

From the beginning, the RMA reform was an effort to integrate economic and environmental concerns. This integration is described by Denise Church, the current Secretary of the Environment as a 'pull and push' dynamic:

> The 'pull' came from government reformers anxious to replace regulations with market-driven approaches to resource policy. The 'push' came from environmental advocates, both within and outside government, who were disappointed with the [previous] Muldoon-led government's environmental record and were demanding superior environmental protection.[13]

An important aspect of the New Zealand stakeholder process was the involvement of the Maori, the country's original Polynesian inhabitants who settled the islands somewhere between 800 and 1,000 years ago. The Treaty of Waitangi, signed by the Maori and English settlers in 1840, is considered the unofficial constitution of New Zealand. In exchange for a recognition of British sovereignty, the treaty recognized the traditional rights of the Maori to their lands and natural resources. The Resource Management Act specifically requires decision makers to respect the principles in the Treaty of Waitangi, the most important of which may be *kaitiakitanga*, or stewardship.

In addition to revamping federal law, the RMA was also undertaken in conjunction with a fundamental restructuring of local government. The eight hundred plus units of local government were condensed into 12 regions and four unitary authorities, based on the ecological boundaries of watersheds. The twelve regions, similar to provinces, in turn contain 74 districts, which are roughly equivalent to municipalities.

While the local government reform involved a considerable integration of government authorities, it also provides a vehicle for the continuity of environmental policies. The structure was described by the American Julie Frieder, an Environmental Protection Specialist from US EPA headquarters who spent most of 1997 studying the implementation of the RMA:

> The RMA serves as a *framework*, not a *blueprint*. Accordingly, it gives local authorities enormous responsibility and flexibility to identify the most efficient means of achieving the goals of the Act and meeting the needs of communities.[14]

Like the Dutch NEPP, New Zealand's RMA moves away from prescriptive command-and-control policies and towards performance-based standards. But again, New Zealand's approach goes much further. Licensing decisions under the RMA are based exclusively on an analysis of cause and effect relationships. Rather than proscribing technologies, or even setting discharge standards, the RMA specifies general quality guidelines for the ambient environment. Parties are free to undertake whatever environmental protection methods they wish, as long as they show they are mitigating adverse effects on the environment. This is similar to the flexibility we strive for in the Dutch covenants, but it is carried to a much larger, basically universal scale.

The same philosophy also applies to land-use planning. In theory, zoning laws are replaced by quality standards. Any activity can be undertaken in any location, as long as the permit applicant can prove that the activity will not violate environmental standards. Securing such a proof essentially involves performing an environmental impact assessment and consulting with neighbours and other interested stakeholders. Although the RMA gives developers considerable freedom, it also strengthens their opponents. Any citizen can contest a licensing decision, and complaints are heard by a special Environmental Court.

The New Zealand approach is interesting to the Netherlands because it is often strong in areas where our policies are weak. The Netherlands, for example, is only now getting a handle on resource issues. In contrast, the New Zealand policy is geared specifically to the management of natural resources – how both renewable and non-renewable resources can be maintained for long-term sustainability. The New Zealanders admit that they cannot plan for sustainable *development*, because they do not know what future generations will desire or need. Instead, their RMA is a plan for sustainable *management* – to maintain the resource base so that all possible options are kept open for future generations.*

Though New Zealand's policies have many strong points, they also have important weaknesses. In her assessment of RMA implementation, Julie Frieder concluded that New Zealand's resource managers are much more focused on bureaucratic efficiency than on long-term environmental performance. The incentives and responsibilities under which they work encourage officials to cut costs and paperwork, but not to address what some call the 'puffery' work of truly integrating environmental policy. Another weakness, according to a 1996 OECD environmental performance review, is the lack of reliable information. The OECD report points out that poor information is especially troublesome because New Zealand's non-prescriptive, activity-based decision making requires an even higher quality of environmental data than a standard command-and-control regime.[15]

Despite all the differences, there are some interesting parallels between the Dutch and New Zealand processes. Both took place against the back-drop of major economic and fiscal restructuring, although the extent of change in New Zealand was much more dramatic. Both countries also had strong political sponsorship. The New Zealand process was led by the Prime Minister (and former Environment Minister), Geoffrey Palmer. Without having the equivalent of a Marius Enthoven, Roger Blakeley had to juggle the roles of driving force and process manager. Both the Dutch and New Zealand processes also gave considerable attention to framing policy discussions and consulting with stakeholders. And both were based on the concept of sustainability.

A New Profession

In the latter half of 1992, my colleagues and I in the Environment Department began thinking of ways to follow up the Canadian and Californian green plan conferences. We decided to get together with some colleagues from the earlier conferences in December of that year to talk about forming a network of environmental professionals. The meeting, held in Washington, was attended by about 15 people from national governments, such as those of Canada and New Zealand, as well as international organizations like the OECD, the World Bank and the United Nations Development Programme (UNDP). The others shared our enthusiasm, and we soon agreed to form an organization which would allow us to meet and exchange ideas on a regular basis.

The hard part was deciding what to call it. After discussing such keynote phrases as 'strategic environmental management', we eventually came back

---

* This is reminiscent of the *multi-functionality* principle which Pieter Winsemius introduced for soil clean-up and later described in the book *Guests in Our Own Home*.

to the term 'green plan'. It had pretty much been taken for granted since the first meeting in Ottawa; but many people, including myself, later had reservations. The word 'green', of course, has some rather strong political connotations, and I didn't want to alienate people who are concerned about the environment but might not consider themselves to be 'green'. There are also problems with the words 'plan' or 'planning', since they remind many people of the failed centrally planned systems in the former eastern bloc nations. For me, 'green planning' also had an elitist tone: 'We are the environmental good guys. Now that we're in charge, we're going to plan the world as we see fit.'

There is yet another problem. When most people hear the word 'plan' they think of a physical document – a set of prescriptions handed down by government bureaucrats. In place of such a traditional *plan,* I advocate a *process* in which information and opinions are shared throughout society, and people reach some consensus on how to shape their world. Such a process will certainly lead to a piece or paper (quite a few, in fact), but any documentation should be a record of what *has* happened in the process, not a prescription for what *should* happen.

The term's appeal wasn't improved by the demise of the Canadian Green Plan in 1993, when Mulroney's Conservatives were replaced by a Liberal government. The plan had always been perceived as a political document of the Conservatives; and the newly elected party was virtually bound to undo the work of its predecessor. The Green Plan's fate was finally sealed by Canada's economic slump of the early 1990s. After a government-mandated 'programme review' for all departments, Environment Canada lost 30 per cent of its funding, and the Green Plan disappeared as a coherent agenda.*

Having set out my critique of the term 'green planning', let me admit that I wasn't able to come up with a better name, and neither was anyone else. In the end, we decided that it was the best possible name, and we dubbed our group the International Network of Green Planners (INGP). Hans van Zijst, who was then Counsellor for Health and Environment at the Dutch

---

* Some remnants of the Green Plan philosophy were preserved in 1996, when the Canadian Parliament passed an amendment to its Auditor General Act establishing a new Commissioner of the Environment and Sustainable Development. The position was filled by the original project leader of the Green Plan, Brian Emmett. The amendment also provides a mechanism for integration by requiring all government departments to prepare three-year sustainable development strategies to be reviewed by the new Commissioner. The first strategies were released in the spring of 1998.

Embassy in Washington, supported the idea of green planning from the start. He emphasizes the word 'planners', explaining that the organization is a network of people all working on the same ideas, but in different circumstances and with different techniques. Despite their differences, all are practitioners of a new profession – green planning.

The INGP's first official meeting was in 1994 at the Dutch border city of Maastricht. Since then, we have met in San Francisco (1995), San José, Costa Rica (1996), and Brussels (1998). The network undertakes some other activities, such as research and producing a small newsletter; but the main event is the (more or less) annual meeting. Hans van Zijst describes it as 'a family that has a reunion every year or two'.[16] Above all, the INGP is a collection of people, many of them good friends, who share ideas and encourage each other in their work.

It soon became clear that the members from every country and every region had something to teach. We have learned not only from affluent countries, such as Canada or New Zealand, but also from countries with developing or transitional economies. Robert Donkers, for example, has been most impressed with the non-European perspectives:

> What I liked most was the experience I had when I was a facilitator at the first meeting [in Maastricht] where I had a group of people mainly from South America, a few from Eastern Europe, and some from Africa.…We [in western Europe] sometimes try to do things the really difficult way – writing programmes, plans, or whatever. We tend to put more emphasis on the product than on the process. The Africans are very much going for the process. I was supposed to be the one from Europe to teach these people how we're doing it, but that was absolutely unnecessary. On the contrary, I learned an enormous amount. And that's the value, I think, of this kind of organization, because we think we have the stone of wisdom, but we don't. They go much more directly and by a much less complicated way to their goals than we do. Believe me!

In hiking, some people have a lot of energy in the morning hours and take the lead, while others save their energy for the afternoon. The morning people get the group going, and the afternoon people keep it going to the end of the day. Everyone contributes something at a critical time. The same could be said of participants in the International Network of Green Planners.

Notes

1 Commission of the European Communities, *Towards Sustainability* (Brussels: Office for Official Publications of the European Communities, 1993), 47.

2 All Robert Donkers quotations are from an interview with the author, Brussels, 11 March 1997.

3 Commission of the European Communities, *Towards Sustainability* (Brussels: Office for Official Publications of the European Communities, 1993), 102.

4 *Ibid.*, 39.

5 Wolfram Tertschnig, personal telephone conversation, 11 August 1997.

6 Organization for Economic Cooperation and Development (OECD), *Environmental Performance Review: Austria* (Paris: OECD, 1995).

7 Vereinigung der Österreichischen Industrie, *Wettbewerbsverzerrungen durch Umweltschutz-auflagen: Tendenzen zur Verlagerung von Unternehmensaktivitäten* (Vienna: 1996).

8 Oliver Dworak, personal telephone conversation, 17 August 1997.

9 *Austrian National Environmental Plan,* English translation (Vienna: 1995), 324.

10 Le Projet de Société, *Canadian Choices for Transitions to Sustainability: Final Draft* (Ottawa: The National Round Table, 1995), 6.

11 Roger Blakeley, 'The Sweeping Change of the Resource Management Act', speech delivered at the first green plan conference in San Rafael, California, 1992.

12 Roger Blakeley, remarks at the conference 'Green Plans for the 21st Century: the Pacific Rim', San Rafael, California, 21–23 October 1993.

13 Julie Frieder, 'Approaching Sustainability: Integrated Environment Management and New Zealand's Resource Management Act', report prepared for the Ian Axford New Zealand Fellowship in Public Policy, December 1997.

14 *Ibid.*, 19.

15 Organization for Economic Cooperation and Development (OECD), *Environmental Performance Review: New Zealand* (Paris: OECD, 1996).

16 All Hans van Zijst quotations are from an interview with the author, The Hague, 19 August 1997.

CHAPTER 12

A Very Big Hiker
The United States

If you're going on a long, difficult hike, it can certainly help to have a big person in your party. Perhaps he or she can carry some of the heavier baggage, for example, or help to cut through thick brush. Small countries, like the Netherlands, New Zealand or Austria, can undertake important environmental measures on their own, but achieving sustainability is a global task. To succeed, we need the bigger athletes to join us on the hike, and one of the biggest is the United States.* Though it has only 5 per cent of the world's population, the US consumes a vast amount of resources and produces a corresponding proportion of pollution. Clearly, the US is critical to achieving global sustainability.

In this chapter, I would like to discuss the strong relationship between the United States and the Netherlands on environmental policy and also evaluate America's progress toward cooperative environmental management. Of course, I can only provide a very general overview and a few examples based on my experiences. A full assessment of the US would require another book, at least.

A Pioneering Role

The US made an important contribution to comprehensive policy with the National Environmental Policy Act (NEPA) of 1969. NEPA may be best known for requiring the preparation of environmental impact statements (EIS) to gauge the negative effects of proposed government projects. Given the US government's considerable role in financing or permitting development, the EIS requirements have had a tremendous influence. NEPA also created the Council on Environmental Quality (CEQ) to develop policies. In

---

* In its 1997 *State of the World* report, for instance, the WorldWatch Institute recognized eight environmental superpowers – based on population, geography, economic might and technology – which it dubbed the 'E-8'. They are: Brazil, China, Germany, India, Indonesia, Japan, Russia, and the United States.

response to NEPA, President Nixon created the country's other main executive body, the Environmental Protection Agency (EPA), to enforce environmental laws and monitor progress.

CEQ was an influential body in the 1970s, under the leadership of dynamic chairpersons such as James Gustave Speth (now Director of the UN Development Programme). In the 1980s, however, the Council was given very low priority, and it almost disappeared. CEQ has regained much of its stature in the 1990s under the six-year chairmanship of Kathleen McGinty, and it has been influential on several key issues, such as climate change.* Because it is so closely associated with the President, however, CEQ is often perceived as a partisan organization, which hinders its ability to forge a national policy consensus.

In the 1970s and early 1980s European environmental policy followed the American lead. US initiatives also inspired us to go a step further. While studying EIS, we asked Professor Larry Susskind of the Massachusetts Institute of Technology to train us in American process management techniques for dispute resolution. We later applied these techniques, not only to individual issues, but to the entire process of developing the National Environmental Policy Plan. In the 1990s, the US continues to introduce important new policy concepts, such as:

- Supporting clear information through the public's 'right to know' about the environmental impacts of industrial facilities in their communities.

- Integration through promoting eco-justice, which examines whether minorities and lower-income communities are exposed to greater environmental risks than other citizens.

- Bringing in more stakeholders by re-examining environmental standards to ensure that they are adequate for children, who are generally more sensitive to pollution than adults.

Unfortunately, there are many drawbacks to being a pioneer. The US developed its environmental policy system in an era of intense conflict, in which every advance was won through hard political struggle. To force a change, activists pushed for strict, punitive laws, and litigation became a primary policy tool. The early battles of the US environmental movement established a confrontational culture which shaped public opinion, legislation and government institutions.

Bureaucratic Limitations

Although the Dutch Environment Department and the EPA are considered

---

* Katie McGinty left the position in October 1998 to accept a fellowship at a research institute in India.

equivalent organizations, they are actually quite different. Our department is a policy-making institution that works with the Prime Minister and other Cabinet members to craft policies which are generally approved by the legislature. In a parliamentary system, the same party controls both the Cabinet and legislature. While the US Executive Branch plays a major role in crafting legislation, the ultimate authority is with the Congress, and EPA policy-making is limited by the detailed requirements of sector-specific environmental laws. 'One of the jokes is that we are the environmental statute implementation agency,' says Paul Cough, the Director of the EPA's Office of International Environmental Policy.[1]

Despite institutional constraints, the EPA has long sought to develop a more strategic policy approach, based on long-term goal setting and accurate measures of environmental progress. In fact, work on environmental performance measures pre-dates the Agency's founding, explains Terry Davies, a long-time EPA official who served as Assistant Administrator and led the Office of Policy, Planning and Evaluation (OPPE) from 1989 to 1991.* In 1990, Terry and his Deputy, Dan Beardsley, proposed using environmental risk reduction as the overall theme for the Agency's work. The EPA Administrator, William Reilly, liked this idea because he wanted a mechanism to prioritize items in the annual budget request.

My first close experience with EPA reform was through Robert Currie, whom I had first met at the Ottawa green plan meeting in 1991. As OPPE's Director of Strategic Planning, Currie headed up the Agency's new programme in comparative risk analysis. He summed up his future vision for the EPA in a 1993 meeting of green planners:

> We need to think strategically …. The goal of the last twenty years has been to administer the statutes, and we're hopefully moving instead toward a goal of administering and managing environmental protection.[2]

Currie was one of the OPPE officials who were enthusiastic about strategic planning in the NEPP. In examining the Dutch approach, Currie worked closely with Hans van Zijst of the Environment Department, whom we had stationed at the Washington Embassy in 1991. One of Hans's duties was to track developments in the United States and Canada. He followed policy, scientific research and technical innovations for the Environment Department. Another duty was to bring the Dutch experience to North America, especially the US.

After the 1992 Presidential election, Bob Currie sensed an opportunity to accelerate reform efforts at the EPA. He focused on the budget for the fiscal year 1994, the first prepared under the Clinton administration. Since its inception, the EPA has made funding requests based on the country's environmental laws, such as the Clean Air Act. Thus, the budgetary process

---

* Davies now directs the Risk Management Center at Resources for the Future, a Washington think-tank.

further tied the EPA to the administration of sector-specific laws.

Using new performance indicators developed at OPPE, Currie proposed restructuring the annual budget request according to environmental goals. Thus, instead of getting money for the Clean Air Act, for example, the EPA would be funded to achieve a certain ambient air quality. Currie also proposed a rolling system of strategic plans which would define general goals for the next four years and more specific policies for the coming year. The similarities to the Dutch IMP programmes of the mid-1980s did not escape us.

Of course, restructuring the budget was a political decision for the new EPA Administrator, Carol Browner. While she understood the merits of Currie's proposal, the risks appear to have been too great for her. Browner had just taken office after difficult confirmation hearings and she was not ready to challenge the Congress with a new policy approach. In the end, she decided to structure the 1994 budget request as her predecessors had done.

According to Paul Cough, the political environment wasn't quite ready for Currie's proposal. 'There was never a strong enough incentive to integrate the strategic planning and budgeting processes in EPA and the other federal agencies at the time,' he explains. 'And without that integration, there was never a strong enough push to do more serious strategic planning.' Cough explains that circumstances began to change in 1993, when Congress passed the Government Performance and Results Act (GPRA). The GPRA requires that agency plans link budget requests and performance results, the same relationship that Currie had promoted. This mechanism has forced all federal agencies to begin adopting a long-term, strategic approach.

In 1997, the EPA presented a three-year strategic plan under the GPRA guidelines. The document begins with a mission statement, ten goals, and eight principles that will guide its work for the plan period and beyond. It goes on to list specific objectives for each goal, and timetables for implementing them. Under the clean air goal, for example, are objectives such as 'By 2010, reduce air toxic emissions by 17 per cent from 1993 levels...'[3]

The ten goals in the Strategic Plan are:*

1 Clean air

2 Clean and safe water

3 Safe food

4 Pollution prevention and risk reduction

5 Waste management, contaminated sites and emergency response

6 Global and cross-border environmental risks

---

* The phrasing is slightly abbreviated here to save space.

7 Expanding the right of access to environmental information

8 Sound science, risk assessment and technical innovation

9 Enforcement and compliance

10 Effective management.

With the exception of 4 and 5, the EPA goals are not comparable to Dutch environmental themes. The first two are traditional media-specific designations. The third focuses almost entirely on controlling pesticide residues and gives no discussion to issues such as soil erosion, groundwater depletion, eutrophication, habitat and biodiversity, or nutrition. The sixth goal recognizes the importance of environmental diplomacy and contains strong language supporting the Kyoto Protocol on climate change. The seventh highlights America's strong tradition of openness and freedom of information. The remaining three goals are a pledge to improve EPA management and procedures.

EPA is still limited in setting integrated goals because of its primary responsibility to implement the country's sector-specific laws. The Strategic Plan indicates the difficulty of integrating US policy by presenting a complex matrix that links the ten goals to the country's many environmental laws and treaty obligations. There is also an on-going debate between the EPA and the some members of Congress who think that any Agency plan should be limited to a strict enforcement of environmental laws.

The Strategic Plan describes a long-term planning cycle for the EPA. Goals set out in the three-year plan will be elaborated in annual plans that serve as the basis for budget requests (thus linking programme and budget). At the end of the year, a performance report will assess progress and provide input for adjustments to the strategic plan. The EPA also receives input from many stakeholders. In preparing the strategic plan, the EPA consulted with 19 members of Congress, 10 Congressional committees, 16 federal agencies, and 17 stakeholder organizations.

The new EPA Strategic Plan resembles the Dutch IMPs of the mid-1980s in many respects. It is a medium-term plan with a mechanism for more detailed annual planning. It consolidates the Agency's work under a handful of major categories, and it includes input from other federal agencies. The plan also states the need for innovative alternatives to end-of-pipe, command-and-control policies, and it encourages better involvement with stakeholders. Perhaps in the coming years the EPA will evolve from this medium-term management plan to a long-term comprehensive policy vision, as the Netherlands progressed from the IMPs to the NEPP. The EPA is at least moving in this direction through a series of experiments in new regulatory structures.

Regulatory Reinvention

During the 1990s, the United States has been grappling with the same dilemma the Netherlands faced after the election of Ruud Lubbers in 1982: how to deregulate the economy and streamline government bureaucracy without sacrificing the progress made under the adversarial approach. As we were completing the first NEPP in the Netherlands, the United States government was beginning to experiment with more flexible alternatives to its strict regulatory approach. The experiments, which began under the Bush Administration, have recently been dubbed 'regulatory reinvention'. By 1998, the EPA had over fifty reinvention projects, ranging from the very general to the very specific. I'd like to highlight just a few of them.

33/50 and the Toxics Release Inventory

The 33/50 programme was announced in February 1991 as a voluntary initiative for the reduction of toxic pollution by US industries, something akin to the Dutch Hydrocarbons 2000 programme. Participating US companies pledged to cut their emissions of 17 chemicals by 33 per cent in 1992 and by 50 per cent in 1995 (with 1988 as the base year). Although there was no legal requirement to participate in the programme, many companies decided it was in their best interests.

In 1988, the EPA published the first results of the Toxics Release Inventory (TRI), a programme which required large industrial facilities to report their annual emissions of 450 toxic chemicals (this had expanded to about 650 chemicals by 1998).* The TRI is a world-renowned example showing the power of clear information in the environmental policy process. In a large, diverse country like America, it is not possible to coordinate the work of all the scientific institutes, as RIVM did in the Netherlands. Instead, the Americans promote citizen access to information and let 'the truth' be decided in open debate.

With the TRI, the magnitude of emissions by many US facilities became clear for the first time. Although the emissions were generally within legal limits, firms faced strong public criticism when the TRI results were published.† Given this pressure to reduce emissions, many companies

* The TRI was created by the 1986 Emergency Planning and Community Right-to-Know Act. The 1990 Amendments to the Clean Air Act also had an important influence on 33/50, since about two-thirds of TRI releases are air emissions.
† In October 1998 Vice-President Al Gore announced a new right-to-know initiative by which companies agreed voluntarily to test the health impacts of the 2,800 most widely used synthetic chemicals. The voluntary approach, in lieu of a regulation to accomplish the same goal, was endorsed by such major players as the Chemical Manufacturers' Association and the American Petroleum Institute.

found they had little choice but to participate 'voluntarily' in 33/50. As with Hydrocarbons 2000, the US programme exceeded its objectives: both the 1992 and 1995 goals were achieved a year ahead of schedule. And 33/50 may be part of a larger trend. The latest TRI data, for 1996, show that toxic chemical releases dropped by 220 million kilograms, or 4 per cent, from 1995 to 1996.[4]

The Common Sense Initiative

In the 1980s, the EPA also began experimenting with structures resembling the Dutch target group approach. Programmes such as Design for the Environment, the Sustainable Industries Project and the Cluster Program focused on the technical and administrative difficulties of select industrial sectors. Building on these earlier efforts, the EPA officials crafted the Common Sense Initiative (CSI) in 1992. CSI most resembles the designation of individual sectors under the Dutch target group for industry. The six sectors are:

- Automobile manufacturing
- Computers and electronics
- Iron and steel
- Metal finishing
- Petroleum refining
- Printing.

CSI convenes broad-based stakeholder groups to identify technical and regulatory hurdles for each sector and propose 'common sense' solutions. The Iron and Steel Subcommittee, for example, has 20 private and non-government members from such diverse organizations as Bethlehem Steel Corporation, Friends of the Earth and the United Steelworkers. The subcommittees have proposed over forty projects to modify environmental regulations, some entailing broad reforms.

Only a handful of subcommittee proposals have been approved for implementation. Not surprisingly, CSI has made the greatest progress in modifying licensing and reporting requirements, areas over which the EPA has direct authority. Unfortunately, the EPA is not authorized to act on many of the bolder suggestions. As Terry Davies and Jan Mazurek of the think-tank Resources for the Future concluded in a 1996 study:

> Ideally, CSI would be a forum to develop projects that would integrate the fragmented air, water, waste, and toxics laws. By all accounts, CSI has not yet fulfilled its promise to achieve greater regulatory reform and integration primarily because EPA lacks the statutory authority to conduct such efforts.[5]

Rather than continue CSI as a peripheral reform project, the EPA recently proposed evolving it into a comprehensive plan to restructure the Agency according to sector-based environmental protection (SBEP). The draft plan explains that:

> SBEP provides an opportunity for integrated multi-media analysis of environmental issues affecting specific sectors and development of solutions that address these issues more cost-effectively and with better environmental results. Because it is comprehensive, SBEP promotes pollution prevention and discourages cross-media pollution transfers.[6]

The document goes on to announce planned actions such as preparing multi-media environmental regulations, encouraging self-auditing by companies, and convening sectoral stakeholder sessions to agree on best practices, benchmarks and performance measures. If the sectoral plan is successful, it may create an integrated structure similar to the Dutch target groups.

Project XL

It's easy to confuse CSI with Project XL. The main difference is that XL targets individual facilities and their surrounding communities, while CSI targets industrial sectors. Another difference is that XL did not originate with the EPA. It emerged from a series of stakeholder discussions convened between 1993 and 1995 by the Aspen Institute in Washington.

The discussions included representatives of federal, state and local government agencies, the US Congress, a broad range of NGOs, and many of the country's major corporations. Participants agreed that the United States should begin an incremental transition to a new environmental policy system which includes: a cooperative relationship between government and business, a shift from end-of-pipe to source-oriented measures, greater emphasis on performance goals, and flexibility for businesses in achieving those goals. To make this transition, the group proposed the 'Alternative Path', a parallel track for testing new approaches to the standard US system. It may be more than coincidence that the Alternative Path so closely resembles the Dutch approach. Many participants in the Aspen Institute discussions were already familiar with the NEPP, especially its covenant approach.

The Clinton Administration accepted the Alternative Path recommendations in 1995 by announcing a new reinvention initiative called Project XL (eXcellence and Leadership). The EPA describes it as an 'enforcement experiment', in which select firms are offered more flexible regulatory treatment if they can show it will allow them to achieve better environmental results. The EPA promised a policy of 'discretionary enforcement'. It could choose not to prosecute XL participants for technical violations of the law as long as those participants demonstrate both commitment and actual progress toward 'superior environmental performance'.

The problem is, the EPA cannot restrict actions by third parties, such as environmental groups. Knowing this, XL participants have shied away from making truly innovative (but risky) proposals. As of October 1998, only ten XL projects had been approved.* As with the Common Sense Initiative, the biggest success under XL has been in streamlining licensing and reporting requirements. With the proposed sectoral reorientation of the EPA, however, XL may help promote more substantive reforms in the future.

The President's Council on Sustainable Development

In addition to the EPA initiatives, there have also been efforts by both the White House and the US Congress to undertake an integrated, fundamental review of environmental policy. One recent attempt was the President's Council on Sustainable Development (PCSD), established by the Clinton Administration in 1993. In the spirit of integration, its membership is fairly broad-based, with representatives from federal agencies, state government, businesses, trade unions and NGOs. The Council's original co-chairs were Jonathan Lash, President of the World Resources Institute think-tank, and David Buzzelli, then Vice President for environment, health and safety at Dow Chemical Company. The first Executive Director was Molly Harriss Olson, who had previously worked in the Department of the Interior. Kathleen McGinty, the Chair of the CEQ, served as special liaison officer to the President.

In early May 1994 Molly Harriss Olson and I attended a meeting of the UN Commission on Sustainable Development in New York City. Afterwards, we shared a cab to the airport and discussed both the mission of the PCSD and the similar work on policy integration that the Dutch had done. I offered to show the Council how things were working out in the Netherlands, and I invited them to visit at the end of the month.

On 29 May, Hans van Zijst accompanied Molly, Katie McGinty, Jonathan Lash and the CEO of Ciba-Geigy, Richard Barth, on their first policy trip to the Netherlands. We also met up with Paul Hofhuis, who had recently been nominated to succeed Hans van Zijst at the Dutch Embassy in Washington. We didn't go hiking, but we did take a long bike ride on their first day. 'This was setting a whole new standard for diplomacy,'

---

* Most are agreements with individual companies to test new management or compliance structures. The largest XL project to date is an agreement with the Massachusetts Department of Environmental Protection to replace individual permits with self-certification by 5,000 small businesses, including dry cleaners, photo processors and printers.

Molly recalls with a laugh. 'It was a great way to get us thinking Dutch.'[7]

In the following days, I took the Council members around the Nether-lands to meet people who had developed or were implementing the NEPP. In a meeting with Pieter Winsemius, for example, Jonathan Lash was very impressed with the Netherlands' use of long-term goals to settle disputes. Molly was also interested in the consensus element of the NEPP:

> I was very enthusiastic and impressed that there had been a creative, non-confrontational approach to designing solutions. To actually examine such a mechanism and a process really influenced the way that we looked at the whole Council's work.

I was excited to see that the Dutch experience could offer some lessons to the Americans. For most of my career, it had been the other way around, and I was glad we had something to offer this time. The PCSD visit started me thinking that the Netherlands should do even more to convey the Dutch experience to other countries, especially the US.

The PCSD leadership worked at framing the process by broadening outreach to stakeholders and deepening the sense of teamwork in the Council. For example, they convened a series of eight task forces with members from around the country. According to Molly, such direct involve-ment of so many outsiders was unusual for a Presidential Council. The PCSD also left Washington for several trips, visiting Seattle, Chicago, Chattanooga and San Francisco, to meet with citizen experts and study local examples of policy innovation. The trips were also an opportunity for the Council members to get to know each other on a personal level, which can be difficult in the formal context of a Presidential commission meeting. 'We couldn't get them all on bicycles,' Molly says, 'but we did our best to get them out of their coats and ties.'*

The PCSD's trips were opportunities for Council members to break out of their official Washington roles and get to know each other better. Of course, greater communication may first result in greater conflict, as people find a means to express their anger or resentment. The American political environment in 1994 was not very hospitable to cooperation and consen-sus. After 12 years of Republican presidents, the Democratic Party had re-taken the White House in 1992 and promised sweeping reforms. Then in 1994, after more than forty years in opposition, the Republican Party won control of the US Congress and announced its own sweeping reform plans. The political tensions finally surfaced at the Council's visit to San Francisco in 1995. During breakfast one morning, the environmentalist

---

* The PCSD was governed by a law called the Federal Advisory Committee Act (FACA), which required that literally every moment of the Council's activities be open to the public. Participants have also cited this requirement as a major hindrance in other reinvention processes, such as the Common Sense Initiative meetings. In fact, one of the PCSD's final recommendations was to review the strict requirements of the FACA.

representatives attacked their colleagues from business, many of whom belonged to trade associations that were lobbying the new Congress to change environmental laws. The environmentalists accused the business representatives of shattering the trust among Council members.

Molly credits Timothy Wirth, a leading environmental official who was then Undersecretary of State for Global Affairs, with pulling the Council back from the brink. Playing the role of process manager, Wirth reminded the members of what they had achieved (they had already completed the second draft of their report); and he proposed they work on building mechanisms to resolve conflicts. According to Jonathan Lash, each side offered something. The business representatives promised to go to their trade associations and make it clear that they did not support the wholesale scrapping of environmental laws. The environmentalists conceded that the current regulatory structure was often a substantial burden. They agreed to put more emphasis on overall environmental objectives and less on inflexible regulatory solutions.

'People left angry,' recalls Jonathan Lash, 'but we thought we heard some really powerful commonalties.'[8] After the meeting, Lash and his co-chair, David Buzzelli, identified the points of agreement they had heard in the discussion and crafted them into a 16-point statement of common beliefs. Agreeing on these points appears to have been the crucial step in framing discussions for the Council.

The PCSD may not have reached a true deal on environmental policy, but it made some progress towards future deals. The Council's 1995 report, *Sustainable America: a New Consensus,* certainly brings up the right topics. Its definition of sustainable development includes not only an integration of environment and economics, but also social issues such as education, equity and civic engagement in policy decisions. The environmental and economic recommendations are similar to those we have seen in other countries. They include: improved information systems, a flexible and goal-oriented approach to regulation, greater responsibility for businesses (covering the entire life cycle of a product), ending harmful subsidies, and shifting the tax burden to encourage sustainable activities.*

One sign of continuity was a statement on climate change issued just before the Kyoto Summit in December 1997. While rather general, the Council's set of 'climate principles' is significant as the first agreement between American environmental NGOs and big industries on the need to address climate change. It may have played a role in changing opinions among key business stakeholders just before Kyoto.

---

* After the release of the PCSD report in 1996, the White House decided to extend its mission to include implementing the plan's recommendations. The current Executive Director is Martin Spitzer; Jonathan Lash remains as co-chair, and he is joined by Ray Anderson, the President and CEO of Interface, Inc.

New Perspectives in 1995

I had several opportunities to learn about the United States in 1995. It began in March, when I was invited by the OECD to participate in an 'environmental performance review' of the country, part of their programme to assess all member states on a regular basis. I travelled with colleagues from several other countries throughout the US, seeing much more than I had on brief visits to Washington, New York City or San Francisco. I developed a better appreciation for the size and diversity of the US, and the scope of the challenge it posed to cooperative environmental management. I also saw many signs that the process was beginning at the state and local levels. This experience reminded me again of the need for more policy exchanges between the Americans and the Dutch.

I returned to the US in June for the second meeting of the International Network of Green Planners in San Francisco. The principle sponsors of the meeting were VROM and the US Environmental Protection Agency, which sent a powerful message that our American colleagues were committed to the 'green plan' idea. At that time, however, I don't think they fully understood what we meant by policy integration. The EPA chose the topic for workshops at the meeting: water management on the San Francisco Bay. I found it strange trying to apply an integrated approach to a sectoral issue. I would have preferred a more interdisciplinary topic, such as rethinking industrial technologies or controlling urban sprawl.

The differing perspectives in San Francisco were a sign that we hadn't described all aspects of the Dutch approach to the Americans. Hans van Zijst had done an excellent job of putting the basics of the NEPP over to the Americans. At first, however, they thought of the NEPP as a green *plan* – a 'strong approach' in which the government explained how the world should work. This image was especially unappealing to American companies who perceived the NEPP as a slightly enlightened form of the old command-and-control regime. Most Americans didn't realize that we had devised the NEPP targets and implementation strategies by framing discussions with stakeholders, including the private sector.

Paul Hofhuis built on the work of his predecessor, Hans van Zijst, and focused on explaining the deal-making elements of the Dutch approach. Paul had extensive experience with the economic and business aspects of the NEPP. As head of Economic Policy Affairs at the Environment Department, he had played a key role in developing the early covenants. Paul's first major project in Washington was a day-long conference in September 1995, 'Innovations in Cooperative Environmental Management'. The conference was an exchange not only for Dutch and American businesses, but also for NGOs and local, state, provincial and national officials from both countries (including the EPA Administrator, Carol Browner and the new Dutch

Environment Minster, Margaretha de Boer). Among nearly 150 participants were high-level representatives from the US Senate and House of Representatives, Akzo Nobel, Amoco, British Petroleum, Du Pont, IBM, Intel, Merck, Monsanto, Philips, the American Enterprise Institute, the US Conference of Mayors, the World Bank, Friends of the Earth, the World Resources Institute and several foundations.

During the conference, the Dutch and American businesspeople realized that they had very similar concerns about environmental regulations. They all wanted predictability via clear, long-term policy goals, and flexibility in finding their own way to meet the goals. The Americans learned how the covenant approach was providing these benefits in the Netherlands, and they expressed great interest in adopting a similar approach in the US. One of the American speakers was Dorothy Bowers, the head of EH&S for the health products company Merck. She admits being rather sceptical of the Dutch approach until she learned the details:

> It seemed to be just so general in addressing the simple problems like acidification … things that we've been working on in the US since 1970…. But when I actually sat down and read through the NEPP, and then had the opportunity to go to Holland and meet with people there, I really got a very different picture of it. In some ways, maybe it's true that they're just getting some of the progress we got by command-and-control in the 1970s. But if we could trade some of our progress for a better process, I think we'd be looking at a brighter future in the US.[9]

The 1995 conference succeeded in linking many important constituencies. It was co-sponsored by two NGOs: the Resource Renewal Institute (RRI) and the Global Environmental Management Initiative (GEMI). John Nelson, RRI's Washington representative at the time, was instrumental in recruiting American companies as both attendees and sponsors. John also brought in GEMI, an environmental association of Fortune 500 companies. The corporate sponsors were Amoco, Sunoco, Sandoz, US Steel, Monsanto and Akzo Nobel.

The Conference also emphasized the existing ties between the White House and Congress, and consequently between environment-minded members of the Democratic and Republican parties. The day featured remarks by EPA Administrator Carol Browner, Molly Harris Olson of the PCSD, and William Reilly, the former EPA Administrator under Republican President George Bush. Senior staff from Democratic and Republican congressional offices attended. Representative John Porter, a Republican from Illinois, sponsored a reception at the Cannon House office building. Much of the Congressional representation was facilitated by Brad Crabtree, a consultant on economic and environmental policy with a flair for bridging the American political divide.

Our Common Journey

As a follow-up to the 1995 conference, Paul Hofhuis and I decided to do a publication that described the Dutch approach for an American audience, something I had been thinking about for some time. Paul asked me who could write the piece, and I surprised him by offering myself. As hikers know, a little distance is often essential for getting a perspective on the landscape, and I wanted a chance to work through presenting the NEPP experience for the Americans. I took a sabbatical from the Environment Department in the summer and autumn of 1996 and became a visiting fellow at the Center for Strategic and International Studies (CSIS) in Washington.

CSIS had just joined with two other organizations, the National Academy of Public Administration (NAPA) and the Keystone Center, on a regulatory reform project called Enterprise for the Environment (abbreviated E4E). The project was partly in reply to a 1995 Congressionally mandated report by NAPA, *Setting Priorities, Getting Results: A New Direction for EPA*. The report identified some of the EPA's classic bureaucratic problems: a plethora of regulations, fragmentation among branches of the agency, and the lack of clear, long-term goals. The E4E project had many of the 'usual suspects' among its members – representatives from businesses and NGOs who had also been involved with the PCSD, XL, CSI and other reinvention projects. But the list of members also included new people, most notably both Republican and Democratic political leaders from national and state governments.

E4E's director was Karl Hausker, who had been an EPA assistant administrator in the first years of the Clinton administration, and the Chairman was William Ruckelshaus, a (twice) former administrator of the EPA and the CEO of Browning-Ferris Industries.* Ruckelshaus made several speeches criticizing the bureaucratic, confrontational atmosphere in the United States. In proposing alternatives, he specifically mentioned the Netherlands as the model for 'a new sort of consensus process, in which all the significant stakeholders are brought together to hammer out a solution to a set of environmental problems'.[10]

In fact, E4E explicitly asked for input from other countries. The staff assisted me in preparing and publishing my paper and asked me to do a formal presentation on the Dutch approach for the E4E members. Similar presentations were given by other international advisers, such as Bo Kjellen, the special adviser for international environmental affairs from the Swedish Environment Ministry. During my Washington time, I began thinking of even more ways to spread information about the Dutch approach. I gave a

---

* Three other former EPA Administrators – Douglas Costle, William Reilly and Lee Thomas – were also members of E4E.

presentation to the World Bank, for example, and I wrote the rough manuscript which eventually became this book.*

The final E4E report, *The Environmental Protection System in Transition*, was released in January 1998. There are no brand-new ideas in the document, and it largely echoes the PCSD report. It does speak, however, to many essential elements of cooperative environmental management, and may have initiated a reform process in the Congress. After publication of the report, a group of Democratic and Republican Representatives have been discussing ways to implement the E4E recommendations.

Innovations in the US States

While we continue to work closely at the US federal level, we have also strengthened our ties with state governments. After all, several American states are the size of European nations. In some respects, they are better exchange partners for a small country like the Netherlands.

Beginning in 1993, Huey Johnson recommended that Hans van Zijst at the Dutch Embassy focus more energy on the state level. Johnson offered help in scheduling trips and identifying key audiences in the states. He arranged a two-year marathon of tours in which Hans went to 14 states, some of them several times. 'If there hadn't been an organization doing it that way, I would have done an occasional speech somewhere,' says Hans. 'But I never would have done it on that scale.'

Many US states have undertaken significant reforms towards cooperative environmental management. Sometimes their work was influenced directly by contact with the Netherlands, sometimes not. Unfortunately, I can only discuss three examples here. But the US is a big country, and there are many other exciting initiatives.

New Jersey

New Jersey may be the US state with the most interest in the Dutch approach because it faces similar environmental challenges. The state is about the same size as the Netherlands, with a fairly high population. It is very densely developed, with similar economic sectors, including a large harbour and airport, manufacturing, and a significant chemical industry. New Jersey also has a strong record of progressive environmental policy.

New Jersey's current policy is founded on two important documents from the early 1990s. In 1991 the state legislature passed a Pollution

---

* When I mentioned my plans to Brad Crabtree, he recommended Seán Captain, a former analyst with the Resource Renewal Institute, as a co-author.

Prevention Act, which required about 700 facilities to prepare environmental plans.[11] Under the Act, facilities can choose any approach they desire, as long as they meet the environmental performance requirements of state and federal laws. The Act also established a pilot programme for integrated licensing. Very similar to the Dutch covenant approach, qualifying facilities have received single-facility permits based largely on the pollution prevention plans they had developed. One facility, for example, was able to consolidate 100 air permits into one. Another combined 75 permits covering various environmental media.*

In 1992, the State Planning Commission unanimously adopted a State Development and Redevelopment Plan (or 'State Plan'), which seeks to prevent urban sprawl, revitalize cities, conserve resources and provide affortable housing. A key element is a mechanism for integrated planning among state agencies, counties and municipalities called 'cross acceptance'. Participation in cross-acceptance planning is completely voluntary, yet all 19 state agencies, 21 counties and 567 municipalities have chosen to take part because they perceive great benefits in coordinating their activities.

In addition to its impressive integration mechanism, the State Plan is also a powerful example of continuity. The legislation was adopted under Republican Governor Tom Kean, and the State Planning Commission and Office of State Planning were established during his term. These institutions have continued their work under the Democratic Governor, Jim Florio, and the current Republican Governor, Christine Todd Whitman.

In 1993, the Resource Renewal Institute invited David Moore, a prominent NGO leader in the state, on a fact-finding trip to the Netherlands. Moore was very impressed with the Dutch approach, and he became a driving force by injecting the idea into the state's upcoming elections for governor. With funding from a private foundation, he offered to take the winning candidate on a similar fact-finding trip. After her electoral victory, Governor Christine Todd Whitman accepted the offer by sending many senior staff people to the Netherlands in early 1994, including her Director of Policy and Planning, her senior environmental adviser, the Commissioners of Environment and Commerce, and the Secretary of Agriculture. Two members of the state legislature also attended. Working with the environmental NGO New Jersey Future, Moore recommended two key elements of the Dutch approach – goal-setting and cooperative relationships – which the state government should study and incorporate into New Jersey policy.

Upon returning from the Netherlands, the governor's staff set up a 'Green and Gold Task Force' as a sounding board for reform projects in the

---

* Unfortunately, the integrated licensing programme virtually ended in 1994 when several key people left the Department of Environmental Protection, possibly due to unrelated political disputes with the Governor.

Department of Environmental Protection. The task force has 15 members representing the NGO and business communities who have wrestled with issues of streamlining and simplifying environmental regulations. The government has also established a unique collaborative effort with New Jersey Future called the 'Sustainable State Project'. Its mission is to carry out a 'green plan' process similar to that of the Dutch NEPP. The project engages both experts and the general public in developing indicators of sustainable development – such as measures of health, pollution, poverty and education. The indicators are used to set goals and objectives for a sustainable development plan that was released in late 1998. The 1992 State Plan continues to provide both the policy basis and the scientific data base for these sustainable development efforts.

In June 1998, the Netherlands and New Jersey further strengthened their relationship by signing a letter of intent to address climate change. The agreement begins discussions to explore several joint initiatives, including a trading system for greenhouse gas emission credits.

Pennsylvania

New Jersey's neighbour, Pennsylvania, has also taken important steps to frame the policy discussion. In 1996, the state government launched a new initiative called strategic environmental management (SEM), which helps companies work with the state government on the most efficient ways to meet high environmental goals. SEM is also promoting continuity of policies as firms realize possible joint earnings and become advocates of future reforms.

SEM came in response to companies requesting regulatory relief in exchange for achieving ISO 14001 certification. The Pennsylvania Department of Environmental Protection felt that environmental management systems have a great potential to enhance performance. Officials felt, however, that they could not offer regulatory relief without assurance that ISO 14001 certification achieved, or exceeded, regulatory compliance. Since 1996, the state has offered numerous technical assistance programmes to help companies voluntarily adopt environmental management systems as a cost-effective alternative to traditional end-of-pipe compliance goals.

Believing that pollution prevention is the most economical way to meet environmental standards, state officials have encouraged businesses to pursue source reduction and even strive for zero emissions. According to Stacy Richards, the state's Deputy Secretary for Pollution Prevention and Compliance Assistance: 'We encouraged the regulated community to view "zero emissions" as a management policy, similar to the management goals of "zero inventory", "zero defects" and "zero accidents" embodied in the total quality management practices of the 1980s.'[12]

The Consensus Approach

The United States is famous for its individualism and confrontational approach to public policy. There are also instances, however, of Americans working together to agree on collective goals for their communities. The North Dakota Consensus Council (NDCC), for example, has worked since 1990 to provide forums in which leaders and citizens can explore common ground and implement the resulting policy agreements. In 1996, Brad Crabtree, who had worked as a consultant to the Dutch Embassy, joined the NDCC. Having spent considerable time in Washington, he decided to create opportunities for leaders in his native North Dakota to learn about the Dutch approach and adapt it to the rural Northern Plains.

As Brad explains, North Dakota and the Netherlands are 'polar opposites' in their history and culture, yet they both have strong incentives to use a cooperative approach. In the Netherlands, people must work together to overcome the difficulties of living in a crowded, resource-poor country. Living in a region with significant resources but very few people and an unforgiving environment, North Dakotans have also needed to work together for their survival. As Brad describes it: 'The American consensus approach is an effort to build on aspects of our cultural tradition which are more like the Dutch and to find policies and approaches that reinforce them.'[13]

In the spring of 1997, record floods and a blizzard devastated the Red River basin, which includes parts of North and South Dakota, Minnesota, and the Canadian province of Manitoba. A wide swath of agricultural land was inundated, while cities such as Grand Forks, East Grand Forks and many smaller communities were severely damaged. Rather than accepting a return to the status quo, Brad and his colleagues believed that the region could develop a consensus vision of how to rebuild in a way that better serves both economic and environmental needs.

In March 1998 the Council organized an international exchange on water management with the Netherlands. A group of public and elected officials, businesspeople, water managers, farmers and environmentalists from North Dakota, Minnesota and Manitoba, along with federal officials from both the US and Canada, came to the Netherlands for a week. They met with their Dutch counterparts and toured local and international flood prevention and water quality projects. The meeting was a fine example of integration, with representatives of three countries and an international watershed, three Dutch ministries, and discussions that linked the environment with water management, agriculture, economic development and recreation.

The visit proved so successful that the US Federal Emergency Management Agency (FEMA) asked the North Dakota Consensus Council to coordinate a regional flood prevention project. The Council is bringing together Canadian and American government, private-sector, and NGO leaders in a consensus-building initiative to develop flood-prevention policies that integrate the region's economic, social and environmental needs.

In addition to the cases in this chapter, many other US states are making important advances towards cooperative environmental management. They include Florida, Idaho, Louisiana, Maryland, Massachusetts, Minnesota, North Carolina and Oregon.

What We Have Learned

The Dutch and Americans have learned a lot from their exchanges in the past decade. We learned that there are alternatives to the traditional adversarial approach, that societies can set long-term goals and work out policy deals to implement them. We also learned that a continental superpower does not work in the same way as a small northern European country. Because the American system is so vast and complex, it cannot be reformed as quickly as the Netherlands, and the process may be very different.

While cooperative environmental management is taking root in the US federal government, it will probably develop more rapidly in American states and cities – smaller entities in which it is easier to bring all the stakeholders together. The US does have a history of developing innovative state and local approaches which later make their way into federal policies.

I was most encouraged by a two-day visit to Chattanooga, Tennessee in 1996. My friend David Gershon had urged me to see how Chattanooga had transformed itself from one of the most polluted places in America to a revitalized city with the official goal of achieving sustainability. On the first day I met citizen EcoTeams and saw that they had played the role of the driving force. In meetings on the second day, I realized that the chamber of commerce had been the process manager, while businesses and local government had been stakeholders.

I gave a short overview of the Dutch approach in a chamber of commerce meeting. Within five minutes, they understood exactly what I was talking about, because they had undertaken a similar process. Like many urban areas, the centre of Chattanooga was disappearing as suburbs were sprawling. The deal between the government and the private sector was to channel investments back to the inner city. It was not a deal about time, as in the Dutch long-term covenants, but about space. If investments were to occur, let them be in the heart of the city. Chattanooga now has a clean, bustling downtown and even a 120-block area planned for only zero-emission businesses.

Chattanooga can be a model for the entire United States because it shows the importance of making a deal. While regulatory reform and better information are important, the US is generally missing the critical element of framing discussions for deal making. Without this focus, parties cannot play distinct policy roles and negotiations will not have clear objectives. The many positive reforms in the US will reach a critical mass when the Americans find their own way to make a 'New Deal' for cooperative environmental management.

Notes

1　All Paul Cough quotations are from a telephone interview with the author, 16 December 1997.

2　Robert Currie, remarks at the conference 'Green Plans for the 21st Century: the Pacific Rim', San Rafael, California, 21–23 October 1993.

3　US Environmental Protection Agency (EPA), *EPA Strategic Plan* (Washington DC: GPO, 1997), 26.

4　US Environmental Protection Agency (EPA), 'US EPA Announces 1996 Toxics Release Inventory'. EPA, 18 June 1998.

5　Terry Davies and Jan Mazurek, 'Industry Incentives for Environmental Improvement: Evaluation of US Federal Initiatives' (Washington, DC: Global Environmental Management Initiative, 1996), 25.

6　US Environmental Protection Agency (EPA), 'Draft Sector-Based Environmental Protection Plan', *Inside EPA,* 16 October 1998.

7　All Molly Harriss Olson quotations are from an interview with the author, Palo Alto, California, 14 November 1997.

8　All Jonathan Lash quotations are from a telephone interview with the author, 3 December 1997.

9　All Dorothy Bowers quotations are from a telephone interview with the author, 18 November 1997.

10　William D. Ruckelshaus, 'Stopping the Pendulum', speech delivered at the Environmental Law Institute's Annual Awards Dinner, October 1995.

11　Dan Beardsley, Terry Davies and Robert Hersh, 'Improving Environmental Management: What Works, What Doesn't', *Environment,* September 1997.

12　All Stacy Richards quotations are from a telephone interview with the author, 30 December 1997 and subsequent correspondence.

13　All Brad Crabtree quotations are from a telephone interview with the author, 22 December 1997 and subsequent correspondence.

CHAPTER 13

Teamwork
International Continuity

The political process of dealing with environmental threats is painfully slow, especially for international issues. The lag time between recognizing a problem and taking action virtually ensures that further damage will occur, and it can be very frustrating to see that our response is often less than it should be. The long view of the international process, however, reveals substantial progress in global consensus building.

As a small country, the Netherlands generally cannot be a 'heavyweight' in the international policy process, such as a sponsor or process manager. Through institutions such as the European Union, the United Nations and the OECD, however, Dutch representatives have often played the role of informer, right hand, and sometimes even driving force, by placing topics on the international agenda.

Towards Global Environmental Policy

Environmental diplomacy can be traced back to the 1972 United Nations Conference on the Human Environment in Stockholm. This meeting, chaired by the Canadian industrialist Maurice Strong, established the rudimentary infrastructure for developing global policies.* It led to the creation of a United Nations Environment Programme (UNEP)† and especially placed the environment on the policy agenda of the so-called 'industrialized nations' – wealthy countries such as the United States, Japan and many western European states. The pace has accelerated constantly since Stockholm, especially in the last ten to fifteen years.

The period from about 1987 to the present is framed by two of the most

---

* The entire globe was not in attendance, however. The eastern bloc countries boycotted the meeting because conference organizers failed to invite the German Democratic Republic (East Germany) as a separate state. Nevertheless, Stockholm established a global framework for environmental policy, which eventually included the eastern bloc countries.
† Maurice Strong also served as UNEP's first Executive Director.

important international environmental agreements: the 1987 Montreal Protocol on Substances that Deplete the Ozone Layer and the fledgling 1997 Kyoto Protocol on climate change. At the beginning of this environmental decade, the global community had great difficulty controlling one class of chemicals whose harmful effects were increasingly obvious.* Today, many nations are considering the need to fundamentally reform their industrial systems to safeguard the planet for future generations.

The Montreal Protocol

The recognition phase of the ozone layer policy life cycle began in 1974. In that year, researchers from the University of Michigan published a study showing that chlorine, if released in the upper atmosphere, would set in motion a series of chemical reactions that destroy large quantities of ozone (O_3). Since ozone acts as a radiation shield by absorbing much of the sun's ultraviolet energy, these findings had potentially dire implications. In the same year, other scientists were examining the properties of chlorofluoro-carbons (CFCs), ubiquitous chemicals used as refrigerants, propellants in spray cans, blowing agents for making plastic foam, and solvents for cleaning electrical components. Their popularity came largely from the belief that they were harmless to the environment. That belief was shaken in 1974, when University of California researchers found that CFCs had the potential to break down in the upper atmosphere, releasing ozone-destroying chlorine.

Although this threat was only theoretical in the mid-1970s, some actions were taken at a very early stage, with the United States in the role of driving force. In 1977, the US Congress added a stratospheric ozone protection amendment to its basic air pollution law, the Clean Air Act. The amendment was an early application of the precautionary principle, because the Environmental Protection Agency was not required to *prove* that a substance would damage the ozone layer. It could take action based simply on a *reasonable expectation* that damage would occur.

The European Union (then the European Community) was much slower to react, and with good reason. Although the United States had once domi-nated the global CFC market, it was overtaken in 1976 by Europe, whose largest producers were Germany, France, the United Kingdom, Italy and the Netherlands. Of these countries, France and the United Kingdom felt especially threatened by efforts to control CFCs; and they originally approached the policy process as adversaries. In 1977, while the US was amending its Clean Air Act, the European Commission shot down a Dutch proposal to label spray cans which used CFCs as a propellant. By 1978 the US had already banned CFC propellants.

---

* For an authoritative discussion of the Montreal Protocol, I recommend a book by the chief US negotiator, Richard Elliot Benedick: *Ozone Diplomacy* (Harvard University Press, 1991).

The United States also played the role of informer. In 1974 the US launched a major research campaign involving a coalition of government agencies and universities. In 1984, US scientists joined forces with several international players, such as UNEP, the World Meteorological Organization (WMO), the European Commission and the West German Ministry for Research and Technology.

Political agreements gradually followed the scientific consensus. Led by UNEP's director, Mostafa Tolba, the United Nations became the sponsor of the process by placing the ozone issue on the international agenda. UNEP also served as right hand by providing a forum for discussion. In 1977, it convened a conference in Washington that produced a World Plan of Action for ozone layer research. In 1981, at Tolba's urging, UNEP began work on an international treaty. In March 1985, the European Commission and twenty countries (representing all major CFC producers, except Japan) signed an agreement in Vienna to promote further cooperative research. The participants also agreed to sign a formal treaty within two years. By signing the Vienna agreement, the European Union and its member countries were leaving the role of adversaries and becoming stakeholders.

The European change of position was probably influenced by internal divisions. While Britain and France were still adversaries of an ozone policy, Germany, Belgium, Denmark and the Netherlands came out in favour of controlling CFCs. As Europe's largest CFC producer (and its largest economic power) Germany could play an effective role as driving force in changing the EU policy. By themselves, small countries like Belgium, Denmark and the Netherlands may not have been very influential; but with German backing, they could play other policy roles, such as right hand.

Meanwhile, the scientific evidence continued to grow. After a year of work by over 150 scientists, the international coalition investigating stratospheric ozone released its report via UNEP and the WMO in 1986. The report documented the ozone-depleting role of CFCs, but also the role of two bromine-based compounds called halons. Furthermore, it touched on the nascent issue of climate change by pointing out that CFCs were thousands of times more effective than carbon dioxide at trapping heat in the atmosphere. The report was influential because of its comprehensive, systemic approach and its support by broad international consensus. It had a similar effect for driving global ozone policy as *Concern for Tomorrow* had for driving development of the NEPP.

As the UNEP/WMO report was nearing completion, British scientists measuring ozone levels over Antarctica released their own dramatic findings. In 1985 they announced that chlorine atoms from the breakdown of CFCs, combined with unique weather patterns of the Antarctic spring (September to November), caused ozone concentrations to drop by 50 per cent. Computer-generated images of a giant 'ozone hole' made an esoteric scientific theory dramatically clear. If the damage over Antarctica was already so severe, how soon would similar holes appear over the other continents?

Despite the growing scientific consensus and public concern, many stakeholders were still reluctant to take action. Companies which manufactured or used CFCs (a US$28 billion/year market) were concerned about the continuity of their operations.[2] Since their introduction in the 1930s, CFCs had been seen as wonder chemicals, and many companies could not imagine a world without them. That world, however, was already emerging. Prohibited from using CFC propellants in spray cans since 1978, American companies had quickly developed economical substitutes for this application.

Reflecting events in the European Union, opposition from the business community also deteriorated when some of its members broke rank. America's Du Pont, the inventor and the world's largest producer of CFCs, announced that it was confident of developing substitutes in five years, provided market or regulatory pressure made the investment worthwhile. Du Pont was approaching the stage of joint earnings by realizing that it could actually profit from environmental policies. If CFCs were to be banned, there would be tremendous financial opportunities for companies that could develop and patent substitutes.

The negotiations leading up to the Montreal Protocol also introduced another group of stakeholders, the so-called 'developing countries' which have not attained the level of prosperity found in the industrialized nations. Foreshadowing today's impasse on climate change, representatives of the developing countries raised an important question about equity. Why were they being asked to help solve a problem that others had created? Industrialized nations had produced and consumed the overwhelming share of CFCs and had enjoyed all the attendant benefits, such as refrigeration, air conditioning and the use of high-tech electronics. An agreement to freeze or reduce CFC use might do some harm in industrialized countries, but it could be much more harmful to developing nations, which saw CFCs as their path to better living standards.

The Montreal Protocol, negotiated in September 1987, did not resolve all issues related to developing countries, but it established a basic framework that enabled them to join the deal. First, developing countries were given a ten-year grace period before they were bound by the same requirements as the industrialized countries. Second, the industrial nations established a multilateral fund to compensate developing countries for adapting to CFC alternatives.* This arrangement proved to be a good deal for both parties. On one hand, developing countries were not economically penalized for the sins of the industrial world. On the other hand, the industrial countries won nearly universal participation in the Protocol, which was a prerequisite for protecting the ozone layer.

*By 1998, the fund had disbursed US$760 million to 100 developing countries.

I attended the last days of the Montreal negotiations and sat in on the discussions between our chief negotiator, Professor Willem Kakebeeke, and Environment Minister Ed Nijpels. Kakebeeke acknowledged that the treaty was not perfect. It only called for a 50 per cent reduction of CFCs by 1998 and a freeze at the 1992 level of production for halons, which, though less common, are 50 times more destructive. It also left out important ozone-depleting chemicals like the fumigant methyl bromide. Nevertheless, Kakebeeke urged Nijpels to sign: his reasoning was that the Montreal agreement would provide a means for framing more ambitious deals in the future.

That's exactly what happened. New science and technological developments soon led to much more ambitious goals. In 1988, NASA scientists announced that a thorough review of ozone levels showed depletion over populated latitudes that was two or three times greater than had been projected. In addition, they found that springtime ozone levels dropped by as much as 95 per cent over Antarctica.[3] Based on such findings, scientists predicted that the ozone layer would continue to deteriorate, even if the Montreal Protocol were fully implemented.

The 50 per cent reduction targets in the Protocol, though inadequate to protect the ozone layer, were enough to encourage the aggressive development of substitutes. Du Pont, for example, announced the development of hydrochlorofluorocarbons (HCFCs) and hydrofluorocarbons (HFCs). HCFCs are much less harmful to ozone and HFCs are harmless. Both, however, are potent greenhouse gases; so they are only interim solutions. More exciting were the fundamental process changes that eliminate harmful chemicals entirely. The electronics industry, for example, quickly found that it could replace CFCs with 'aqueous cleaning solutions', in other words, good old soap and water.

As Willem Kakebeeke had predicted, the Montreal Protocol created a mechanism for the continuity of ozone policy and the incorporation of new information. At a June 1990 follow-up meeting in London, the parties to the original agreement decided to accelerate the process radically by completely phasing out both CFCs and halons in the year 2000. They also agreed to address previously unregulated chemicals, such as methyl chloroform and carbon tetrachloride. At a 1992 Copenhagen meeting, phase-out dates were set for methyl chloroform and carbon tetrachloride; and those for halons and CFCs were further accelerated. In addition, production caps were set for methyl bromide and HCFCs. These caps were replaced with phase-out dates at a 1995 Vienna conference.[4]

There is still considerable progress to be made, but the progress of the past decade is astounding. Before the tenth meeting of parties to the Montreal Protocol in 1998, UNEP's Klaus Töpfer announced that global production of CFCs was down 80 per cent from its peak in 1988.[5] Scientists predicted that the ozone layer might recover fully by the middle of the next century. In just over ten years, the world has moved through the policy life cycle from recognition of a problem to the final phase of control.

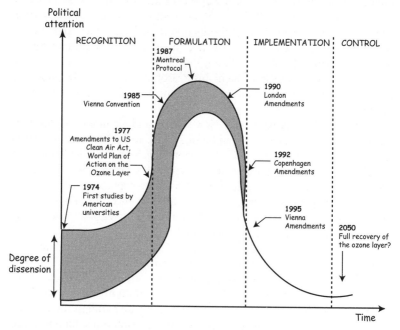

Figure 40 The policy life cycle of ozone layer protection

From Brundtland to Rio

1987 was also the year of the Brundtland Commission's report *Our Common Future*. Brundtland's theory of sustainable development argued that the environment and the economy were mutually supportive, not exclusive. While the report was important for an industrialized country like the Netherlands, its main purpose was to bring developing nations into a global environmental deal.

Although we live in a world of constant and increasingly rapid change, our economic thinking is remarkably stagnant. We assume, for example, that a certain amount of resources or energy is required for a certain quality of life. Yet technological advances constantly show that we can attain more by using less, if we improve efficiency, recycle materials and search for substitute resources. When the Montreal Protocol forced drastic cuts in CFC use, for example, industry quickly found other chemicals to provide the same services. Montreal showed that there are several means to any economic goal, and that society can choose the means which are least harmful to the environment.

While Brundtland acknowledges an absolute limit on the earth's carrying capacity, it also recognizes that intelligent use of resources can improve conditions within this carrying capacity. Furthermore, Brundtland gave special emphasis to raising living standards in developing countries:

> The satisfaction of human needs and aspirations is the major objective of development.... A world in which poverty and inequality are endemic will always be prone to ecological and other crises. Sustainable development requires meeting the basic needs of all and extending to all the opportunity to satisfy their aspirations for a better life.[6]

The Brundtland philosophy can be traced back to discussions on linking environment and development issues at the OECD in the 1980s. Originally set up to administer the US Marshall Plan, the Paris-based OECD later became a forum for exchanging information and policy ideas among the industrialized countries. Although originally it had a narrow focus on economic development, the OECD later expanded to cover social and environmental issues, and an Environment Directorate was established in 1971.

In 1984 the Netherlands and other countries began a discussion about linking the environment and development work in the OECD.* The issue was raised, for example, by our Deputy Director General Frans Evers, who also served on the OECD's environmental policy committee. The desire to link environment and development issues was also shared by Jim MacNeill, a Canadian who headed the OECD Environment Directorate. In 1983, MacNeill had been invited to serve as Secretary of the Brundtland Commission. While Ms Brundtland served as sponsor of the Commission, Jim MacNeill was a driving force who influenced the report's content.

More than a collection of platitudes, Brundtland provided an agenda of action items for the world community, including some of the thorniest issues in the developing world. Brundtland recognized the spiralling financial situations in countries that are pressed to extract more and more natural resources to finance ever higher foreign debts. At the same time, depressed world commodity prices are bringing these countries less and less export revenue. The environmental consequences of excessive resource extraction had long been discussed, but Brundtland also addressed the economic consequences, which are often the first concerns of impoverished, debt-ridden countries. Furthermore, Brundtland placed much of the responsibility for solving these problems on international institutions, such

---

* The Netherlands actually sent an American, Bill Kennedy, to lead this effort. We first hired Bill, who had formerly worked for the US EPA, as a consultant on developing environmental impact assessments. In 1984, we charged him with spearheading the integration of trade and the environment at the OECD.

as the World Bank and the International Development Association, which are funded and largely controlled by industrialized nations.

The report also raised the problem of overpopulation, although it was careful not to prescribe a standard solution. As the text explains: 'Though the issue is not merely one of population size but of the distribution of resources, sustainable development can only be pursued if demographic developments are in harmony with the changing productive potential of the ecosystem.'[7]

Brundtland recommended addressing the challenge of sustainable development through an international conference. In 1989, the United Nations General Assembly took up this recommendation, and Brazil offered to host the event in Rio de Janeiro in 1992. Clearly showing the link to Stockholm, the UN chose Maurice Strong to serve as the meeting's secretary general. The United Nations Conference on Environment and Development (also known as UNCED, the Rio Conference, or the Earth Summit) was not only the world's largest environmental meeting, but the largest gathering of national political leaders in history. Nearly 100 heads of state attended the final segment of the two-week conference.

Some critics of Rio have called the huge, sprawling conference a 'circus'. Perhaps it was, but I think that was one of its strong points. The whole world was literally in one room – a giant conference centre with booths representing all the participating countries and institutions. I found this diplomatic village – with a restaurant in the middle – to be an effective means for bringing the world together on an informal, personal level.

Several major agreements were negotiated at Rio, including conventions on climate change and biological diversity. Unfortunately, the last item consumed most media attention because of objections raised by the United States. While not necessarily opposed to protecting biodiversity, the US administration was very concerned about the language of the convention and its implication for intellectual property rights in biotechnology. The US had not worked through its position on the biodiversity convention; and the discussions quickly turned into a storm of ill-feeling from which the US emerged as the environmental bad guy. With such negative energy, it was hard for the world community to feel good about UNCED. Yet the biodiversity agreement was only one of the items on the Rio agenda. Perhaps the defining product of Rio was a massive document called Agenda 21, which proposed strategies for coping with literally all environment and development issues.

In addition to recommending actions, Agenda 21 also provided a cost estimate: approximately US$600 billion annually from 1993 to the year 2000. About 80 per cent of this money would come from developing countries, but the other 20 per cent, or $125 billion, would have to come from industrialized nations through overseas development assistance (ODA). At the time, annual ODA totalled only US$55 billion, so the industrialized nations were asked to more than double their development assistance efforts. Some countries, including the Netherlands and the Nordic countries, took up this challenge and agreed to meet the formula of raising average donations from 0.35 to 0.7 per cent of gross domestic product (GDP). Many other countries were reluctant to endorse the proposal, however, and simply pledged their 'best efforts' to increase ODA.

The Rio implementation time is almost over, and funding is nowhere near the prescribed levels. In fact, ODA had fallen to an average of 0.3 per cent of GDP by 1996.[8] Based on the funding shortfalls, it could be said that the world community broke the Rio deal. I believe, however, that Rio was the wrong deal, because it only focused on the amount of ODA in relation to 'the environment'.

The flow of ODA from the North to the South is minor in comparison with the total global flow of money and investments, so the proper deal should have been about environmental and investment strategies from public and private organizations. Not only did the old ODA approach hide the more important money flows around the world (and the missing investments in the South), it also placed the developing world in the neo-colonial position of beggars for Northern money. Instead, developing countries should be recognized as suppliers of valuable commodities in the form of resources and ecological amenities.

The Agenda 21 assumption was that 'poor countries' needed aid from industrial nations. But developing countries don't want hand-outs; they want opportunities. ODA is a dying instrument of global economic policy. In 1996, developing nations received US$244 billion – most of the money to come their way – through private investment. Achieving sustainable development will depend more on influencing private capital flows than on providing development assistance.

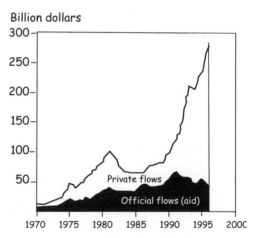

Billion dollars

Private flows

Official flows (aid)

Figure 41 ODA vs private investment, 1970–96
Source: World Bank.

Yet Rio scarcely touched on issues of international trade and investment, even though they were being negotiated at the same time by the General Agreement on Tariffs and Trade (GATT). In 1995 GATT negotiators established a new institution, called the World Trade Organization (WTO), to regulate international trade relations. In typical institutional fashion, there was no connection between Agenda 21 and the work of the WTO. Agenda 21 fails to consider how sustainable development affects trade, and the WTO fails to consider how international trade affects the environment.

The results have been devastating. While a few hundred million dollars are provided for pilot environmental projects in developing countries, hundreds of *billions* are spent on exploiting natural resources, often without proper regard for sustainable development principles. Deforestation, desert-ification, over-fishing and industrial pollution are continuing; and many 'developing' countries are not developing at all. They are simply scrambling to exploit and export resources to gain hard currency for paying off foreign debts. Unfortunately, the assessment of the Brundtland report still holds:

> Two conditions must be satisfied before international economic exchanges can become beneficial for all involved. The sustainability of ecosystems on which the global economy depends must be guaranteed. And the economic partners must be satisfied that the basis of exchange is equitable. For many developing countries, neither condition is met.[10]

My criticisms of Rio do not mean it is a failed process, but rather an incomplete one. Brundtland and Rio brought the world to the recognition phase of the policy life cycle by pointing out the connection between environment and development problems. Agenda 21 did an excellent job of identifying the problems, and its approval by the world community shows that we have found acceptable terms to frame the sustainable development debate. But we still have a long way to go in making a deal. First of all, we have to work on integrating our view of development. As long as economic policies are separated from environmental and social concerns, we will not find the right balance. Integration will provide clear information to show how economic decisions affect the environment, and vice versa.

There have been some positive recent developments towards integration. Environment, labour and human rights organizations have been campaign-ing for years to expose the harmful effects of trade and investment regimes which do not consider sustainable development. In 1998 US activists helped derail their country's expansion of a free trade area into South America because they feared the agreement would not address environmental and labour concerns. That same year, international pressure forced the OECD to adjourn its first round of negotiations for a Multilateral Agreement on Investment. Activists were concerned that the liberal terms of the agreement would allow foreign investors to circumvent any country's labour, environ-mental or social welfare laws.

Advocates of sustainable development may be winning a role as stakeholders in future trade and investment deals. In November 1998 the European Commission announced its intention to include consumer and environmental concerns in the 'Millennium Round' of negotiations for the World Trade Organization. European Trade Commissioner Sir Leon Brittan said that 'A Millennium Round of trade talks should not just benefit business. We can and should ensure that consumers and the environment also gain.'[11] The Commission initiated a study of the Millennium Round's impacts on sustainable development and called for greater transparency in the WTO, including NGO access to its proceedings.

While Rio has not delivered the systemic reforms it promised, it did set up a framework to continue the policy process on the global, national and local levels. One of the most important mechanisms is the United Nations Commission on Sustainable Development (CSD) which was established to clarify the broad mandate of Agenda 21 and monitor its implementation. Although the world community endorsed Agenda 21 at Rio, probably no one knew exactly what they were approving. The final Rio document contained hundreds of passages in 'square brackets', diplomatic parlance for disputed text.

The CSD's job is to work through Agenda 21, clarifying vagueness and eliminating square brackets. I have experienced this tedious but rewarding process first-hand as co-chair of the Commission in 1996. Take, for example, our work on the square bracket text about changing production and consumption patterns. At Rio, this was strongly opposed by the United States, which feared any intervention in the free market or international control over its domestic economy. In the years since Rio, we have clarified this text to mean greater energy and material efficiency and product quality, rather than a 'war economy' of austerity. By 1995, the American view on production and consumption had so changed that it became an official goal of the President's Council on Sustainable Development.

My colleague Joke Waller worked intensively on the preparation for Rio and was instrumental in getting production and consumption into Agenda 21. She has continued to play a big role in implementing the Rio agreements. In 1994, Joke left her position as head of Strategic Planning in the Environment Department and became Director of the CSD Secretariat in New York. In building up her staff, Joke brought in other experts on the Dutch approach, such as Erik Brandsma and the British consultant Emily Mattews, who had both worked on the NEPP 2. In 1998, Joke left the CSD to become Secretary of the OECD Environment Directorate.

Although the work in New York has been very positive, I think the CSD's biggest impacts have been in national capitals and communities around the world. In their preparation and follow-up to the UNCED conference, many countries have built up environmental competencies in their governments. The CSD reinforces this process with its requirement of yearly updates on each country's progress. In addition, the Rio agreement encourages community involvement by urging the adoption of 'local Agenda 21s' – translations of the Rio deal down to the local level.

In the spring of 1997 the UN General Assembly met to assess progress since Rio. The general tone at this meeting was disappointment and criticism of the failure of nearly all countries to fulfil obligations. Nevertheless, the Rio Plus Five meeting, as it was called, served the cause of continuity by affirming that the UNCED agreements still hold and by keeping the pressure on national governments to take them seriously.

Climate Change: From Noordwijk to Buenos Aires

Climate change was one of the major topics addressed at Rio and is perhaps the most contentious international environmental issue. The burning of coal, oil and gas now provides 85 per cent of the world's energy.[12] Scientific evidence increasingly shows, however, that combustion, by releasing heat-trapping carbon dioxide into the air, may substantially alter the world's climate. Possible results of this 'greenhouse effect' include catastrophic storms, rising sea levels, droughts, habitat loss and the spread of tropical diseases into formerly temperate regions. Although there are many other heat-trapping gases – such as methane, CFCs and halons – climate change is essentially an issue of carbon dioxide (CO_2) emissions, owing to their central role in all industrial economies. Since 1880 the atmospheric CO_2 concentration has risen by 30 per cent.[13]

While there may always be scientific uncertainty about climate change, mounting evidence indicates that something must be done to minimize it. A study released in September 1998 by the US National Oceanic and Atmospheric Administration (NOAA) reports that each of the preceding eight months set a new global high temperature record. This conclusion was based on data collected since 1880, when thermometers were first widely used to measure temperatures. Using proxy data from tree rings and ice cores, another team of researchers announced that the twentieth century was the warmest in 600 years. The chief author of the latter report, Professor Michael E. Mann from the University of Massachusetts, had no doubt about the causes: 'the warming of the past few decades appears closely tied to emission of greenhouse gases by humans and not any of the natural factors'.[14]

There also appears to be a frightening link between climate change and ozone depletion. As more heat is trapped in the lower atmosphere, the upper atmosphere has been cooling. The lower temperatures produce ice crystals which catalyze ozone destruction. Thus, even though ozone-destroying emissions are falling, they are becoming more potent. In October 1998 NASA and NOAA scientists announced that the Antarctic ozone hole was bigger than ever, larger than all of North America.[15] Even more frightening, the November 1997 issue of *Geophysical Research Letters* reported that ozone loss over the North Pole has been occurring regularly since 1993. Researchers predict that Arctic ozone loss will peak in the decade 2010 – 2019, with up to two-thirds depletion over populated parts of the northern hemisphere for part of the year.[16]

The recognition phase for climate change has been extremely difficult, given the psychological barriers involved. Yet we seem to have progressed through this stage relatively quickly; and we are already entering the phase of policy formulation. If the predictions about climate change are accurate, we are still not doing nearly enough to head off the problem. In terms of the policy process, however, our progress is quite impressive.

In 1987, the year of Brundtland and the Montreal Protocol, climate change was still poorly understood or appreciated. By 1989, however, public concern for the issue had already risen considerably; and the Netherlands could designate climate change as one of the NEPP's eight themes. Of course, the Netherlands CO_2 emissions are inconsequential on a global scale. Furthermore, the Netherlands would have a competitive disadvantage if CO_2 reduction policies were not adopted by our major trading partners, at least the other European Union countries. Thus, we had no choice but to play the role of driving force on climate change policy.*

We began with an international conference. In October 1989 representatives of 75 countries met in the Dutch town of Noordwijk for the first discussions on global climate change policy. In the process, they nudged the issue from the recognition to the implementation phase of the policy life cycle. Queen Beatrix played a sponsoring role by delivering the opening address at the conference. She also delivered to Ed Nijpels what he later called 'the perfect end of my time as a minister'. Because the Queen was travelling to Noordwijk in the morning, the ceremonial installation of the new Cabinet at the Royal Palace had to be postponed until later in the day. Thus Ed Nijpels introduced the conference as the Dutch Environment Minster, though he closed it as a member of the opposition party.

Ed's successor, Hans Alders, helped keep climate change on the agenda for both the European Union and the Rio process. Alders had important allies in Klaus Töpfer, the environment minister from Germany, and Sven Auken, his counterpart from Denmark.† In the first half of 1991 they proposed that the Union adopt the goal of stabilizing its CO_2 emissions at their 1990 levels by the year 2000. At the time, however, the Union was lacking some key roles needed to enter a policy process on climate change. Alders and Auken played driving force, and Töpfer played process manager. There was no strong sponsor, however, few engaged stakeholders, and a great many adversaries.

Most people saw no room for a deal because they believed that limiting CO_2 emissions meant limiting economic performance. This sentiment was

---

* To facilitate this role, Pier Vellinga, a specialist in physical modelling at the Water Hydraulics Institute, became head of a small section on climate change in the Environment Department.
† Alders and Töpfer both later went on to the UN. Alders headed the European branch of UNEP from 1994 to 1996, and Töpfer became UNEP's Executive Director in 1998.

especially strong among the less-developed 'cohesion' countries. To allay such fears, Bert Metz, the Dutch Deputy Director for Air Policy, worked out a formula by which the growth of emissions in some countries would be offset by reductions in others. The key to this formula was the newly unified Germany. It could offer about a 20 per cent emission reduction, mainly by ending the use of lignite fuel in its new eastern provinces. The only policy option for implementing this formula appeared to be an energy tax, which the Commission proposed a few days before the Rio conference. A proposal from the Commission, however, does not always indicate support from the member states. Some countries – such as Germany, Belgium, Denmark and the Netherlands – were in favour. France said it could accept the tax under certain conditions. Italy was ambivalent, while Britain and the cohesion countries were opposed.

In 1994 the Netherlands tried to drum up support for energy taxes by visiting the capitals of the EU member states. In the process, we found that few national governments had begun to tackle the issue by attempting to integrate the work of their various departments, such as those for environment, trade, economic affairs and energy policy. We were often the first people to bring those departments together. For many countries, climate change was still in the recognition phase of policy, and they were not prepared to formulate concrete measures.

Although we were not successful in 1994, I think the Netherlands advanced the recognition of climate change in the Union and laid the foundation for stronger policies. In the spring of 1997 the Dutch Environment Minister at the time, Margaretha de Boer, proposed not just stabilization but a 15 per cent *reduction* in CO_2 emissions (compared with 1990 levels) by the year 2010. This time, the member states were prepared to take strong action, and the 15 per cent target was adopted as the Union's official negotiating position for an international agreement on climate change that year. The Union essentially adopted Bert Metz's formula, by which emission cuts in some countries would leave enough room for growth in others, an approach later called the 'European Bubble'.

The 15 per cent reduction was the European Union's opening bid for an international protocol on climate change negotiated in the Japanese city of Kyoto in December 1997. The meeting was part of the Framework Convention on Climate Change which emerged from UNCED in 1992. Under the Framework Convention, signatories agreed to cooperate on research into climate change, with the goal of signing a binding treaty in five years. The developments from Rio to Kyoto were quite similar to those between the Vienna Convention and the Montreal Protocol: the first agreement was a framing process for bringing the parties together, the second was an attempt to close a deal. Because the European Union had the most ambitious position going into the Kyoto negotiations, it played the role of driving force.

A global agreement could only succeed with the participation of the United States, because it is the largest contributor to climate change, with 25 per cent of the world's greenhouse gas emissions. In the beginning, few people expected much from the United States, given its energy-intensive economy and poor reputation after the Rio conference. For many, these expectations were reinforced when President Clinton announced that the US only intended to *stabilize* CO_2 emissions at 1990 levels sometime in the period between 2008 and 2012. Nevertheless, the Clinton proposal represented a considerable change in American attitudes. With a business-as-usual strategy, American CO_2 emissions probably would have climbed to 35 per cent over 1990 levels by the year 2010:[17] against that background, even stabilization would be quite a feat. Furthermore, by simply setting a goal for limiting CO_2 emissions the United States was recognizing climate change as a legitimate concern.

In general, President Clinton played the role of sponsor in the United States. Like a typical sponsor, the President did not make bold proposals himself but allowed other parties, such as NGOs and alternative energy companies, to play the role of driving force in calling for more ambitious targets. One NGO, Redefining Progress, sponsored an Economists' Statement on Climate Change in early 1997 which called on the United States to pursue market-based approaches to reduce greenhouse gas emissions. The statement was signed by over 2,500 economists, including six Nobel Laureates.

Despite a lot of scepticism in the US and internationally, it appears that the American attitude is changing. At the start of 1997, US businesses were almost universally opposed to a binding climate treaty. Many of them joined forces in the 'Global Climate Coalition', which spent millions on advertising and public relations to turn opinion against the Kyoto process. By the autumn, however, the anti-Kyoto coalition was beginning to break up. In September, British Petroleum (BP) pulled out of the coalition and its CEO, John Browne, became the first executive of the petroleum industry to acknowledge that CO_2 emissions cause climate change.

While his peers still considered climate change policy a threat to their continuity, Browne was already perceiving joint earnings. In announcing its exit from the Global Climate Coalition, BP also announced that it would be investing about a billion dollars a year in its solar power subsidiary over the next decade. Shortly afterwards, Shell announced that it planned to invest half a billion dollars in alternative energy development over the next five years. An official from the company left little doubt that the motivation was joint earnings: 'We're not doing this for the hell of it. We think there are commercially viable opportunities.' In the autumn of 1998, both BP and Shell announced that they would voluntarily cut their CO_2 emissions by 10 per cent below 1990 levels.

Meanwhile, new investments in alternative energy have driven rapid growth in the sector. Sales of photovoltaic cells have grown by an average of 16 per cent each year since 1990, and sales expanded by 40 per cent in 1997. This rate of expansion is only topped by wind power, which is the world's fastest-growing energy source. A 1998 study by Royal Dutch/Shell concluded that renewable sources could supply half of the world's energy by the year 2050.[18] In October 1998 US researchers announced that precisely such a development would be needed to stabilize atmospheric CO_2 levels.[19]

At the end of November 1997 several US businesses joined with American environmental organizations to produce a set of 'Climate Principles'. The document, released by the President's Council on Sustainable Development, called for international commitments, flexible implementation measures, and strong incentives for business to take early action. In 1998, America's Pew Charitable Trusts established a Center on Global Climate Change, supported by a number of Fortune 500 companies with combined annual revenues of over US$340 billion. By acknowledging the need for some kind of climate change policy, many businesses have moved from the role of adversaries to stakeholders. In advocating new, clean technological development, some may even become driving forces.

Banks and insurance companies are among the major business backers of a climate treaty. Insurers could be wiped out by paying claims on properties lost to storms and rising sea levels. The eastern coast of the United States alone, for example, has more than US$2 trillion of insured assets which may be at risk.[20] Most bank loans are long-term investments, so their bottom line will be affected by events a generation or more in the future. In 1996 the Assistant Director of the British Bankers' Association,

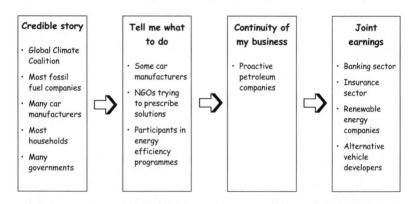

Various sectors work their way through the policy life cycle of an issue at different rates. This figure shows the stakeholder concerns for climate change policy in late 1998.

Figure 42 Stakeholders' concerns for climate change, autumn 1998

Peter Blackman, stated that half of all bank lending is affected by environmental factors. In the 20- to 40-year lifetime of today's loans, he explained,
'climate change is forecast to have a dramatic impact....'[21] Not only do
banks and insurance companies perceive joint earnings from a climate
change treaty; they see failure to secure a treaty as a threat to the continuity
of their operations.

Given its economic power and new support for climate change policy,
the US took the role of process manager, and sometimes even sponsor, at
the Kyoto summit. The process manager role was especially clear near the
end of the summit when Vice President Al Gore dashed off to Kyoto to help
break a deadlock in the talks. The results of that last-minute deal making
were impressive. In the end, the US went well beyond its original goal of
stabilization and proposed a 7 per cent emissions cut (compared with 1990
levels) in the time period 2008–2010. Japan also upped its offer to 6 per
cent reductions (it had originally been 5 per cent), and the EU settled for an
8 per cent cut.[22]

All the parties have taken some steps at least towards fulfilling their
obligations. Already in late 1997 the European Commission had called for
doubling the Union's share of co-generation (combined heat and electricity
generation) by the year 2010. This development alone is expected to cut
CO_2 emissions by 4 per cent. Despite opposition in Congress, the US
administration is pushing for tax incentives to encourage clean energy
investments. It also proposed requiring US utilities to generate 5.5 per cent
of their electricity from renewable sources by 2010, more than doubling the
current share. Meanwhile, the Japanese set industry-specific targets for CO_2
reductions. The automobile industry, for example, is to cut emissions by 20
per cent, the electronic machinery industry by 18 per cent, and the steel
industry by 10 per cent.

Many companies are trying to anticipate future legal requirements by
taking their own 'voluntary' initiatives. In October 1998 European electricity
producers announced plans to reduce emissions slightly as a way to stave off
prescriptive government regulations. Eurelectric's secretary general, Paul
Bulteel, explained: 'Our expectation is that the more industry shows it can
deliver ... the less need there will be for government intervention.'[23]

Although it was a considerable step forward, Kyoto did not represent a
final deal on climate change because all the stakeholders were not involved.
Echoing a major concern of the Montreal Protocol, developing nations
argued that they should not have to pay for a problem which the wealthy
nations had caused. Industrialized nations are estimated to have produced
86 per cent of the world's carbon dioxide emissions from 1870 to 1986. 'We
need to see leadership from those who have been historically responsible for
the majority of emissions,' said Mark Mwandosya, a Tanzanian who chairs
the 'Group of 77' developing nations (its actual membership has grown to
129).[24] The United States, however, made it clear that it would not ratify the

agreement unless developing countries participated, and without the US, the Kyoto Protocol cannot enter into force.

Participation by developing nations was the major issue at the follow-up meeting to Kyoto, held in Buenos Aires in November 1998. For example, delegates agreed to establish guidelines for a clean development mechanism (CDM) of technology transfer and green investments in developing countries. In a symbolic show of support, the US signed the Kyoto Protocol but made clear that it would not submit the treaty for ratification in the Senate (where it would face certain doom) until developing countries also joined the agreement. A few developing nations chose to become stake-holders. Argentina, the conference host, agreed to make voluntary emission cuts and encouraged other developing countries to participate. Khazakstan also joined the agreement. Unfortunately, major CO_2 emitters China and India refused to consider emission reductions for at least a decade.

Because they control most of the world's technological and economic resources, the industrialized countries must bear most costs of imple-menting a climate change policy. Joint implementation and international emissions trading may provide such a mechanism. Under joint implementa-tion, companies from industrialized countries make direct investments for cleaning up pollution in developing nations. The industrial countries will

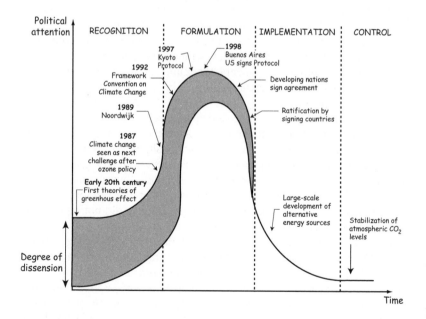

Figure 43 Climate change policy life cycle: present trends and possible outcomes

save by making their environmental investments where the marginal costs of pollution reduction are much cheaper than at home.* If developing countries receive an equitable allotment of pollution credits, they would have considerable flexibility in deciding how to expand their economies. They could choose to grow, up to a point, with traditional technologies, in which case industrialized countries would have to cut emissions (similar to the trade-offs of the European bubble). They could also choose to maintain or lower their emissions, sell pollution credits to industrialized nations, and invest the proceeds in clean technologies or debt reduction.

Where Do We Go From Here?

Developments from the past decade show that the international community is on the path towards better integration of environmental policies. There has been a process of continuity in two directions. National initiatives, such as the American push for a CFC agreement and the Dutch push for climate change policy, have brought new stakeholders into deals on global policy. At the same time, international events have brought in more stakeholders at the national and local levels, as evidenced by the profusion of national environmental plans and 'local Agenda 21s' developed since Rio. In Chapter 14 I will preview the major challenges of global environmental policy for the future.

* A 1998 study by the US Council of Economic Advisers predicts, for example, that international emissions trading could cut the US compliance costs for the Kyoto Protocol by 80 per cent.

Notes

1 Richard Elliot Benedick, *Ozone Diplomacy: New Directions in Safeguarding the Planet* (Cambridge, Mass.: Harvard University Press, 1991), 26.

2 WorldWatch Institute, *State of the World 1997*, ed. Linda Starke (New York: Norton, 1997), 158.

3 *Ibid.*, 155.

4 *Ibid.*

5 United Nations Environment Programme, 'Government to Meet in Cairo 18–24 November 1998' (http://www.unep.org), 4 November 1998.

6 World Commission on Environment and Development, *Our Common Future* (Oxford: Oxford University Press, 1987), 43–4.

7 *Ibid.*, 44.

8 WorldWatch Institute, *State of the World 1997*, ed. Linda Starke (New York: Norton, 1997), 6.

9 WorldWatch Institute, *State of the World 1998*, ed. Linda Starke (New York: Norton, 1998), 149.

10 World Commission on Environment and Development, *Our Common Future* (Oxford: Oxford University Press, 1987), 7.

11 Environmental News Service (ENS), 'Environment on Board for Millennium Trade Talks' (http://ens.lycos.com/), 18 November 1998.

12 Environmental News Network (ENN), 'Professor Predicts Oil's Demise', 10 November 1998.

13 United States Environmental Protection Agency (EPA), 'US Greenhouse Gas Emissions and Sinks: 1990–1996' (Washington, DC, 1998), ES-1.

14 *New York Times,* 'New Evidence Finds This Is the Warmest Century in 600 Years', 28 April 1998.

15 *Washington Post,* 'Ozone Hole Is Biggest Ever', 7 October 1998.

16 Jim Scanlon, 'Silenced Science: Arctic Ozone Loss', *Earth Island Journal* (San Francisco, autumn 1998), 23.

17 Environmental News Network (ENN), 'UN Climate Change Talks Cool to Clinton', 23 October 1997.

18 Canadian Institute for Business and Environment, 'The Gallon Environment Letter', 14 August 1998.

19 Environmental News Service (ENS), 'Tenfold Boost in Power Alternatives by 2050 Urgently Needed', 28 October 1998.

20 Mark Hertsgaard, 'The Cost of Global Climate Change', *Perspectives on Business and Global Change* (San Francisco), Vol. 10, No. 4 (1996), 11.

21 *Ibid.*

22 Environmental News Network (ENN), 'Kyoto Accord Key Turning Point on Climate, US Says', 11 December 1997.

23 Environmental News Service (ENS), 'European Power Firms Plan Voluntary Climate Action', 27 October 1998.

24 Environmental News Network (ENN), 'Poor Nations Stand Firm on No Emissions Cuts', 2 December 1997.

CHAPTER 14

The Trail Ahead
Five Global Challenges

In 1975 I attended an international seminar, 'Man and Environment', in the once peaceful seaside town of Dubrovnik, Yugoslavia. The problems of environment and sustainable development (though we didn't use the term then) were still very fuzzy at the time, and the differences of opinion were extreme. Some participants said we should use technology to remake nature for our purposes. Others argued that humanity had been going downhill ever since the Middle Ages, precisely because technology allowed us to misuse the environment.

However complex and twisted the logic may have been, the world around us appeared relatively simple. There was East and West, North and South. Since then, the East has disappeared, leaving the West with the illusion of having 'won' the Cold War. The South has also disappeared, at least in the way we thought of it twenty years ago: poor and weak countries heavily influenced by the East–West conflict. Now, many parts of the 'South' have had their own rapid economic development, and recently their own rapid economic recession.

The main socio-economic differences in the world are no longer based on countries or regions but on the various lifestyles within them. A homeless man in New York City lives pretty much the same life as a homeless man in any other big city of the world. The CEOs of global corporations have essentially the same lifestyle, whether they live in Rotterdam or Buenos Aires. Young people going to a House party in Moscow have much in common with their counterparts in Madrid.

In a global economy and global culture, sustainable development must be a global challenge. Yet our national and international policies are still based on regional identity, and environmental consciousness will always be rooted in local concerns. The old slogan 'think globally, act locally' still describes the key challenge of sustainable development: relating global issues to the perspective of individuals.

In 1999, the world is at a mid-point in the journey toward sustainability. Looking back along the trail, we realize how much we have learned along the way. Looking ahead, we can only dimly perceive the challenges that await us. The question is, will the lessons from the first part of the journey help us through the next part? We can't answer with a simple 'yes' or 'no', but we can begin to explore the possibilities of applying cooperative environmental management to the future challenges of sustainable development.

As an exercise, let's examine five possible themes for global environmental policy and a few strategies to address them. For each theme, I will choose the one element of cooperative environmental management that I think poses the greatest challenge. We will eventually have to work out all the elements for all the themes, but I'm just giving a rough picture of future tasks, as I see them. It's up to all of us to complete this exercise.

My proposed global themes are:

1 Biodiversity and nature protection

2 Population, migration and the distribution of wealth

3 Eco-efficiency

4 Water supply

5 Climate change.

Biodiversity and Nature Protection: Integration

Despite all their amazing abilities and attributes, humans are just one among countless species on the earth. I say 'countless' because scientists have only a vague notion of how many species there are. Very rough estimates range from 4 million to 40 million, and scientists have only catalogued about 1.8 million so far. Scientists will never have the chance to study all the remaining species. Approximately 1,000 species disappear every year, up to 999 of which are driven to extinction by human activities.[1]

Humans are utterly dependent on other species and the natural ecosystems that sustain them. The indiscriminate destruction of these ecosystems is a blow not only to 'nature' but to ourselves. While we may never calculate the full economic benefits of biodiversity, many economists have made rough estimates. Recently, Professor Robert Costanza at the University of Maryland synthesized over 100 of these studies and came up with a range of US$16–$54 trillion per year, which probably exceeds the US$28 trillion stacked up in economic activities measured by the gross world product.[2] In *State of the World 1997*, the WorldWatch Institute listed some of the major services provided by nature.

A few examples demonstrate our utter dependence on natural services. Take pollination, for example. Though humans may think they control food production through modern agriculture, 80 per cent of the world's 1,330

NATURE'S SERVICES

- Raw materials production (food, fisheries, timber and building materials, non-timber forest products, fodder, genetic resources, medicines, dyes)

- Pollination

- Control of pests and diseases

- Habitat and refuge

- Water supply and regulation

- Waste recycling and pollution control

- Nutrient cycling

- Soil building and maintenance

- Disturbance regulation

- Climate regulation

- Atmospheric regulation

- Recreation

- Cultural, educational and scientific values

Source: WorldWatch Institute.

crop species rely on natural pollinators, such as honey bees, to reproduce. Another example is the value of retaining and purifying rainwater. New York City recently faced the following choice regarding its drinking water supply: it could spend US$7 billion dollars on treatment facilities or one tenth as much to protect the land around its reservoirs. The decision was easy.[3]

Despite the tremendous value of biodiversity, humans are destroying it at an amazing rate. A recent compilation by the WorldWatch Institute, for example, estimates that 25 per cent of all species face likely extinction. In most cases, the main cause is habitat loss. As the human economy and population grow at exponential rates, they demand more and more space for factories, transportation and housing. Furthermore, this growth often consumes the best land. In the United States for example, over half of the most fertile cropland is at the edge of fast-growing urban centres.

Even if nature is not paved over, it can be lost to resource extraction, such as clearcutting natural forests or mining. Even farmland, often considered a natural setting, represents a great loss of biodiversity. Monocrops of wheat or corn, for example, replace wide genetic diversity with a single plant species, eliminate habitat for animals, and absorb less carbon dioxide than the native grasslands or forests they replaced.

To preserve biodiversity and natural systems, the world will have to set some ambitious targets. Just for the sake of discussion, I suggest we protect 90 per cent of the seas and oceans, 99 per cent of the North and South Poles, and 60 per cent of the remaining land areas. By protection, I mean to leave that area unaffected by development, apart from *genuinely* sustainable harvesting of resources. To some this might sound like an unacceptable burden which would shackle economic development. To others it may sound as if we are giving up almost half the planet.

Both fears come from our failure to take an integrated view of biodiversity and nature preservation. By protecting 60 per cent of the land from development, I do not propose giving up all economic values from these areas, nor do I propose giving up all environmental values in developed areas. Several studies from around the world show that land often has more economic value in its natural state. A study of forests on Indonesia's Bintuni Bay, for example, found that non-timber products and services – such as fish, plants and erosion control – contribute more to the local economy than timber harvesting. If logged, the forest would yield US$3,600 per hectare. If preserved, it would yield US$4,800 per hectare, and continue producing economic value in perpetuity.[4]

To integrate economic and natural values, we must first integrate the responsibility for preserving nature. Along with a 'polluter pays' principle for industry, we need an 'exploiter pays' principle for nature protection. So far, nature is considered a free good. Aside from a few zoning requirements, people can use nature much as they please. Most of my day-to-day work in nature protection comes from the fact that we don't recognize individual responsibility. Why should the government have to subsidize nature by purchasing land for parks and reserves? Why not make every landowner responsible for preserving his or her own piece of nature?

Though the area in national parks and other protected areas has continued to grow worldwide, habitat loss and species extinction proceed even faster. We simply can't buy up all the land that needs to be protected, nor would it help much if we could. In India, for example, forests began deteriorating when the government took control of them from local communities in the last century, and forest health has improved since some control was given back to communities in the 1980s. When people have a stake in a resource, they tend to value it more highly and take measures to ensure it will be available for their children. By setting clear, comprehensive targets and providing a mechanism of shared responsibility, we may be able to integrate the natural values of the local, regional and global economies.

Population, Migration and the Distribution of Wealth: Presenting Clear Information on Causes and Effects

There are two aspects of our impact on the natural environment. On one hand, individuals are demanding more and more natural resources. On the other hand, there are more and more individuals making these demands. This theme addresses the number and distribution of individuals.

It took aeons, from the dawn of the species until 1804, for the human population to reach one billion people. The next billion came just 123 years later, in 1927. The next billion came in 1960. By late 1999, the human population will reach 6 billion, and by 2050, there will be 9 billion.[5] These new individuals will require more food, although agricultural land is shrinking. They will require more water, though global freshwater reserves are nearly tapped out. They will need more energy for heating and lighting and more consumer goods, further depleting global fuel reserves, pumping more carbon dioxide into the atmosphere, and using up more precious forest and mineral reserves.

Along with overall growth in population, there are also significant shifts in its distribution. The United Nations estimates that between 4 and 50 million people are 'internally displaced' within their countries due to political upheavals, such as the million Colombians driven from their homes by military clashes. Others move for economic reasons, such as the 100 million Chinese workers who have moved to the country's southern provinces in search of jobs.

One major trend is the migration to cities. For all of human history, most people have lived in rural areas. By the year 2000, more than half the population will live in cities.[6] The explosive growth of urban areas produces major environmental stress. Large cities produce substantial air pollution and water pollution, for instance, and they gobble up farmland and natural areas for factories, housing developments and transport infrastructure.

Many other migrants cross international borders, such as the 15 million political refugees in places like Central Africa or the Middle East. In addition, there are about 42 million temporary migrants who seek work opportunities, such as Filipinos in Saudi Arabia or Mexicans in the United States.[7] Migration has an important impact on regional population pressures. In the United States, for example, half of the country's population growth is from immigration.

There must be a limit to the number of people the earth can sustain, and there must be a way to keep population within this limit. There must also be ways to address the causes of migration and reduce its social and environmental impacts. At this point, however, the policy debate lacks the clear information to address these issues, especially their cause and effect relationships. While we have an overflow of information about the globalization of economic and monetary developments, and spend much energy promoting trade liberalization, we don't analyze their impact on the structure of society. Economic globalization leads to social globalization, which we see in migration and other impacts. Whatever our ideological bent, we cannot deny that people follow wealth, as they always have.

Even the information we do have can be misleading. For example, we know there is a clear difference in population growth between industrialized and developing countries. The population of industrialized countries is actually beginning to fall. The United Nations estimates it will drop from 1.18 billion in 1998 to 1.16 billion in 2050. Meanwhile, the population of developing countries will soar from 4.75 billion to 8.2 billion in the same time period.[8] These statistics seem to indicate that families in the developing world are having more and more babies, but that isn't entirely true. In fact, fertility rates have been dropping around the world, from an average of six children per woman to three per woman in the past 30 years.[9] So there have been substantial changes in population trends which we don't appreciate when we only hear that numbers are going up.

We also need better information on why fertility is dropping and how to reinforce the trend. Certainly contraception has played an important role, but it cannot function in a social vacuum. Many communities have shunned birth control because of religious beliefs or cultural norms. Many parents also have children for economic reasons, so there will be more people to help with household work and to care for them in their old age. In fact, economics may be the most important factor in family planning. Families with more financial security tend to have fewer children, as seen in the stagnant or even falling birth rates in wealthy European nations.

Economic opportunity is especially important for women. Many examples show that women who have better prospects for economic and educational advancement choose to have fewer children. In Bangladesh, for example, the Grameen Bank has provided approximately US$2 billion dollars in 'micro-credit' loans, averaging just US$180, to women entrepreneurs since 1976. Bangladeshi women who receive Grameen Bank loans are twice as likely to practise family planning.[10] The issue of economic and social opportunity also demonstrates the blurring of regional differences. The world's wealthiest country, the United States, also has a high rate of teenage pregnancies, mostly among poorer women who have fewer opportunities for advancement.

Migration is also poorly understood by most people. Developed countries have always made a distinction between political and economic refugees. They have recognized the legitimate needs of political refugees to leave their homelands but have treated economic refugees like criminals. In many cases, however, economic refugees also have very legitimate motivations for leaving their homes. In a globalizing economy, capital can move freely, but labour may not. Economic opportunities move, but workers are not expected to follow.

Massive migrations rob already poor regions of their youngest and strongest workers and overwhelm wealthier regions with an influx of new people. But barbed wire and guard posts are effect-oriented measures and not the best means to control immigration. To address the causes, we have to examine the global economic systems that promote such wide divergence in opportunities among countries.

Eco-Efficiency: Recognizing Policy as a Process with Roles to Be Played

While the *number* of people living on Earth is important, the *way* they live is equally important. India may have a higher birth rate than the United States, for example, but the world could sustain many more Indians than Americans. The 2.6 million new Americans born each year will produce greater environmental strains than the 17 million Indians born the same year.[11] In almost all cases, however, humans could achieve the same material benefits using fewer resources.

Eco-efficiency is a general term describing efforts to reduce our material and energy needs radically. An important goal for eco-efficiency is 'factor ten', identified by Ernst Ulrich von Weizsäcker of Germany's Wuppertal Institute and Wouter van Dieren from the Institute for Environment and Systems Analysis in Amsterdam. They propose that society can and must reduce resource use by a factor of 10 – that is, 90 per cent – to achieve a sustainable world.* Though it may sound daunting, there are enough examples to prove that factor 10 is quite feasible. The electronics industry, for example, has gone well beyond factor 10 through miniaturization – producing smaller and smaller components that run on less and less energy.

Eco-efficiency means more than just limiting resources. It means using them more wisely, and re-using them. The concept of quality from the Dutch NEPP plays a role here. If a product lasts twice as long, it provides the same level of service with only half the resources. If it lasts 10 times as long, it meets the factor 10 goal. If the product can be recycled at the end of its useful life, it saves even more resources.

Eco-efficiency also takes a new view of waste, by asking if is necessary at all. Some forward-thinking companies are now adopting the goal of zero waste by substituting harmful substances with natural materials or using wastes as inputs for other operations. Industrial ecology, for example, clusters facilities together so that the wastes from one process can be used as raw material for another – just as in nature. The most famous industrial ecosystem may be the city of Kalundborg, Denmark. The Asnaes coal-fired power plant, for example, supplies steam to the Novo Nordisk

---

* This is the same order of magnitude called for in the NEPP, with the overall goal of about a 90 per cent reduction in pollution.

pharmaceutical plant and the Statoil refinery. The refinery filters sulphur from its natural gas and sells it to Kemira, which manufactures sulphuric acid. Asnaes also sells its fly ash to a cement plant and waste gypsum to a wallboard plant. Meanwhile, Novo Nordisk sells its sludge as fertilizer for local agriculture.[12]

One of the leading thinkers in environmental design is the American architect William McDonough, who says that even eco-*efficiency* is not enough. McDonough believes that products or buildings should not only do no harm to nature, but even do some good. He points out in a 1997 interview that

> a tree distils water, produces food, uses solar energy, creates a habitat, a micro-climate, and gives us healthy soil. Why can't a building do that? We must design habitats that are intrinsically connected to nature. We need to redesign our lives to have more of the natural flow of life on Earth.[13]

McDonough's ideas are more than nice theories: they work. Together with the German eco-chemist, Michael Braungart, McDonough developed a new fabric whose production uses no toxic input and produces no pollution. In fact, inspectors found that the 'waste water' coming out of their operations was cleaner than the water going in. Apparently the fabric actually filtered the water.

Despite all the technological wonders, the most important development in eco-efficiency will be the continued evolution of roles in the process. Originally, the driving forces were scientists and research centres such as the Wuppertal Institute. They are now growing into the more appropriate role of informers, as new driving forces emerge in the business world.

Ray Anderson, CEO of the Interface carpet company and a co-chair of the US President's Council on Sustainable Development, has committed his US$1-billion company to the goal of zero emissions. Interface has undertaken over 400 eco-efficiency initiatives, including the 'evergreen carpet lease.' Instead of selling carpet, the company leases carpeting services. Interface carpets come in square sections, or 'tiles' which can be replaced individually as they wear out. For an annual fee, the company maintains the carpets, replacing only the worn sections and recycling them into new carpet. Alongside its environmental initiatives, Interface is equally impressive for its financial performance. It controls 40 per cent of the global market for carpet tile and plans on doubling revenues in the next ten years. Interface is showing that eco-efficiency can also be profitable in the shift from a resource-oriented economy to a service-oriented economy.

Other companies are also recognizing combined financial and economic benefits. The Xerox Corporation, for example, is a leader in 'remanufacturing', building machines whose components can be disassembled easily and re-used in new machines. Eastman Kodak is also seeing the benefits of remanu-facturing. Davan Kelsey, the company's manager of design for health, safety and environment, explains: 'We're finally convincing designers that it doesn't matter if a part is twice as expensive if you can use it again and again.'[14]

The challenge for the future will be to convert many more companies, some of which are currently adversaries, into stakeholders or even driving forces. For many, it should not be such a hard sell. Not only can manufacturers save money on raw materials and energy, they can also save on the environmental compliance costs of collecting and treating waste. There will be more difficulty with the suppliers of raw materials, who will experience – one hopes – declining demand for their commodities. It may also be possible, however, to convert these adversaries into stakeholders. Forestry companies facing reduced demand for wood may realize that forests often provide greater economic benefits when trees are left standing. Mining companies will have less business providing virgin materials for industry – but perhaps they will convert into suppliers of recycled materials by mining old landfills!

We must also develop more sponsors and process managers. Some governments, for example, act as sponsors through 'green purchasing policies' that target the least environmentally harmful products. Because governments are such large purchasers, they create a substantial market demand for fledgling environmental technologies. Chambers of commerce and business associations can also play a sponsoring role by recognizing that eco-efficiency is in their members' best interest.

At an international level, we can look for sponsors and process managers among organizations such as the ISO, the OECD, the UN and the World Trade Organization (WTO). The ISO has already taken this role by developing ISO 14000. The standards do not say exactly how a company should change its operations, but rather state the importance of making this change by requiring the preparation of an environmental management system. The OECD played process manager by giving members like the Netherlands and the Nordic countries a forum in which to advocate eco-efficiency. In their 1996 meeting of Environment Ministers, the members endorsed eco-efficiency and factor 4. A year and a half later, the member states agreed to work towards the goal of factor 10. The OECD should build on this experience and continue playing a role as process manager for future developments.

The next important step will be to approach the World Trade Organization. The WTO has really been an adversary to environmental concerns, which it sees only as hindrances on the way to freer trade. The challenge will be to reform its policies to recognize the economic benefits of environmental measures. Perhaps some day it could even serve as a process manager for harmonizing eco-efficiency standards in its member states. Those who think such a transformation is impossible need only consider the gradual but undeniable changes in the World Bank, which was an environmental adversary a decade ago. Another example is the European Union, which began as a strictly free-market organization, but is now providing a framework for improving and harmonizing environmental standards throughout Europe.

Water Supply: Framing the Policy Debate and Making Deals

One of the worst things that can happen on a hiking tour is to get really thirsty and run out of water. Once hikers experience that, they never forget how important water is. Perhaps more policy makers should go hiking, so that water issues would receive more recognition.

Despite various efforts in the United Nations and conflicts from California to Israel, water is still not a main focus for international deal making. Indeed, water issues are often kept behind the scenes even when they play a vital role in developments. The Israeli–Palestinian conflict is as much about water as about land. The West Bank aquifer, for example, is a tremendous resource that could transform living conditions for the parched Palestinians living on top of it. But Israel, which draws 25 per cent of its freshwater from the aquifer, prevents the Palestinians from tapping it. Other conflicts are brewing between Egypt and Ethiopia on the Nile, between Turkey and its downstream neighbours Iraq and Syria along the Euphrates, and among southwestern US states along the Colorado River.

The earth's water supply is paradoxical. While most of the planet is covered with water, less than 1 per cent of this resource is freshwater suitable for most human uses.[16] Yet even this tiny fraction would be plenty if it were shared equitably, used efficiently and kept free of pollution. Unfortunately, it is not. The United Nations estimates that one billion people, one sixth of the earth's citizens, lack access to clean water, and the number will double in 30 years as both population and pollution grow.[17] At the same time, water demand is decoupling from economic growth in relative and even absolute terms in many places. In Europe, for example, water demand has levelled off in recent years. In the United States, water demand actually dropped by 10 per cent between 1980 and 1995.[18] Providing everyone with adequate clean water is not so much a technological or economic as a political challenge. The most important aspect of this theme is framing a deal that will provide everyone with the resources they need.

Water nourishes agriculture and natural habitats and regulates local climate. It also carries pollution very effectively and serves as an indicator for regional environmental health. In working to clean up water resources like the River Rhine of Europe or Chesapeake Bay of the United States, people soon realized that they had to address the full range of environmental issues in their watershed – from industrial pollution to road-building, soil erosion and pesticide use. Watersheds are natural units to use in making regional deals on overall environmental issues, and establishing watershed authorities may provide process managers for these deals.

A deal must be brokered between economic growth and health concerns. Especially in newly industrializing countries, investments in water treatment lag far behind investment in housing and industry. The United Nations estimates that about 90 per cent of all waste water is discharged untreated into local water bodies.[19] This deal should ensure that industrial growth is accompanied by commensurate growth in pollution control.

Another deal will need to be struck between natural and human uses of water resources. Just as we need to keep a large portion of the land in its natural state, so we need to preserve a large portion of natural water resources. This is far from the case in many areas. The Colorado River, for example, is so tapped by US states and Mexico that it generally dries up long before reaching its delta in the Gulf of California. The same fate is befalling the Yellow River in China, which has been running dry an average of 70 days per year for the past 12 years.[20]

Agriculture is the largest water consumer. While food production is certainly an essential use of water, it could easily consume much less. In some cases, half of all irrigation water is lost to run-off and evaporation.[21] This waste will persist as long as agricultural water is subsidized to hold prices well below market levels. Despite its traditional dominance in water consumption, however, agriculture is now losing out as more and more water is diverted to growing cities.

Sandra Postel of the Global Water Policy Project has proposed a deal to solve both agricultural and urban water problems. If traditional users, such as farmers, were given property rights to water, they could sell the resource to cities, using the extra income to invest in conservation technologies. Meanwhile cities, paying a market price for water, would have more incentive to use it wisely. Such a framing of the political and economic reality is needed to develop deals on managing water supply around the world. A system of local and regional water boards may be set up for this purpose.

Climate Change: Continuity and the Use of Time

I have discussed the problem of climate change at length in previous chapters. While there is still considerable uncertainty about the extent of changes we can expect, it is reasonable to assume that human activities are altering the climate in potentially dangerous ways.

The Kyoto Protocol of 1997 and the Buenos Aires follow-up of 1998 provide some focus for climate change policy. There is now a rough deal with some targets for reducing greenhouse gas emissions. We have not reached a phase, however, in which we fully understand the economic and political consequences of a real climate change policy for the world. Without this understanding, we cannot guarantee the continuity of the deal and its translation to the relevant stakeholders. So far, the discussions have been restricted to the environmental world, with only minimal input from other parts of government and no full-scale societal debate.

The discussion can be strengthened by considering the relation between the final target and responsibility for achieving it, rather than by quarrelling about countries' fair shares in achieving the intermediate targets. The debate should focus on the long-term, global target, something of the order of a 90 per cent reduction of emissions in 50 or 100 years. Using a century as our time frame, we can envision the systemic changes that will be required. We can focus our efforts on developing revolutionary technologies and new paradigms, rather than bean-counting emission reductions of a few percentage points. Intermediate targets are helpful, of course, but only as mileposts along the policy trail, not to be confused with the actual destination.

A long-term, global perspective on climate change makes more sense than having a 'CO_2 discussion' about an airport expansion, as we now have in the Netherlands. Yet we cannot blame environmentalist for putting CO_2 on the airport expansion agenda, if that's the only agenda available. The same happens in other sectors, such as road transport or electricity generation. If we had an overall global target, and a breakdown of responsibilities by sector, we would have a much more orderly means for assessing the climate change impacts of a new airport or industrial expansion.

A Glimpse into the Future

This chapter has tried to provide a glimpse into the future of the sustainable development challenge. At this stage, we can only begin to discern the issues that will face our world in the next century of rapid economic, technological, demographic and cultural change. As I have said, identifying the major themes of global sustainability and working out policy solutions will be a complex challenge for all of us. I humbly offer cooperative environmental management as a framework in which to begin the process.

Notes

1 WorldWatch Institute, *State of the World 1998*, ed. Linda Starke (New York: Norton, 1998), 41–2.
2 *Ibid.*, 37.
3 *Ibid.*, 101–5.
4 WorldWatch Institute, *State of the World 1997*, ed. Linda Starke (New York: Norton, 1997), 99.

5 Environmental News Network (ENN),'World Population Growth Slows a Bit', 4 November 1998.

6 WorldWatch Institute, *State of the World 1997*, ed. Linda Starke (New York: Norton, 1997), 48.

7 Michael Parfit, 'Human Migration', *National Geographic,* October 1998, 16.

8 Erla Zwingle, 'Women and Population', *National Geographic,* October 1998, 42.

9 *Ibid.,* 38.

10 *Ibid.,* 39.

11 WorldWatch Institute, *State of the World 1997,* ed. Linda Starke (New York: Norton, 1997), 19.

12 Gil Friend, 'Industrial Ecology in Motion (3): Eco-Industrial Parks', *New Bottom Line* (www.igc.org/eco-ops/nbl) (Berkeley, 21 November 1995).

13 Diane Wintroub Dalmenson, 'From Generation to Generation: a Conversation with William McDonough', *IS Magazine* (www.isdedignet.com), April 1997.

14 'Second Time Around, and Around', *New York Times,* 14 July 1998.

15 Elaine Robbins, 'Water, Water Everywhere', *E Magazine* (Norwalk, CT) September/October 1998, 31.

16 Jim Motavalli, 'Water Fight', *E Magazine* (Norwalk, CT) September/October 1998, 4.

17 Elaine Robbins, 'Water, Water Everywhere', *E Magazine* (Norwalk, CT) September/October 1998, 29.

18 Wayne B. Solley, Robert R. Pierce, Howard A. Perlman, 'Estimated Use of Water in the United States in 1995', United States Geological Survey (Reston, VA), 1998: abstract.

19 Elaine Robbins, 'Water, Water Everywhere', *E Magazine* (Norwalk, CT) September/October 1998, 33.

20 Jim Motavalli, Elaine Robbins, 'The Coming Age of Water Scarcity' (interview with Sandra Postel), *E Magazine* (Norwalk, CT), September/October 1998, 12.

21 Elaine Robbins, 'Water, Water Everywhere', *E Magazine* (Norwalk, CT) September/October 1998, 31.

Working on this book reminded me of looking through a photo album. Showing happy pictures of past hikes to friends and relatives, I remembered the hike from the perspective of the photos I had shown so many times. In describing the development of cooperative environmental management, the good moments stay in memory, the bad moments disappear. Whatever difficulties we faced, however, the important thing is that we learned from our experiences and can prepare better for future hikes.

Though there have been many lessons along the way, one of them is clearly most important: *people* have to take the steps toward sustainable development. First they take steps in their minds, then steps to prepare, steps to start and, most important, steps to keep going. Each step is an individual decision – sometimes easy, sometimes painful, but never without risk. Everyone in this book could have made other choices: to stay in a safe position rather than take action, to avoid risk rather than to seek it, to let other people go their way and just hope the goals would be achieved somehow. Fortunately, individuals decided to step forward into the process, and they made everything happen. That is why I have emphasized the people involved and not simply written a theoretical reflection on sustainable development.

But it took more than individuals willing to walk on their own. It was their ability to walk together that made the hike possible. Reflecting on the events in this book, I cannot help but think that everyone played his or her role in the cooperative process perfectly: what a wonderful group we were in the different teams, in the combined efforts of politicians and civil servants, in the meetings between industrialists, bureaucrats and environmental groups! It would be a very sad mistake, however, to conclude that success was only possible with these particular people in these particular groups and situations.

It would be too easy simply to wait and see whether the right people stand up and start the hike. The call for 'leadership', which I heard quite often in the United States and many other places, sounds like an alibi for people not to take their own steps: as long as the 'leader' isn't moving, we can sit with our backpacks and wait. That is not the moral of the stories in this book. We can all take initiatives, and when we truly appreciate the challenges and opportunities of sustainable development, we realize that we *must* all take initiatives.

In every journey there is a point where people realize that going back is no longer an option. Maybe it is too late to find a safe camp site on the way back. Maybe there are so many people committed to the hike that even the organizers cannot call it off. Let's presume that the journey towards sustainable development is at such a point. Going backwards (forgetting about the environment) is not an alternative any more.

This doesn't mean that finishing the journey will be easy. In fact, the last part is often the hardest. It is quite possible to imagine the darkest scenarios for our future – with starvation, war (for water, space and resources), economic collapse, social disintegration, devastating natural disasters, mass extinction. Even without turning back, simply taking a rest increases the chance that these scenarios will come true. We know that resting in the middle of a snowstorm or heavy rain is the worst thing to do. When you're stuck out in bad weather, you have to keep going until you reach shelter.

But to 'keep going' doesn't mean we should stop thinking and move forward the way we always did. The solutions of the past might not work for the problems of the future. The financial–economic crisis of 1998 asks for new approaches, as does the successful implementation of environmental policies in a rapidly changing world.

When we do reach the peak of our environmental journey, we will see new peaks ahead of us. Even with a clean environment, we will not have a sustainable world unless we also achieve economic justice, universal access to education and health care, and social tolerance. The environmental journey will condition us and give us many of the skills we will need in the future, as we continue on our common journey.

Industry Covenants in the Netherlands

Agreements on the implementation of environmental policy for industrial sectors	DATE Start, extension
Primary metals industry	1993
Chemical industry	1993
Printing industry	1990, 1993
Wood preservation	1992
Metal working and electrical engineering industry	1994
Dairy industry	1994
Textile industry	1995
Paper and cardboard industry	1996
Oil and gas production	1995

Declaration on energy efficiency improvement	DATE Start, extension
Metal working and electrical engineering industry	1992
Bakeries	1993
Flowerbulb storage and preparation sector	1994
Mushroom nurseries	1995
Biscuits, chocolate and confectionery industry	1995
Housing associations	1992
Supermarkets	1995
Electric installation companies	1995
Electro-technical companies	1995
Technical consultants	1995
Transport sector	1995
Netherlands Railways	1997

Agreement on energy efficiency improvement	DATE Start, extension
Iron and steel industry	1992, 1995
Cement industry	1992, 1998
Textile industry	1992, 1996
Calcium-silicate brick industry	1992, 1997
Glass industry	1992
Greenhouse horticulture	1993
Paper and cardboard industry	1993, 1996
Margarine, fats and oil industry	1993, 1996
Sugar industry	1993
Meat processing industry	1993
Breweries	1993, 1998
Fruit and vegetable processing industry	1993
Non-ferrous metals industry	1993, 1996
Construction ceramics industry	1993
Chemical industry	1993
Industrial laundries	1994
Solar industry	1994
Dairy industry	1994
Coffee-roasting plants	1994, 1996
Fine-grained ceramics industry	1994
Rubber processing industry	1994
Oil refineries	1995
Institutions for secondary vocational training	1994
Institutions for higher vocational training	1996
Chilling and freezing houses	1996
Surface treatment plants	1996
Asphalt industry	1995
Plastic processing industry	1994
Iron foundries	1995
Institutional health care	1993
Carpet industry	1996
Potato-processing industry	1996
Soft drink industry	1996
Banking sector	1996
Individual companies: Philips	1993
KLM Royal Dutch Airlines	1994
Schiphol Airport	1994
TDV, STORK, etc	1996, 1997
Mushroom nurseries	1998
Insurance sector	1998
Flower bulbs	1998

Agreements on waste recycling refund systems	DATE Start, extension
Plastic film in agriculture	1996
Car recycling	1994
Plastic window frames	1996

Miscellaneous	DATE Start, extension
Mercury oxide batteries	1985
Beverage containers	1985
PETP bottles	1987
Air pollution from trucks and buses	1987
Mercury in batteries	1987
Phosphates in detergents	1987
CFCs	1988
Cadmium in crates	1988
Packaging of crop protection agents	1989
Asbestos in cars and trucks	1989
Nickel-cadmium batteries	1989
Packaging waste I	1991
Packaging waste II	1997
Plastic film in industry	1993
Plastic film in agriculture and market gardening	1993
Waste management of cable residues	1993
Tropical timber	1993
Wooden stairways	1993
Implementation of long-term crop protection policy plan	1993
Recycling of plastic window frames	1993
Volatile organic compounds of storage tanks (VOTOB)	1989
SO_2 and NO_x emissions of power stations (SEP)	1990
Policy plan 'Volatile organic compounds 2000' (KWS 2000)	1988
Clean-up of contaminated soil of petrol stations (Subat scheme)	1991
Environmental advertising	1991
Waste transport	1987
Inland shipping of waste	1989
Construction industry, environmental targets 1995	1993
Cargo residues from barges	1991
Environmental measures for road transport	1989
Green label for cow-houses	1993

Miscellaneous cont.	DATE Start, extension
Sustainable development contract	1994
Set of agreements Environmental Action Plan utilities	1997
PV (photovoltaic)-agreement	1997
Energy efficiency improvement and sustainability in housing	1997
Green houses and the environment	1997

Source: VNO/NCW.

Select Bibliography

Amsterdamse Gemeenteraad. 'Beleidsnotitie Het Amsterdamse bodemsanieringsbeleid: herzien'. Amsterdam: Gemmenteblad 1996, bijlage A.

Aspen Institute. 'The Alternative Path: a Cleaner, Cheaper Way to Protect and Enhance the Environment'. Washington, DC: The Aspen Institute, 1996.

Association of the Dutch Chemical Industry, State of the Netherlands. 'Declaration of Intent on the Implementation of Environmental Policy for the Chemical Industry' (English translation). The Hague: 2 April 1993.

Austrian Federal Ministry of the Environment. *National Environmental Plan* (English translation). Vienna: Austrian Federal Government, 1995.

Bastmeijer, Kees. 'Provisional Code of Conduct for Concluding Environmental Covenants'. The Hague: Ministry of Housing, Land Use Planning, and the Environment, 1994.

— 'The Covenant as an Instrument of Environmental Policy in the Netherlands: a Case Study for the OECD'. The Hague: Ministry of Housing, Land Use Planning, and the Environment, 1994.

Beardsley, Dan, Terry Davies and Robert Hersh. 'Improving Environmental Management: What Works, What Doesn't'. *Environment,* September 1997.

Benedick, Richard Elliot. *Ozone Diplomacy: New Directions in Safeguarding the Planet.* Cambridge: Harvard University Press, 1991.

Beverdam, H. W. and W. Vlieger. 'Horeca in de Binnenstad: milieuvriendelijk en gezellig'. Amsterdam: Milieudienst Amsterdam, 1995.

Biekart, Jan Willem. 'Environmental Covenants Between Government and Industry: a Dutch NGO's Experience'. *Review of European Union and International Environmental Law.* Oxford: Blackwell Publishers, 1995.

— 'Negotiated Agreements in EU Environmental Policy'. In *New Instruments for Environmental Policy in the EU.* Ed. Jonathan Golub. London: Routledge, 1998.

— 'Wij kunnen hetzelf wel: Industrie heeft milieubeleid met regels en wetten niet nodig'. *Natuur en Milieu* (Utrecht), November 1993.

— 'De basismetaalindustrie en het doelgroepenbeleid industrie: analyse van process en resultaten op weg naar 2000'. Utrecht: Stichting *Natuur en Milieu,* 1994.

Blakeley, Roger. 'The Sweeping Change of the Resource Management Act'. Speech delivered at the first green plan conference in San Rafael, California, 1992.

Caldwell, Lynton Keith. *International Environmental Policy: Emergence and Dimensions,* 2nd ed. Durham, NC: Duke University Press, 1990.

Canadian House of Commons. Bill C-83: An Act to Amend the Auditor General Act. 28 November, 1995. First Session, thirty-fifth Parliament, 42–43-44 Elizabeth II, 1994–95.

Canadian Office of the Auditor General. '1997 Report of the Commissioner of the Environment and Sustainable Development'. Hull, Quebec: 1998.

Captain, Seán. 'The Green Plan Guide: A Sustainability Theory Based on the Strategies of The

Netherlands and New Zealand, Supported by Examples from Other Select Countries' (unpublished report). San Francisco: Resource Renewal Institute, 1996.

Cleij, Jan. 'Balancieren op de rand van de wet.' *Bodem*, Jaargang 7, nr. 1 (1997).

— 'De Steden als Bron van Welvaart en Duurzamheid'. Presented at the Sixth Conference on Public Housing. Amsterdam, 19–20 September 1996.

Commission of the European Communities. 'Progress Report from the Commission on the Implementation of the European Community Programme of Policy and Action In Relation to the Environment and Development'. Brussels: Office for Official Publications of the European Communities, 1996.

— 'Taking European Environment Policy into the 21st Century'. Brussels: Office for Official Publications of the European Communities, 1996.

— *Towards Sustainability*. Brussels: Office for Official Publications of the European Communities, 1993.

Confederation of Netherlands Industry and Employers (VNO-NCW). 'Environmental Policy in the Netherlands: The Role of Industry.' The Hague: 1995.

Consultative Group for the Chemical Industry. 'Annual Report 1994'. The Hague: 1995.

Davies, Terry and Jan Mazurek. 'Industry Incentives for Environmental Improvement: Evaluation of US Federal Initiatives'. Washington, DC: Global Environmental Management Initiative, 1996.

De Graaf, John and Jack Hamann. *GreenPlans*. Produced and directed by John de Graaf and Jack Hamann, 60 min. KCTS-TV, Seattle, 1995.

De Graeff, Jan Jaap. 'Environmental Cooperation Between Government and Industry in the Netherlands'. Speech deliverd for the Resource Renewal Institute, San Francisco, 1994.

De Jongh, Paul. 'The Development of Integrated Environmental Polices in the Netherlands' (unpublished manuscript). 1996.

— 'The Netherlands Approach to Environmental Polices: Integrated Environmental Policy Planning as a Step Towards Sustainable Development'. Washington, DC: Center for Strategic and International Studies, 1996.

Den Bosch, Malmberg. 'The Netherlands in Brief'. The Hague: Ministry of Foreign Affairs, 1990.

Earth Island Journal. Numerous articles (San Francisco: Earth Island Institute).

Enterprise for the Environment. 'The Environmental Protection System in Transition'. Washington, DC: Center for Strategic and International Studies, 1998.

Environmental News Network (ENN). Numerous articles from 1996–8. www.enn.com.

Environmental Protection Agency (EPA). 'States Reach new Deal to Foster Regulatory "Reinvention" Projects'. *EPA Weekly Report*, Vol. 18, No. 36 (5 September 1997).

— *EPA Strategic Plan*. Washington, DC: Government Printing Office (GPO), 1997.

European Environment Agency. 'Environment in the European Union: 1995'. Copenhagen, 1996.

Foundation of the Primary Metals Industry, State of the Netherlands. 'Declaration of Intent on the Implementation of Environmental Policy for the Primary Metals Industry' (English translation). The Hague, 10 March 1992.

Frieder, Julie. 'Approaching Sustainability: Integrated Environmental Management and New Zealand's Resource Management Act'. A report prepared for the Ian Axford New Zealand Fellowship in Public Policy, December, 1997.

Gardner, Richard N. *Negotiating Survival: Four Priorities After Rio*. Washington DC: The Council on Foreign Relations, 1992.

General Accounting Office (GAO). Various Environmental Reports. Washington, DC: GAO, 1996–8.

Gow, Lindsay. 'Implementing Sustainability: New Zealand's Experience with Its Resource Management Act'. Speech delivered at the New Zealand Embassy, Washington DC, 6 June 1995.

Hagedorn, Nanette. 'Verzuring blijft heet hangijzer in basismetaalindustrie', *Natuur en Milieu*

(Utrecht), July/August, 1997.

Hammond, Jeff et al. *Tax Waste, Not Work*. San Francisco: Redefining Progress, 1997.

Hertsgaard, Mark. 'The Cost of Global Climate Change'. *Perspectives on Business and Global Change* (San Francisco), Vol. 10, No.4 (1996).

Johnson, Huey D. *Green Plans: Greenprint for Sustainability*. Lincoln, NB: University of Nebraska Press, 1995.

KPMG Milieu/IVA Tilburg. 'National Environmental Policy Plan 2: Evaluation of Industry'. The Hague: 1993.

Le Projet de Société. 'Canadian Choices for Transitions to Sustainability: Final Draft'. Ottawa: National Round Table, 1995.

Liefferink, Duncan. 'The Dutch National Plan for Sustainable Society'. In *International Environmental Law, Institutions, and Polices,* eds N.J. Vig and R. S. Axelrod. Washington, DC: CQ Press, 1999 (forthcoming).

Mattews, Emily. 'Environmental Policy in Action' (series of six briefing papers). The Hague: Ministry of Housing, Land Use Planning and the Environment, 1994.

— 'Towards a Sustainable Netherlands'. The Hague: Ministry of Housing, Land Use Planning and the Environment, 1994.

Ministry of Economic Affairs. 'Third White Paper on Energy Policy' (English translation). The Hague: 1996.

Ministry of Foreign Affairs. *History of the Netherlands*. Maastricht: Netherlands Institute for the Development and Support of Educational Projects, 1995.

Ministry of Housing, Land Use Planning, and the Environment (VROM). *National Environmental Policy Plan* (English translation). The Hague: SDU Publishers, 1989.

— 'Environmental Management: A General View'. The Hague: Directory for Information and External Relations, 1997.

— *Environmental News from the Netherlands* (various editions) (The Hague), 1996–8.

— *Environmental Programme* (3 consecutive editions, English translation). The Hague: SDU Publishers, 1995, 1996, 1997.

— 'Environmental Programme of the Netherlands: 1985–9' (English translation). The Hague: SDU Publishers, 1984.

— 'Final Report: Cleaner Production Programme: 1992–1995' (English translation). The Hague: SDU Publishers 1995.

— 'Indicatief Meerjaren Programma Milieubeheer: 1987–91'. The Hague: SDU Publishers, 1986.

— 'National Environmental Policy Plan Plus' (English translation). The Hague: SDU Publishers, 1990.

— 'Netherlands' National Communication on Climate Change Policies.' The Hague, 1994.

— 'Netherlands' Regulatory Tax on Energy: Questions and Answers'. The Hague: Ministry of Housing, Land Use Planning and the Environment, 1996.

— 'Report: Recommendations on and Responses to the NEPP' (English translation). The Hague: SDU Publishers, 1990.

— *National Environmental Policy Plan 2* (English translation). The Hague: SDU Publishers, 1993.

— *National Environmental Policy Plan 3* (English translation). The Hague: SDU Publishers, 1998.

— (with) Ministry of Agriculture, Nature Protection, and Fisheries, Ministry of Traffic and Transportation. 'White Paper on Environment and Economy' (English translation). The Hague: 1997.

Moons, Cees. 'Experiences with the Dutch Approach'. Paper presented at the conference 'The Significance of ISO-14000 for Government's Policies Towards Sustainable Industrial Development', Beijing, 6 November 1996.

N. V. Samenwerkende Elektriciteits-Produktiebedrijven, De Staat der Nederlanden. 'Covenant over de bestrijding van SO_2 en NO_x'. 's-Gravenhage, 12 June 1990.

— '3e Voortgangsrapportage: betreffend de Bestrijding van SO_2 en NO_x Emissies in de Elektriciteits-Produktiebedrijven in de jahren 1994 en 1995 in het kader van het Covenant'. Arnhem: January, 1997.

National Geographic. Washington, DC: October, 1998.

National Institute of Public Health and Environment (RIVM). *Concern for Tomorrow* (English translation). Bilthoven: RIVM, 1989.

— *National Environmental Outlook*. Editions 2–4. Bilthoven: RIVM, 1992, 1994, 1997.

New Jersey Future (bi-monthly newsletter of organization by the same name). Trenton, NJ: November/December 1997, January/February 1998.

Organization for Economic Cooperation and Development (OECD). *Environmental Performance Review: The Netherlands*. Paris: OECD, 1995.

— *Environmental Performance Review: Austria*. Paris: OECD, 1995.

— *Environmental Performance Review: New Zealand*. Paris: OECD, 1996.

— *Environmental Performance Review: United States*. Paris: OECD, 1996.

— *Environmental Performance Review: Canada*. Paris: OECD, 1995.

— *The OECD Observer* (Special Edition on Sustainable Development). Paris: June 1997.

Pennsylvania Department of Environmental Protection. 'Strategic Environmental Management in Pennsylvania: New Tools for Gaining Environmental and Economic Efficiencies'. Harrisburg, PA: 1997.

President's Council on Sustainable Development. *Sustainable America: a New Consensus*. Washington, DC: US GPO, 1995.

Resource Renewal Institute. Proceedings from the conference 'Green Plans for the 21st Century: the Pacific Rim', San Rafael, California, 21–23 October 1993.

Robbins, Elaine. 'Water, Water Everywhere'. *E Magazine*. Norwalk, CT, September/October, 1998.

Royal Netherlands Embassy. 'Innovations in Cooperative Environmental Management: Netherlands and the United States'. Videotaped proceedings of a 1995 conference at the Netherlands Embassy. 60 min. Washington, DC.

Ruckelshaus, William D. 'Stopping the Pendulum', Speech delivered at the Environmental Law Institute's annual awards dinner, October 1995.

Second Chamber of the Netherlands Estates-General. Environmental Management Act. 1 October 1995.

Sitarez, Daniel. *Agenda 21: The Earth Summit Strategy to Save Our Planet*. Boulder, CO: Earth Press, 1993.

Tweede Kamer der Staten-Generaal. 'Besluitvorming financiering Nationaal Milieubeleidsplan: Brief van de Minister-President, Minister van Algemene Zaken'. 's Gravenhage, 1 May 1989. Vergaderjaar 1988–1989, 21 120, nr. 1.

Vereinigung der Österreichischen Industrie. 'Wettbewerbsverzerrungen durch Umweltschutz-auflagen: Tendenzen zur Verlagerung von Unternehmensaktivitäten'. Vienna, 1996.

Whitman, Governor Christine Todd. Inaugural address. Trenton, NJ: 20 January 1998.

Winsemius, Pieter. *Guests in our Own Home* (English translation). Amsterdam: McKinsey and Company, 1990.

World Commission on Environment and Development. *Our Common Future*. Oxford: Oxford University Press, 1987.

WorldWatch Institute. *State of the World 1997*, ed. Linda Starke. New York: Norton, 1997.

— *State of the World 1998*, ed. Linda Starke. New York: Norton, 1998.

Recommended Further Reading

Adriaanse, Albert. 'Environmental Policy Performance Indicators: A Study on the Development of Indicators for Environmental Policy in the Netherlands'. The Hague: SBU State Publishing Ltd, 1993.

Benedick, Richard Elliot. *Ozone Diplomacy: New Directions in Safeguarding the Planet*. Cambridge: Harvard University Press, 1991.

Buitenkamp, M., H. Venner and T. Wams. 'Action Plan, Sustainable Netherlands'. Friends of the Earth Netherlands, Amsterdam, 1993.

Choucri, Nazli (ed.). *Global Accord: Environmental Challenges and International Responses*. Cambridge, Mass: MIT Press, 1993.

Dalal-Clayton, Barry. *Getting to Grips with Green Plans: National-level Experience in Industrial Countries*. London: Earthscan Publications, Ltd., 1996.

De Boer, Margaretha. *The Environment, Space, and Living Quality: Time for Sustainability*. The Hague: Ministry of Housing, Land Use Planning and the Environment, 1995.

Dutch Committee for Long-term Environmental Policy. *The Environment: Towards a Sustainable Future*. Dordrecht: Kluwer Academic Publishers, 1994.

European Commission. 'Potential Benefits of Integration of Environmental and Economic Policies: an Incentive-Based Approach to Policy Integration'. Report prepared by Graham and Trotham Ltd. London, 1994.

Friend, John and Allen Hickling. *Planning Under Pressure: The Strategic Choice Approach*. Oxford: Pergamon Press, 1987.

Fussler, Claude with Peter James. *Driving Eco-Innovation: A Breakthrough Discipline for Innovation and Sustainability*. London: Pitman Publishing, 1996.

Gerald T. Gardner and Paul C. Stern. *Environmental Problems and Human Behavior*. Boston: Allyn and Bacon, 1996.

Hammond, Jeff *et al*. Tax Waste, Not Work. Redefining Progress, 1997.

Johnson, Huey D. *Green Plans: Greenprint for Sustainability*. University of Nebraska Press, 1995.

MacNeill, Jim, Pieter Winsemius and Taizo Yakushiji. *Beyond Interdependence: The Meshing of the World's Economy and the Earth's Ecology*. Oxford: Oxford University Press, 1991.

Jonathan Golub (ed.). *New Instruments for Environmental Policy in the EU*. London: Routledge, 1998.

Organization for Economic Cooperation and Development (OECD). *Environmental Performance Review: The Netherlands*. Paris: 1995.

— *Environmental Performance Review: United States*. Paris: 1996.

Ritter, Don and Bruce Piasecki. *Reinventing the Vehicle for Environmental Management*. Washington, DC: National Environmental Policy Institute, 1995.

Rorty, Richard. *Contingency, Irony and Solidarity*. Cambridge: Cambridge University Press, 1989.

Rotmans, Jan and Bert de Vries. *Perspectives on Global Change: The Targets Approach*. Cambridge University Press, 1997.

Susskind, Lawrence and Jeffrey Cruikshank. *Breaking the Impasse*. New York: Basic Books, 1987.

Susskind, Lawrence and Patrick Field. *Dealing With An Angry Public*. London: The Free Press, 1996

Susskind, Lawrence *et al*. *The Consensus Building Handbook*. London: Sage Publishers, 1999 (forthcoming).

Wallace, David. *Environmental Policy and Industrial Innovation: Strategies in Europe, the USA and Japan*. London: Earthscan Publications, Ltd., 1995.

Weale, Albert. *The New Politics of Pollution*. Manchester: Manchester University Press, 1992.

Winsemius, Pieter. *Guests in Our Own Home: Thoughts on Environmental Management*. Amsterdam: McKinsey and Company, 1990.

WorldWatch Institute. *State of the World 1998*, ed. Linda Starke. Norton, 1998.

World Commission on Environment and Development. *Our Common Future*. Oxford: Oxford University Press, 1987.

Index